Practical Reinforcement Learning

Develop self-evolving, intelligent agents with OpenAI Gym, Python, and Java

Dr. Engr. S.M. Farrukh Akhtar

BIRMINGHAM - MUMBAI

Practical Reinforcement Learning

First published: October 2017

Production reference: 1131017

Published by Packt Publishing Ltd.
Livery Place
35 Livery Street
Birmingham
B3 2PB, UK.

ISBN 978-1-78712-872-9

www.packtpub.com

Credits

Author
Dr. Engr. S.M. Farrukh Akhtar

Reviewers
Ruben Oliva Ramos
Juan Tomás Oliva Ramos
Vijayakumar Ramdoss

Commissioning Editor
Wilson D'souza

Acquisition Editor
Tushar Gupta

Content Development Editor
Mayur Pawanikar

Technical Editor
Suwarna Patil

Copy Editors
Vikrant Phadkay
Alpha Singh

Project Coordinator
Nidhi Joshi

Proofreader
Safis Editing

Indexer
Tejal Daruwale Soni

Graphics
Tania Dutta

Production Coordinator
Aparna Bhagat

About the Author

Dr. Engr. S.M. Farrukh Akhtar is an active researcher and speaker with more than 13 years of industrial experience analyzing, designing, developing, integrating, and managing large applications in different countries and diverse industries. He has worked in Dubai, Pakistan, Germany, Singapore, and Malaysia. He is currently working in Hewlett Packard as an enterprise solution architect.

He received a PhD in artificial intelligence from European Global School, France. He also received two master's degrees: a master's of intelligent systems from the University Technology Malaysia, and MBA in business strategy from the International University of Georgia. Farrukh completed his BSc in computer engineering from Sir Syed University of Engineering and Technology, Pakistan. He is also an active contributor and member of the machine learning for data science research group in the University Technology Malaysia. His research and focus areas are mainly big data, deep learning, and reinforcement learning.

He has cross-platform expertise and has achieved recognition for his expertise from IBM, Sun Microsystems, Oracle, and Microsoft. Farrukh received the following accolades:

- Sun Certified Java Programmer in 2001
- Microsoft Certified Professional and Sun Certified Web Component Developer in 2002
- Microsoft Certified Application Developer in 2003
- Microsoft Certified Solution Developer in 2004
- Oracle Certified Professional in 2005
- IBM Certified Solution Developer - XML in 2006
- IBM Certified Big Data Architect and Scrum Master Certified - For Agile Software Practitioners in 2017

He also contributes his experience and services as a member of the board of directors in K.K. Abdal Institute of Engineering and Management Sciences, Pakistan, and is a board member of Alam Educational Society.

Skype id: farrukh.akhtar

About the Reviewers

Ruben Oliva Ramos is a computer systems engineer with a master's degree in computer and electronic systems engineering, teleinformatics, and networking, with a specialization from the University of Salle Bajio in Leon, Guanajuato, Mexico. He has more than 5 years of experience in developing web applications to control and monitor devices connected with Arduino and Raspberry Pi, and using web frameworks and cloud services to build Internet of Things applications.

He is a mechatronics teacher at the University of Salle Bajio and teaches students of master's in design and engineering of mechatronics systems. Ruben also works at Centro de Bachillerato Tecnologico Industrial 225 in Leon, teaching subjects such as electronics, robotics and control, automation, and microcontrollers.

He is a technician, consultant, and developer of monitoring systems and datalogger data using technologies such as Android, iOS, Windows Phone, HTML5, PHP, CSS, Ajax, JavaScript, Angular, ASP.NET databases (SQlite, MongoDB, web servers, Node.js, IIS), hardware programming (Arduino, Raspberry Pi, Ethernet Shield, GPS, and GSM/GPRS), ESP8266, and control and monitor systems for data acquisition and programming.

He has written a book called *Internet of Things Programming with JavaScript*, published by *Packt*.

I would like to thank my savior and lord, Jesus Christ, for giving me strength and courage to pursue this project. Thanks to my dearest wife, Mayte, our two lovely sons, Ruben and Dario, my father, Ruben, my dearest mom, Rosalia, my brother, Juan Tomas, and my sister, Rosalia, whom I love. This is for all their support while reviewing this book, for allowing me to pursue my dreams and tolerating not being with them after my busy day's work.

Juan Tomás Oliva Ramos is an environmental engineer from the University of Guanajuato, Mexico, with a master's degree in administrative engineering and quality. He has more than 5 years of experience in management and development of patents, technological innovation projects, and development of technological solutions through the statistical control of processes. He has been a teacher of statistics, entrepreneurship, and technological development of projects since 2011. He became an entrepreneur mentor and started a new department of technology management and entrepreneurship at Instituto Tecnologico Superior de Purisima del Rincon.

Juan is an *Alfaomega* reviewer and has worked on the book *Wearable designs for Smart watches, Smart TVs and Android mobile devices*.

He has developed prototypes through programming and automation technologies for the improvement of operations, which have been registered for patents.

> *I want to thank God for giving me the wisdom and humility to review this book. I thank Packt for giving me the opportunity to review this amazing book and to collaborate with a group of committed people. I want to thank my beautiful wife, Brenda; our two magic princesses, Regina and Renata; and our next member, Angel Tadeo; all of you give me the strength, happiness, and joy to start a new day. Thanks for being my family.*

www.PacktPub.com

For support files and downloads related to your book, please visit www.PacktPub.com.

Did you know that Packt offers eBook versions of every book published, with PDF and ePub files available? You can upgrade to the eBook version at www.PacktPub.com and as a print book customer, you are entitled to a discount on the eBook copy. Get in touch with us at service@packtpub.com for more details.

At www.PacktPub.com, you can also read a collection of free technical articles, sign up for a range of free newsletters and receive exclusive discounts and offers on Packt books and eBooks.

https://www.packtpub.com/mapt

Get the most in-demand software skills with Mapt. Mapt gives you full access to all Packt books and video courses, as well as industry-leading tools to help you plan your personal development and advance your career.

Why subscribe?

- Fully searchable across every book published by Packt
- Copy and paste, print, and bookmark content
- On demand and accessible via a web browser

Customer Feedback

Thanks for purchasing this Packt book. At Packt, quality is at the heart of our editorial process. To help us improve, please leave us an honest review on this book's Amazon page at https://www.amazon.com/dp/1787128725.

If you'd like to join our team of regular reviewers, you can e-mail us at customerreviews@packtpub.com. We award our regular reviewers with free eBooks and videos in exchange for their valuable feedback. Help us be relentless in improving our products!

Table of Contents

Preface

This book is divided into three parts. The first part starts with defining reinforcement learning. It describes the basics and the Python and Java frameworks we are going to use it in this book. The second part discusses learning techniques with basic algorithms such as temporal difference, Monte Carlo and policy gradient with practical examples. The third part applies reinforcement learning with the most recent and widely used algorithms with practical applications. We end with practical implementations of case studies and current research activities.

What this book covers

Chapter 1, *Reinforcement Learning*, is about machine learning and types of machine learning (supervised, unsupervised, and reinforcement learning) with real-life examples. We also discuss positive and negative reinforcement learning. Then we see the trade-off between explorations versus exploitation, which is a very common problem in reinforcement learning. We also see various practical applications of reinforcement learning like self driving cars, drone autonomous taxi, and AlphaGo. Furthermore, we learn reinforcement learning frameworks OpenAI Gym and BURLAP, we set up the development environment, and we write the first program on both frameworks.

Chapter 2, *Markov Decision Process*, discusses MDP, which defines the reinforcement learning problem, and we discuss the solutions of that problem. We learn all about states, actions, transitions, rewards, and discount. In that context, we also discuss policies and value functions (utilities). Moreover, we cover the practical implementation of MDP and you also learn how to create an object-oriented MDP.

Chapter 3, *Dynamic Programming*, shows how dynamic programming is used in reinforcement learning, and then we solve the Bellman equation using value iteration and policy iteration. We also implement the value iteration algorithm using BURLAP.

Chapter 4, *Temporal Difference Learning*, covers one of the most commonly used approaches for policy evaluation. It is a central part of solving reinforcement learning tasks. For optimal control, policies have to be evaluated. We discuss three ways to think about it: model based learning, value-based learning, and policy-based learning.

Chapter 5, *Monte Carlo Methods*, discusses Monte Carlo approaches. The idea behind Monte Carlo is simple: using randomness to solve problems. Monte Carlo methods learn directly from episodes of experience. It is model-free and needs no knowledge of MDP transitions and rewards.

Chapter 6, *Learning and Planning*, explains how to implement your own planning and learning algorithms. We start with Q-learning and later we see the value iterations. In it, I highly recommend that you use BURLAP's existing implementations of value iteration and Q-learning since they support a number of other features (options, learning rate decay schedules, and so on).

Chapter 7, *Deep Reinforcement Learning*, discusses how a combination of deep learning and reinforcement learning works together to create artificial agents to achieve human-level performance across many challenging domains. We start with neural network and then discuss single neuron feed-forward neural networks and MLP. Then we see neural networks with reinforcement learning, deep learning, DQN, the DQN algorithm, and an example (PyTorch).

Chapter 8, *Game Theory*, shows how game theory is related to machine learning and how we apply the reinforcement learning in gaming practices. We discuss pure and mixed strategies, von Neumann theorem, and how to construct the matrix normal form of a game. We also learn the principles of decision making in games with hidden information. We implement some examples on the OpenAI Gym simulated in Atari. and examples of simple random agent and learning agents.

Chapter 9, *Reinforcement Learning Showdown*, we will look at other very interesting reinforcement learning frameworks, such as PyBrain, RLPy, Maja, and so on. We will also discuss in detail about Reinforcement Learning Glue (RL-Glue) that enables us to write the reinforcement learning program in many languages.

Chapter 10, *Applications and Case Studies – Reinforcement Learning , covers advanced topics of reinforcement learning. We discuss Inverse Reinforcement Learning and POMDP's.*

Chapter 11, *Current Research – Reinforcement Learning*, describes the current ongoing research areas in reinforcement learning, We will discuss about hierarchical reinforcement learning; then we will look into reinforcement learning with hierarchies of abstract machines. Later in the chapter we will learn about MAXQ value function decomposition.

What you need for this book

This book covers all the practical examples in Python and Java. You need to install Python 2.7 or Python 3.6 in your computer. If you are working on Java, then you have to install Java 8.

All the other reinforcement-learning-related toolkits or framework installations will be covered in the relevant sections.

Who this book is for

This book is meant for machine learning/AI practitioners, data scientists, engineers who wish to expand their spectrum of skills in AI and learn about developing self-evolving intelligent agents.

Conventions

In this book, you will find a number of text styles that distinguish between different kinds of information. Here are some examples of these styles and an explanation of their meaning.

Code words in text, database table names, folder names, filenames, file extensions, pathnames, dummy URLs, user input, and Twitter handles are shown as follows: "We need to initialize our environment with the reset() method."

A block of code is set as follows:

```
for _ in range(1000):
  env.render()
  env.step(env.action_space.sample())
```

Any command-line input or output is written as follows:

```
cd gym
pip install -e .
```

New terms and **important words** are shown in bold.

Words that you see on the screen, for example, in menus or dialog boxes, appear in the text like this: "In order to download new modules, we will go to **Files** | **Settings** | **Project Name** | **Project Interpreter**."

Warnings or important notes appear like this.

Tips and tricks appear like this.

Reader feedback

Feedback from our readers is always welcome. Let us know what you think about this book-what you liked or disliked. Reader feedback is important for us as it helps us develop titles that you will really get the most out of. To send us general feedback, simply email feedback@packtpub.com, and mention the book's title in the subject of your message. If there is a topic that you have expertise in and you are interested in either writing or contributing to a book, see our author guide at www.packtpub.com/authors.

Customer support

Now that you are the proud owner of a Packt book, we have a number of things to help you to get the most from your purchase.

Downloading the example code

You can download the example code files for this book from your account at http://www.packtpub.com. If you purchased this book elsewhere, you can visit http://www.packtpub.com/support and register to have the files emailed directly to you. You can download the code files by following these steps:

1. Log in or register to our website using your email address and password.
2. Hover the mouse pointer on the **SUPPORT** tab at the top.
3. Click on **Code Downloads & Errata**.

4. Enter the name of the book in the **Search** box.
5. Select the book for which you're looking to download the code files.
6. Choose from the drop-down menu where you purchased this book from.
7. Click on **Code Download**.

Once the file is downloaded, please make sure that you unzip or extract the folder using the latest version of:

- WinRAR / 7-Zip for Windows
- Zipeg / iZip / UnRarX for Mac
- 7-Zip / PeaZip for Linux

The code bundle for the book is also hosted on GitHub at https://github.com/ PacktPublishing/Practical-Reinforcement-Learning. We also have other code bundles from our rich catalog of books and videos available at https://github.com/ PacktPublishing/. Check them out!

Errata

Although we have taken every care to ensure the accuracy of our content, mistakes do happen. If you find a mistake in one of our books-maybe a mistake in the text or the code- we would be grateful if you could report this to us. By doing so, you can save other readers from frustration and help us improve subsequent versions of this book. If you find any errata, please report them by visiting http://www.packtpub.com/submit-errata, selecting your book, clicking on the **Errata Submission Form** link, and entering the details of your errata. Once your errata are verified, your submission will be accepted and the errata will be uploaded to our website or added to any list of existing errata under the Errata section of that title. To view the previously submitted errata, go to https://www.packtpub.com/ books/content/support and enter the name of the book in the search field. The required information will appear under the **Errata** section.

Piracy

Piracy of copyrighted material on the internet is an ongoing problem across all media. At Packt, we take the protection of our copyright and licenses very seriously. If you come across any illegal copies of our works in any form on the internet, please provide us with the location address or website name immediately so that we can pursue a remedy. Please contact us at copyright@packtpub.com with a link to the suspected pirated material. We appreciate your help in protecting our authors and our ability to bring you valuable content.

Questions

If you have a problem with any aspect of this book, you can contact us at questions@packtpub.com, and we will do our best to address the problem.

1
Reinforcement Learning

In this chapter, we will learn what machine learning is and how reinforcement learning is different from other machine learning techniques, such as supervised learning and unsupervised learning. Furthermore, we will look into reinforcement learning elements such as state, agent, environment, and reward. After that, we will discuss positive and negative reinforcement learning. Then we will explore the latest applications of reinforcement learning. As this book covers both Java and Python programming languages, the later part of the chapter will cover various frameworks of reinforcement learning. We will see how to set up the development environment and develop some programs using open-air gym and **Brown-UMBC Reinforcement Learning and Planning (BURLAP)**.

Overview of machine learning

In this era of technological advancement, the utilization of machine learning is not like the way it used to be in the past. The purpose of machine learning is to solve the problems such as pattern recognition or perform specific tasks that a computer can learn without being programmed. Researchers are interested in algorithms that a computer can learn from data. The repetitive way of machine learning is vital because as models get new data with time, they are also able to independently adjust. They learn from past performances to produce more reliable results and decisions. Machine learning is not a new subject, but nowadays it's getting fresh momentum.

What is machine learning?

Machine learning is a subject that is based on computer algorithms, and its purpose is to learn and perform specific tasks. Humans are always interested in making intelligent computers that will help them to do predictions and perform tasks without supervision. Machine learning comes into action and produces algorithms that learn from past experiences and make decisions to do better in the future.

Arthur Samuel, way back in 1959, said: *"Machine Learning is the field of study that gives computers the ability to learn without being explicitly programmed"*.

Can a computer learn from experience? The answer is yes and that is what precisely machine learning is. Here, past experiences are called data. We can say that machine learning is actually a field that gives computers the capability to learn without being programmed.

For example, a telecom company is very much interested in knowing which customers are going to terminate their service. If they are aware or can predict those customers, they can offer them special deals to retain them. A machine learning program always learns from past data and improves with time. In simpler words, if a computer program improves on a certain task based on a past experience, then we can say that it has learned.

Machine learning is a field that discovers structures of algorithms that enable learning from data. These algorithms build a model that accepts inputs, and based on these inputs, they make predictions or results. We cannot provide all the preconditions in the program; the algorithm is designed in such a way that it learns itself.

Sometimes the words, machine learning and **Artificial Intelligence (AI)**, are used inter-changeably. However, machine learning and AI are two distinctive areas of computing. Machine learning is solely focused on writing software that can learn from past experiences.

Applications of machine learning include sentiment analysis, email spam detection, targeted advertisements (Google AdSense), recommendation engines used by e-commerce sites, and pattern mining for market basket analysis. Some real-life examples of machine learning are covered in the next section.

Speech conversion from one language to another

This Skype feature helps break the language barrier during voice/video calling. It translates a conversation into another language in real time, allowing both sides of speakers to effectively share their views in their native languages.

Suspicious activity detection from CCTVs

This is a wonderful example of how an application of machine learning can make society a safer place. The idea is to have a machine learning algorithm capture and analyze CCTV footage all the time and learn from it the normal activities of people, such as walking, running, and so on. If any suspicious activity occurs, say robbery, it alerts the authorities in real time about the incident.

Medical diagnostics for detecting diseases

Doctors and hospitals are now increasingly being assisted in detecting diseases such as skin cancer faster and more accurately. A system designed by IBM picked cancerous lesions (damage) in some images with 95 percent accuracy, whereas a doctor's accuracy is usually between 75—84 percent using manual methods. So, the computing approach can help doctors make more informed decisions by increasing the efficiency of recognizing melanoma and spotting cases where it is difficult for a doctor to identify it.

Machine learning can be divided into three categories:

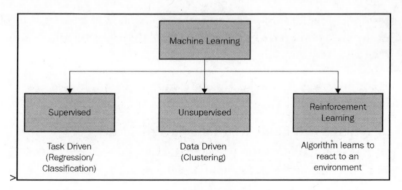

Figure 1.1: Types of machine learning

Supervised learning

Supervised learning is a type of machine learning where we have input and output variables and we use an algorithm to learn the mapping from the input variable to the output variable.

$$Y = f(X)$$

The goal here is to understand the mapping very well, and that enables us to transform the input into the output. When our program receives the input data, it runs the mapping function to generate output data.

Why is this called supervised learning? Actually, the algorithm that is used to learn from the training dataset is similar to a teacher supervising the process. For each run, the algorithm makes predictions on the training dataset and the teacher is doing the correction. Once we get an acceptable level of correct predictions, the learning will stop and the algorithm will move on to the production environment.

 In supervised learning, there are dependent and independent variables. We need to understand the effect of each variable used in the mapping and see the effect on the output variable.

We can further group supervised learning into classification and regression problems:

- **Classification**: A classification problem is when we need to predict a category. For example, we have a patient's history record in a hospital and we want to predict how many people have high chances of a heart attack. Here, the output variable will be yes or no.
- **Regression**: A regression problem is when we need to predict a number or value. For example, when predicting a stock value, it always results in a real number.

There are further divisions of classification and regression problems that include time series predictions or recommendations and so on. Some famous examples of supervised learning algorithms are as follows:

- Random forest (classification or regression problems)
- Linear regression (regression problems)
- **Support Vector Machines (SVM)** (classification problems)

Now we will learn supervised learning from a real-life example. Let's say we are in a garden and we have a bag full of different types of fruits. Now we need to remove all the fruits from the bag and put the same types of fruits together. That's an easy task because we're already aware of the physical characteristics of each fruit. For example, we know which one is a mango and which is an apple. So, it's very easy to arrange them in groups. Here, our previous memory is working like training data. We've already learned the fruit names from the training data; here, the fruit names are actually output or decision variables. *Table 1.1* shows the fruit characteristics:

No.	Color	Size	Shape	Fruit Name
1	Green	Small	Round to oval	Grape
2	Green	Big	Half moon	Banana
3	Red	Small	Heart	Cherry
4	Red	Big	Round with slight curves on both sides	Apple

Table 1.1: Characteristics of fruits

Let's say we take out a new fruit from the bag and now we need to place it into the correct group. We will check the color, size, and shape of the new fruit and take a decision based on the results to put it into the correct group. For example, if the fruit size is big, the color is red, and the shape is round with slight curves, then we can easily say it's an apple and place it in an apple group.

This is called supervised learning because we've already learned something from training data and then we apply that knowledge to the new data (test data). The technique used for this type of problem is called classification. Why? It is a classification problem because we are predicting a category; here, the category is fruit name.

Unsupervised learning

Unsupervised learning is a type of machine learning in which we have only input variables and no output variables. We need to find some relationship or structure in these input variables. Here, the data is unlabeled; that is, there is no specific meaning for any column.

It is called unsupervised learning because there is no training and no supervision. The algorithm will learn based on the grouping or structure in the data, for example, an algorithm to identify that a picture contains an animal, tree, or chair. The algorithm doesn't have any prior knowledge or training data. It just converts it into pixels and groups them based on the data provided.

In unsupervised learning, we group the parts of data based on similarities within each other. The data in unsupervised learning is unlabeled, meaning there are no column names. This is not important because we don't have any specific knowledge/training of the data.

Unsupervised learning problems can be further grouped as clustering and association problems:

- **Clustering**: A clustering problem is for discovering a pattern or understanding the way of grouping from the given data. An example is a grouping of customers by region, or a grouping based on age.
- **Association**: Association is a rule-based learning problem where you discover a pattern that describes a major/big portion of the given data. For example, in an online book shop, the recommendation engine suggests that people who buy book *A* also buy certain other books.

Some popular examples of unsupervised learning algorithms are:

- Apriori algorithm (association problems)
- K-means (clustering problems)

Now take up the same fruit grouping example again from the earlier section. Suppose we have a bag full of fruits and our task is to arrange the fruits grouped in one place.

In this instance, we have no prior knowledge of the fruits; that is, we have never seen these fruits before and it's the first time we will be seeing these fruits. Now, how do we perform this task? What are the steps we will do to complete this task? The first step is to take a fruit from the bag and see its physical characteristics, say the color of this particular fruit. Then arrange the fruits based on color. We end up with a grouping as per *Table 1.2*:

Color	Fruit Name
Red group	Cherries and apples
Green group	Grapes and bananas

Table 1.2: Grouping based on color

Now we will group them based on size and color. See the result in *Table 1.3*:

Size and color	Fruit Name
Big and red	Apple
Small and red	Cherry
Big and green	Banana
Small and green	Grapes

Table 1.3: Grouping based on size and color

It's done now! We've successfully grouped them.

This is called unsupervised learning and the approach is called **clustering**.

Note that in unsupervised learning, we don't have any training data or past example to learn from. In the preceding example, we didn't have any prior knowledge of the fruits.

Reinforcement learning

Reinforcement learning is a type of machine learning that determines the action within a specific environment in order to maximize a reward. One of the characteristics of reinforcement learning is that the agent can only receive a reward after performing the action, and thus must continue to interact with the environment in order to determine the optimal policy through trial and error.

Let's take an example. How did you learn to ride a cycle? Was somebody telling you how to ride a cycle and you just followed those instructions? What kind of learning is it? Some people have a misconception that it is supervised learning and they give the reasoning that *my uncle held me while I started cycling*, he *was telling me what to do*, and so on. At best, what they could tell you is *Watch out, don't fall down from the cycle, be careful*, or some other instruction. That does not count as supervision. As you know, supervised learning means that you are ready to ride a cycle and someone gives you the exact steps, such as *Push down your left foot with 5 pounds of pressure*, or *Move your handle to 80 degrees*.

Someone has to give you the exact control signals in order for you to ride a cycle. Now you may think that if someone gave instructions of this kind, a child would never learn to cycle. So, people immediately say that it is unsupervised learning. The justification they now give is that no one tells them how to ride a cycle. But let's analyze this. If it is truly unsupervised learning, then what that means is that kids watch hundreds of videos of other cyclists and how they ride, figuring out the pattern, and then get down to cycle and repeat it. That is essentially unsupervised learning; you have lots of data and you figure out the patterns and try to execute those patterns. Cycling does not work that way! You have to get down to cycling and try it yourself. *How to learn cycling?* is neither supervised nor unsupervised learning. It's a different paradigm. It is reinforcement learning, one that you learn by trial and error.

During this learning process, the feedback signals that tell us how well we do are either pain... *Ouch! I fell! That hurts! I will avoid doing what led to this next time!*, or reward... *Wow! I am riding the bike! This feels great! I just need to keep doing what I am doing right now!*

Introduction to reinforcement learning

Have you seen a baby learn to walk? The baby readily succeeds the first time it stands up, tries to walk a few steps, then falls down, and again stands up. Over time, the baby learns to walk. There is no one really teaching it how to walk. Learning is more by trial and error. There are many learning situations where humans, as well as biological systems, do not get detailed instructions on how to perform a task. However, they undertake those tasks by evaluation and try to improve with behavior based on scans of evaluations. Reinforcement learning is actually a mathematical structure that captures this kind of trial-and-error learning. The goal here is to learn about the system through interaction with the system.

Reinforcement learning is inspired by behavioral psychology. In the year 1890, a Russian physiologist named Ivan Pavlov was doing an experiment on salivation in dogs when they are being fed. He noticed that whenever he rang the bell, his dog began to salivate. Even when he was not bringing them food and just rang the bell, the dog started to salivate. Pavlov had started from the theory that there are some elements that a dog does not need to learn. Let's say dogs do not learn to salivate whenever they see food. This reaction is hard-wired into the dog. In behavioral science terms, it is an undefined response (a stimulus-response is a connection that requires no learning). In behavioral psychology terms, we write: *Undefined Stimulus > Undefined Response.*

The dog actually forms an association with the bell and the food. And later on, without serving the food you ring the bell, the dog starts salivating to digest the food it expects to be delivered. Essentially, the food is the pay-off, like a reward to it, and it forms an association between the signals (in this case, ringing a bell and the reward the dog is going to get).

After this experiment, there were more and very complex experiments on animals and people came up with lots of theories. Lots of papers on reinforcement learning are taken from the behavioral psychology journals.

There are a few terms in reinforcement learning that are used in this book several times: agent, environment, states, actions, and rewards. Let me explain these terms briefly here and later, we will go into the details of each term in Chapter 2, *Markov Decision Process*.

An agent in reinforcement learning always takes actions. Let me give you an example. A plane moving left and right in a video game is an agent. Or if the character is moving left, right, up, and down in the *Pac Man* game, then the character is actually an agent.

A state is the place or the situation in which the agent finds itself. Let's say our plane's game is a state or the *Pac Man* game is a state.

An action, as the name implies, is some work based on certain scenarios. An agent can perform certain actions. In the *Pac Man* game, he can move left, right, up, or down. In our other example of the plane in the video game, it can go left or right.

A reward is a feedback signal; it can be plus or minus. For example, in the *Pac Man* game, if the agent goes left and it avoids the enemy, it gets a plus reward. In the same way, if our plane goes right or left and dodges a bomb, it gets a reward.

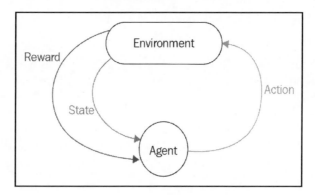

Figure 1.3: Reinforcement learning elements

Reinforcement learning is all about learning from the environment and learning to be more accurate with time. There are two types of reinforcement learning, called positive reinforcement learning and negative reinforcement learning. We will discuss both the approaches in the next section.

Positive reinforcement learning

Positive reinforcement learning means getting a positive reward. It is something desirable that is given when you take an action. Let me give you an example to understand the concept. Let's say after studying hard, you've secured the first position in your class. Now that you know your good action results in a positive reward, you'll actually try more to continue such good actions. This is called **positive reinforcement learning**.

Another example, continued from the previous section on riding a bicycle, is of someone clapping for you when you are finally able to ride a cycle. It's a positive feedback and is called positive reinforcement learning.

Negative reinforcement learning

On the other hand, negative reinforcement learning means getting negative rewards, or something undesirable given to you when you take an action. For example, you go to a cinema to watch a movie and you feel very cold, so it is uncomfortable to continue watching the movie. Next time you go to the same theater and feel the same cold again. It's surely uncomfortable to watch a movie in this environment.

The third time you visit the theater you wear a jacket. With this action, the negative element is removed.

Again, taking up the same ride-a-cycle example here, you fall down and get hurt. That's a negative feedback and it's called **negative reinforcement learning**.

The goal here is to learn by interacting with the system; it's not something that is completely offline. You have some level of interaction with the system and you learn about the system through the interaction.

Now we will discuss another example from a game of chess. One way is to sit with the opponent and make a sequence of moves; at the end of the game, either you win or lose. If you win, you will get a reward; someone will pay you $80. If you lose, you have to pay the opponent $80. That's all that happens and the maximum feedback you get is, either you win $80 or you lose $80 at the end of the game. No one will tell you that given this position this is the move you have to take; that's the reason I said it is learning from reward and punishment in the absence of detailed supervision.

A dog can be trained to keep the room tidy by giving him more tasty food when he behaves well and reducing the amount of his favorite food if he dirties the room.

The dog can be considered as an agent and the room as the environment. You are the source of the reward signal (tasty food). Although the feedback given to the dog is vague, eventually his neural networks will figure out that there is a relation between good food and good behavior.

The dog will possibly behave well and stop messing up with his room to maximize the goal of eating more tasty food. Thus we've seen reinforcement learning in non-computer issues.

This reinforces the idea that reinforcement learning can be a powerful tool for AI applications. Self-driving cars are a good example of AI applications.

With reinforcement learning, we aim to mimic biological entities.

Another example can be of a robot as an agent with a goal to move around in a room without bumping into obstacles. A negative score (punishment) on bumping into an obstacle and positive score (reward) on avoiding an obstacle will define the final score for the author. The reward can be maximized by moving around in the room avoiding obstacles. Here, we can say that the goal is to maximize the score.

An agent can maximize the reward by acting appropriately on the environment and performing optimum actions. Reinforcement learning is thus also used in self-adapting systems, such as **AlphaGo**.

Applications of reinforcement learning

Reinforcement learning is used in a wide variety of applications.

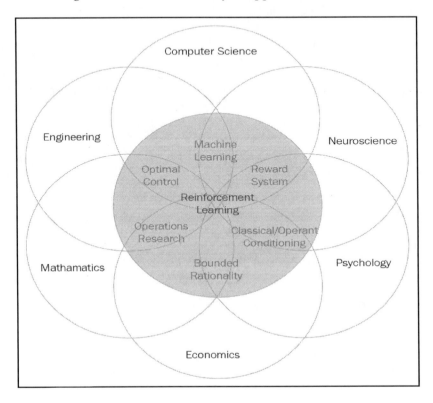

Figure 1.4: The many faces of reinforcement learning

Self-driving cars

Self-driving cars are not science fiction anymore. Companies such as Toyota and Ford have invested millions of dollars for R&D in this technology. Taxi services such as Uber and Lyft, currently paying human drivers, may soon deploy entire fleets of self-driving cars. In the next two to three years, hundreds of thousands of self-driving cars may be sold to regular consumers.

Google is also taking a lead in this. The Google self-driving car project is called **Waymo**; it stands for a new way forward in mobility.

 Now, Waymo is an autonomous car development company.

Thirty-three corporations are working on autonomous vehicles and over $450 M is invested across 36 deals to date; auto tech start-ups are on track for yearly highs in both deals and dollars.

Many influential personnel from automobile and technology industries predict that this will happen. But the big question behind this is, *when will this actually happen?* The timing is the key here; by 2020 many relevant companies are planning to launch autonomous cars. Refer to the following predictions by motor companies:

Motor company	Launch prediction
Audi	2020
NuTonomy (Singapore)	2018
Delphi and MobiEye	2019
Ford	2021
Volkswagen	2019
General Motors	2020
BMW	2021
Baidu	2019
Toyota	2020
Elon Musk	2019
Jaguar	2024
Nissan	2020
Google	2018

Autonomous cars are the core and long-term strategy. IEEE predicts that 75 percent of vehicles will be fully autonomous by 2040.

Planning for a self-driving car is done via reinforcement learning. The car learns to continuously correct its driving capability over time through trial and error when training.

We will learn how to create a self-driving car using a simulator in upcoming chapters.

Drone autonomous aerial taxi

While people are still debating about the safety of self-driving cars, the United Arab Emirates is actually preparing to launch an autonomous aerial taxi or drone taxi.

It is one of the finest examples of applying reinforcement learning.

The **Road and Transport Authority (RTA)**, Dubai employs the Chinese firm Ehang's 184, which is the world's first passenger drone. It's capable of a range of about 30 miles on a single charge and can carry one person weighing up to 220 lbs, as well as a small suitcase. The entire flight is managed by a command center; all you need to do is hop in and choose from the list of predetermined destinations where you want to land.

Riders can use a smartphone app to book their flights to pick them up from the designated zones. The drone taxi arrives at the designated place and the rider will go inside and get into a seat and select the pre-programmed designation using a touchscreen. They will just sit and enjoy the flight. All the flights are monitored in the control room remotely for passenger safety.

This drone autonomous taxi can carry a weight of 110 kg, and it uses eight motors to fly at a speed of up to 70 kilometers/hour.

Aerobatics autonomous helicopter

Computer scientists at Stanford have successfully created an AI system that can enable robotic helicopters to learn and perform difficult stunts watching other helicopters performing the same maneuvers. This has resulted in autonomous helicopters which can perform a complete airshow of tricks on its own. Controlling the autonomous helicopter flight is the most challenging problem.

Autonomous helicopter flight is widely regarded to be a highly challenging control problem. Despite this fact, human experts can reliably fly helicopters through a wide range of maneuvers, including aerobatic maneuvers.

How does it work? By using reinforcement learning for the optimal control problem, it optimizes the model and reward functions.

We will look into all these reinforcement learning algorithms practically in the upcoming chapters.

TD-Gammon – computer game

TD-Gammon is a widely played computer backgammon program developed in 1992. TD-Gammon is a neural network which teaches itself to play backgammon and improves its strategies by playing the game with itself and learns from the results. It is a good example of reinforcement learning algorithm. It begins with random initial weights (and hence a random initial strategy), TD-Gammon eventually develops a strong level of play. While raw description of the board state is given, but with zero information built-in, the system teaches itself and develops strong ability to play at intermediate level. Moreover, with additional hand-crafted features the systems performs stunningly well.

Figure 1.5: A backgammon game

The current version of TD-Gammon is very close to the level of the best human player of all time. It explored a lot of strategies that humans had never used, and that is the reason for the advancement in current TD-backgammon play.

AlphaGo

The game of *Go* originated in China more than 3,000 years ago. The rules of the game are simple. Players take turns to place white or black stones on a board, trying to capture the opponent's stones or surround empty space to make points out of territory. As simple as the rules are, *Go* is a game of profound complexity. There are more possible positions in *Go* than there are atoms in the universe. That makes *Go* more complex than chess.

The game of *Go* is a classic and very challenging game. Computer scientists have been trying for decades to at least achieve a beginner level of performance with a computer as compared to a human. Now, with advancements in deep reinforcement learning, the computer learns a network policy (which selects actions) and also a network value (which predicts the winner) through self-play.

AlphaGo uses a state-of-the-art tree search and deep neural network techniques. It is the first program that beat a professional human player in Oct 2016. Later on, AlphaGo also defeated Lee Sedol, one of the strongest players with 17 world titles. The final score of the game was 4 to 1; this match was seen by 200 million viewers.

The agent environment setup

Reinforcement learning is learning from interaction with the environment. Here the learner is called the **Agent**. Everything outside the **Agent** is called the **Environment**. The **Agent** performs actions continuously and the **Environment** responds to all those actions and presents new situations to the **Agent**. Furthermore the environment gives feedback for all the actions, called a **reward**; it is a numeric value. The **Agent** goal is to maximize this **reward**. A complete specification of an **environment** defines

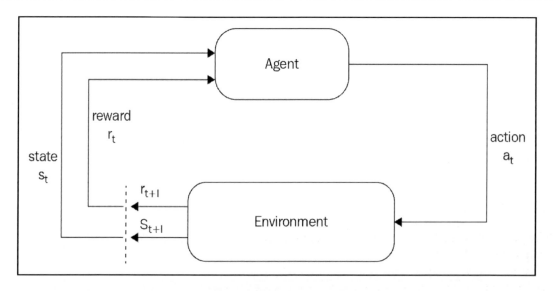

Figure 1.7: Reinforcement learning environments

Moreover, the **Agent** and **Environment** interact at discrete time steps $t=0,1,2,3,...$ At each time step t, the **Agent** receives some representation of the **Environment** state, S_t E S, where S is the set of possible states. On that basis, it selects an **action**, A_t E $A(S_t)$, where $A(S_t)$ is the set of actions available in **state** S_t. One time step later, in part as a consequence of its **action**, the **Agent** receives a numerical **reward**, R_{t+1} E R, and finds itself in a new **state**, S_{t+1}:

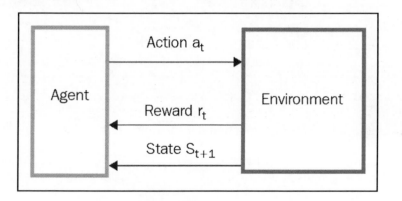

Figure 1.8: Reinforcement learning example

Let's take an example of GridWorld; people who are into reinforcement learning love to think about it. This GridWorld shown in *Figure 1.9* is a 3 X 4 grid. For the purpose of this discussion, think that the world is a kind of game; you start from a state that is called **start state** and you are able to execute actions, in this case, up, down, left, and right. Here, the green square represents your goal, the red square represents failure, and the black square is where you cannot enter. It actually acts as a wall. If you reach the green square (goal), the world is over and you begin from the start state again. The same holds for the red square. If you reach the red square (failure), the world is over and you have to start over again. This means you cannot go through the red square to get to the green square.

The purpose here is to roam around this world in such a way that eventually you reach the goal state and under all circumstances you avoid the red spot. Here you can go up, down, left, and right but if you are on the boundary state such as **(1,3)** and you try to go up or left, you just stay where you are. If you try to go right, you actually end up in the next square **(2,3)**:

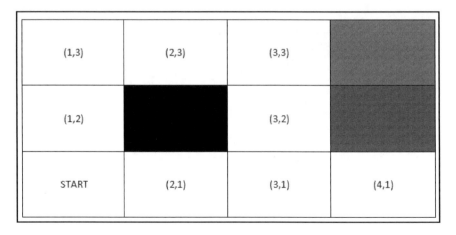

Figure 1.9: GridWorld

What is the shortest sequence of actions that gets us from start state to goal state? There are two options:

- Up, up, right, right, right
- Right, right, up, up, right

Both the answers are correct, taking five steps to reach the goal state.

The previous question was very easy because each time you take an action, it does exactly what you expected it to do. Now introduce a little bit of uncertainty into this GridWorld problem. When you execute an action, it executes correctly with a probability of **0.8**. This means 80 percent of the time when you take an action, it works as expected and goes up, down, right, or left. But 20 percent of the time, it actually (incorrectly) causes you to move by a right angle. If you move up, there is a probability of **0.1** (10 percent) to go left and **0.1** (10 percent) to go right.

Now what is the reliability of your sequence of up, up, right, right, right in getting you to the goal state given?

↑ (P=0.1) → (p=0.8) (1,3)	↑ (P=0.1) → (p=0.8) (2,3)	→ (p=0.8) (3,3)	+1
↑ (P=0.8) → (p=0.1) (1,2)		(3,2)	-1
↑ (P=0.8) → (p=0.1) Start	(2,1)	(3,1)	(4,1)

Figure 1.10: GridWorld with probabilities

To calculate it, we need to do some math. The correct answer is *0.32776*. Let me explain how this value is computed. From the **Start** state we need to go up, up, right, right, right. Each of those actions works as it is supposed to do with a probability of *0.8*. So: $(0.8)^5 = 0.32768$.

Now we have the probability that the entire sequence will work as intended. As you noticed, *0.32768* is not equal to the correct answer *0.32776*. It's actually a very small difference of *0.00008*.

Now we need to calculate the probability of uncertainties, it means we need to calculate the probability that the intended sequence of events will not work as it is supposed to.

Let's go through this again. Is there any way you could have ended up falling into the goal from that sequence of commands by not following the intended path? Actions can have unintended consequences, and they often do. Suppose you are on the start state and you go up in the first step; there is a probability of *0.1* that you will actually go to the right. From there, if you go up, there is again a probability of *0.1* that you will actually go to the right. From there, the next thing we do is take the right action as per our intended sequence, but that can actually go up with a probability of *0.1*. Then another *0.1* to get to the next right action can actually cause an up to happen. And finally, that last right might actually execute correctly with a probability of *0.8* to bring us to the goal state:

$$0.1 X 0.1 X 0.1 X 0.1 X 0.8 = 0.00008 ;$$

Now add both of them and you get the correct answer:

$$0.32668 + 0.00008 = 0.32776$$

What we did in the first case is to come up with a sequence of up, up, right, right, right where it is sort of planned out what we do in a world where nothing could go wrong; it's actually like an ideal world.

But once we introduce this notion of uncertainty or the randomness, we have to do something other than work out in advance what the right answer is, and then just go. Either we have to execute the sequence and once in a while we have to drift away and re-plan to come up with a new sequence wherever it happened to end up or we come up with some way to incorporate these uncertainties or probabilities that we never really have to rethink of in case something goes wrong.

There is a framework that is very common for capturing these uncertainties directly. It is called **Markov Decision Process (MDP)**; we will look into it in Chapter 2, *Markov Decision Process*.

Exploration versus exploitation

Exploration implies firm behaviors characterized by finding, risk taking, research, search, and improvement; while exploitation implies firm behaviors characterized by refinement, implementation, efficiency, production, and selection.

Exploration and exploitation are major problems when you learn about the environment while performing several different actions (possibilities). The dilemma is how much more exploration is required, because when you try to explore the environment, you are most likely to keep hitting it negative rewards.

Ideal learning requires that you sometimes make bad choices. It means that sometimes the agent has to perform random actions to explore the environment. Sometimes, it gets a positive, or sometimes it gets a reward that is less rewarding. The exploration—exploitation dilemma is really a trade-off.

The following are some examples in real life for exploration versus exploitation:

- Restaurant selection:
    - **Exploitation**: Go to your favorite restaurant
    - **Exploration**: Try a new restaurant
- Online banner advertisements:
    - **Exploitation**: Show the most successful advert
    - **Exploration**: Show a different advert
- Oil drilling:
    - **Exploitation**: Drill at the best-known location
    - **Exploration**: Drill at a new location
- Game playing:
    - **Exploitation**: Play the move you believe is best
    - **Exploration**: Play an experimental move
- Clinical trial:
    - **Exploitation**: Choose the best treatment so far
    - **Exploration**: Try a new treatment

Neural network and reinforcement learning

How do neural networks and reinforcement learning fit together? What is the relationship of both these topics? Let me explain it, the structure of a neural network is like any other kind of network. There are interconnected nodes, which are called neurons and the edges that join them together. A neural network comes in layers. The layers are called **input layer**, the **hidden layer** and the **output layer**.

In reinforcement learning, convolutional networks are used to recognize an agent's state. Let's take an example: the screen that Mario is on. That is, it is performing the classical task of image recognition.

Don't be confused by a convolutional network with unsupervised learning. It is using different classifications from images in reinforcement learning. On the other hand, in supervised learning, the network is trying to match to an output variable or category to get a label of the image. It is actually getting the label of the image to the pixel:

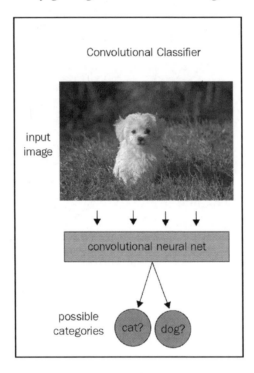

Figure 1.11: Convolutional classifier

In supervised learning, it will give the probability of the image with respect to labels. You give it any picture and it will predict in percentages the likelihood of it being a cat or a dog. Shown an image of a dog, it might decide that the picture is 75 percent likely to be a dog and 25 percent likely to be a cat.

However, in reinforcement learning, given an image that represents a state, a convolutional network can rank the actions likely to happen in that state; for example, it might predict that running right will return 5 points, jumping 7, and running left none.

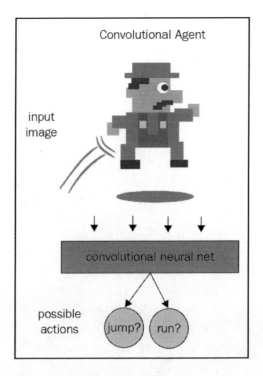

Figure 1.12: Convolutional agent

Reinforcement learning frameworks/toolkits

As the title of this book is *Practical Reinforcement Learning*, this book will cover a lot of practical examples and case studies. We will focus on both Python and Java. The first framework we will look at is OpenAI.

OpenAI Gym

OpenAI is a non-profit AI research company. OpenAI Gym is a toolkit for developing and comparing reinforcement learning algorithms. The gym open source library is a collection of test problems—environments—that can be used to work out our reinforcement learning algorithms. Shared interface of these environments allow us to write general algorithms.

Getting Started with OpenAI Gym

The first step: we need to have Python 2.7 or Python 3.5 installed. I suppose you have Python already installed.

Next, you need to have Git; it is a free and open source version control system. If you don't have it, then download it from https://git-scm.com/downloads.

After installing Git, you need to clone the gym directory in your computer. Execute the following command to create a new directory named gym in your current location:

```
git clone https://github.com/openai/gym
```

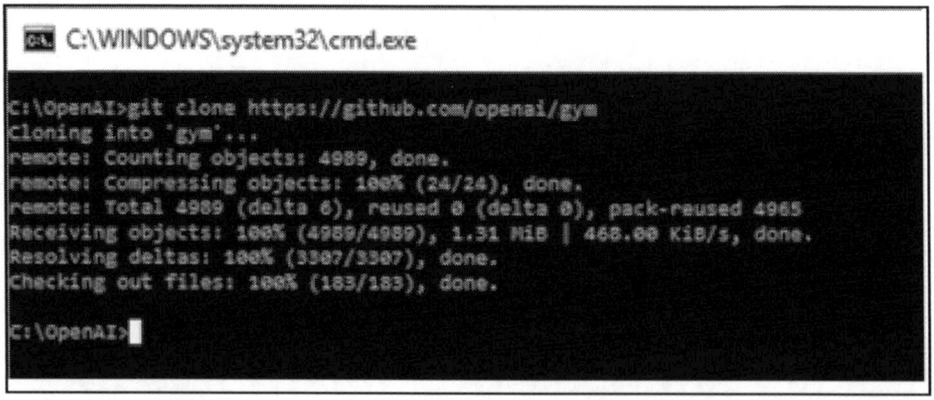

Figure 1.13: Clone directories to your local computer

Now go to the gym directory and install it:

```
cd gym
pip install -e .
```

```
C:\OpenAI>cd gym

C:\OpenAI\gym>pip install -e .
Obtaining file:///C:/OpenAI/gym
Collecting numpy>=1.10.4 (from gym==0.7.4.dev0)
  Downloading numpy-1.12.0-cp36-none-win32.whl (6.7MB)
    100% |████████████████████████████████| 6.7MB 93kB/s
Collecting requests>=2.0 (from gym==0.7.4.dev0)
  Downloading requests-2.13.0-py2.py3-none-any.whl (584kB)
    100% |████████████████████████████████| 593kB 669kB/s
Collecting six (from gym==0.7.4.dev0)
  Downloading six-1.10.0-py2.py3-none-any.whl
Collecting pyglet>=1.2.0 (from gym==0.7.4.dev0)
  Downloading pyglet-1.2.4-py3-none-any.whl (964kB)
    100% |████████████████████████████████| 972kB 408kB/s
Installing collected packages: numpy, requests, six, pyglet, gym
  Running setup.py develop for gym
Successfully installed gym numpy-1.12.0 pyglet-1.2.4 requests-2.13.0 six-1.10.0

C:\OpenAI\gym>
```

Figure 1.14: Installing gym

Now we need to have Docker installed because OpenAI Gym has a large number of environments and each environment is packaged as a Docker image. The next section covers what Docker is and how to install it:

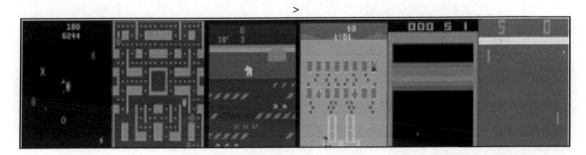

Figure 1.15: OpenAI Gym environments

Docker

Docker is a famous tool designed for developers to create an application, deploy it, and run it using containers. A container will give you the luxury to package an application with all the dependencies and libraries required and create one package to ship it. By doing this, the life of the developer is much more comfortable. They are sure that the same program developed in their machine will run on any other machine without any customization. It is widely used because it is very easy to package and ship programs.

Docker automates the repetitive tasks of setting up and configuring development environments so that developers can focus on what matters: building great software.

Docker installation on Windows environment

You can download the binaries from this URL:

`https://www.docker.com/products/overview.`

Run the binaries and follow these steps:

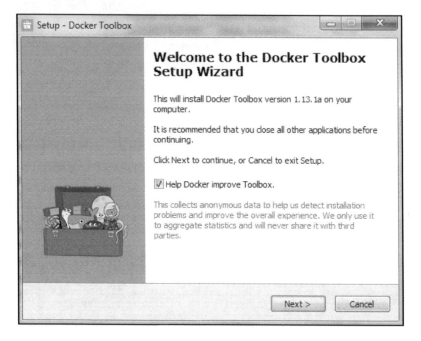

Figure 1.16: Docker installation

Then select the directory to install Docker:

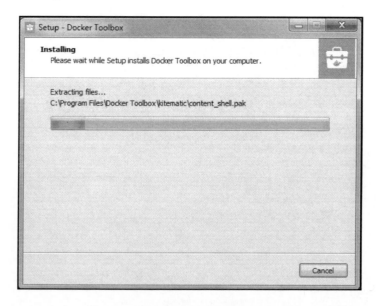

Figure 1.17: Docker install location

Then select the components you want to install; we don't need to change anything here:

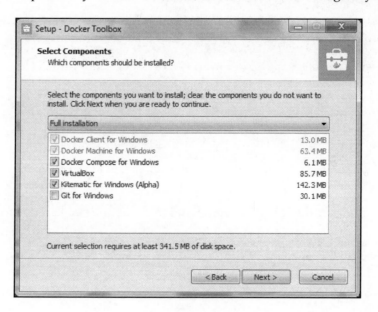

Figure 1.18: Docker components

Now just click on **Next** and use all the default values:

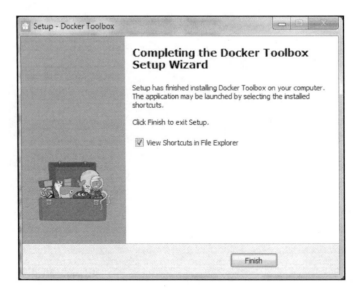

Figure 1.19: Docker installation completed

Docker installation on a Linux environment

First, we need to create a Docker repository. Afterwards, we can install and update Docker from that repository:

1. To install packages, `apt` is allowed to use a repository on HTTPS:

   ```
   $ sudo apt-get install apt-transport-https ca-certificates curl
   software-properties-common
   ```

2. Then add Docker's official GPG key:

   ```
   $ curl -fsSL https://download.docker.com/linux/ubuntu/gpg | sudo
   apt-key add -
   ```

3. After that, use the following command to set up the stable repository:

   ```
   $ sudo add-apt-repository "deb [arch=amd64]
   https://download.docker.com/linux/ubuntu $(lsb_release -cs) stable"
   ```

4. The next step is to update the `apt` package. This step completes the Docker installation:

```
$ sudo apt-get update
```

5. Now we are ready to test the installation:

```
$ sudo docker run helloworld
```

If you see the message `helloworld`, then it means your installation is working perfectly.

Let me explain how this `helloworld` message is actually generated:

1. The CLI client of Docker Engine calls the Docker Engine daemon.
2. The Docker Engine daemon fetches `helloworld` from the Docker Hub.
3. The Docker Engine daemon also creates a new container from `helloworld` that runs the `.exe` and displays the output.

Now our environment is completely set up.

Running an environment

We are ready to write our first program with OpenAI Gym. Here's a simple minimum example of getting something running. This will run an instance of the `CartPole-v0` environment for 1,000 time steps, rendering the environment at each step. You will be able to see a window pop up, rendering the classic cart-pole problem.

First we have to import `gym`, and then we need to select an environment; the second line in the following code snippet creates an environment of `CartPole-v0`. The `gym` already has more interface, making it possible to write generic algorithms that can be applied to many differ then 2,600+ environments; we just pass the environment name and it creates an environment in our program. These environments expose a common intent environment:

```
import gym
env = gym.make('CartPole-v0')
```

After that, we need to initialize our environment with the `reset()` method:

```
env.reset()
```

Then we will run the environment for 1000 timestamps and it will render the environment and take some random action at each time stamp:

```
for _ in range(1000):
    env.render()
    env.step(env.action_space.sample())
```

Here is the complete program:

```
import gym
env = gym.make('CartPole-v0')
env.reset()
for _ in range(1000):
    env.render()
    env.step(env.action_space.sample())
```

Save this program into Demo.py and run the program:

python Demo.py

The output should look something like this:

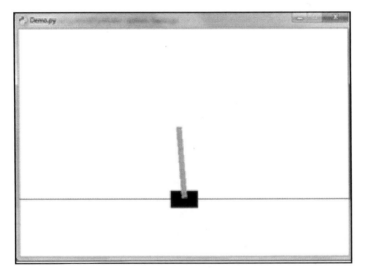

Figure 1.20: Output of the first program

The preceding snippet does not include any learning or training—that would require much more code.

If you are interested to see the working of other environments all you need to do is replace `CartPole-v0` with something like `MsPacman-v0`or `MountainCar-v0` .

Gym's provides a large collection of environments that expose a common interface and are versioned to allow for comparisons. You can find a listing of them as follows:

```
from gym import envs print(envs.registry.all())
```

In this book, we will implement various algorithms using OpenAI Gym environments.

Brown-UMBC Reinforcement Learning and Planning

BURLAP is licensed under the permissive Apache License 2.0. BURLAP is a Java library used to implement reinforcement learning algorithms. It is used for the development of single- or multi-agent planning and learning algorithms and domains to supplement them. BURLAP is a highly flexible and customizable API for defining the state and action in different forms, such as discrete, continuous, and relational domains. It also includes analysis tools for visualization of agent and domain performance.

Walkthrough with Hello GridWorld

In this walkthrough, we'll get started with BURLAP. We assume that you already have Maven installed since it will make managing dependencies very easy. If you don't have Maven installed, please install it from `https://maven.apache.org/download.cgi`.

It is highly recommended you to use any IDE; it will make working with libraries and directory structure substantially easy. If you don't have any IDE, we recommend Eclipse or IntelliJ. Both have the tools to use Maven. For this walk-through, we will use the command line and any text editor. Those who already have an IDE can follow along in the IDE.

Hello GridWorld project

To start with a project, the first thing is to create a new directory in your filesystem. Then we need to create `pom.xml` using any text editor and write the following code:

```xml
<?xml version="1.0" encoding="UTF-8"?>
<project>
    <modelVersion>4.0.0</modelVersion>
    <groupId>com.mycompany.app</groupId>
    <artifactId>myProj</artifactId>
```

```
<version>1</version>
<dependencies>
    <dependency>
        <groupId>edu.brown.cs.burlap</groupId>
        <artifactId>burlap</artifactId>
        <version>3.0.0</version>
    </dependency>
</dependencies>
<build>
    <plugins>
        <plugin>
            <groupId>org.codehaus.mojo</groupId>
            <artifactId>exec-maven-plugin</artifactId>
            <version>1.2.1</version>
            <executions>
                <execution>
                    <goals>
                        <goal>java</goal>
                    </goals>
                </execution>
            </executions>
        </plugin>
    </plugins>
</build>
</project>
```

As you can see, we should set `groupId` to any name that we wish, and the same goes for `artifactId`. The `<dependencies>` section requires any dependency for this project; it actually tells Maven that this project requires BURLAP libraries.

Now we need to create the directory structure of the project, `com/book/java/project`. In the `project` folder, we will create two java files named `HelloWorld.java` and `TestPlor.java`.

Now let's write the code for the `HelloWorld.java`:

```
package project;
import burlap.shell.visual.VisualExplorer;
import burlap.mdp.singleagent.SADomain;
import burlap.domain.singleagent.gridworld.GridWorldDomain;
import burlap.domain.singleagent.gridworld.GridWorldVisualizer;
import burlap.domain.singleagent.gridworld.state.GridWorldState;
import burlap.domain.singleagent.gridworld.state.GridLocation;
import burlap.domain.singleagent.gridworld.state.GridAgent;
import burlap.mdp.core.state.State;
import burlap.visualizer.Visualizer;
```

```java
public class HelloWorld
{
 public static void main(String[] args)
 {
//11x11 grid world
GridWorldDomain gridworld = new GridWorldDomain(11,11);

//layout four rooms
gridworld.setMapToFourRooms();

//transitions with 0.9 success rate
gridworld.setProbSucceedTransitionDynamics(0.9);

//now we will create the grid world domain
SADomain sad= gridworld.generateDomain();

//initial state setup
State st = new GridWorldState(new GridAgent(0, 0), new GridLocation(10,
10, "loc0"));

//now we will setup visualizer and visual explorer
Visualizer vis = GridWorldVisualizer.getVisualizer(gridworld.getMap());
VisualExplorer ve= new VisualExplorer(sad, vis, st);

//now setup the control keys move the agent to "a w d s"
ve.addKeyAction("a", GridWorldDomain.ACTION_WEST, "");
ve.addKeyAction("w", GridWorldDomain.ACTION_NORTH, "");
ve.addKeyAction("d", GridWorldDomain.ACTION_EAST, "");
ve.addKeyAction("s", GridWorldDomain.ACTION_SOUTH, "");

ve.initGUI(); } }
```

Now, the directory structure should be as follows:

```
pom.xml

src/
    main/
        java/
            project/
                HelloWorld.java
```

We are ready to compile and run the program. Make sure that in the command-line tool, you are in the `project` directory where your `pom.xml` is located:

```
mvn compile
```

Once you run the command, Maven will download BURLAP and the required libraries.

To run the `HelloWorld` code:

```
mvn exec:java -Dexec.mainClass="project.HelloWorld"
```

Once you run the command, the output will display as per *Figure 1.21*:

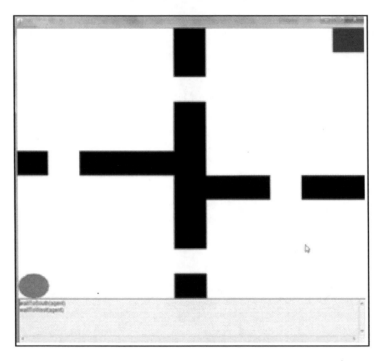

Figure 1.21: Output of the GridWorld program

Now you can move the agent with the *A, S, D, W* keys and control its movement. As this program makes the stochastic GridWorld, it means some time agent will not work as expected.

In this walkthrough, we compiled and set up a project that uses BURLAP using the command line. We strongly suggest you use the IDE.

Summary

In this chapter, we learned about machine learning and discussed the types of machine learning with real-life examples. Reinforcement learning is learning from interactions with the environment. We also briefly discussed agents, states, actions, environments, and rewards. An agent is an actual body that takes action. Everything outside the agent is called environment. The state is the place or the situation in which the agent finds itself. The action is some work done based on certain scenarios, but agents choose actions from a list of possible actions. The reward is a feedback signal, it can be positive or negative.

We also learned about positive reinforcement learning; it is something desirable that is given to the research subject after it performs an action. On the other hand, negative reinforcement learning results when an undesirable thing happened after an action is performed.

Then we also discussed the trade-off between explorations versus exploitation. The dilemma is between when to start and end exploration. It is about selecting what we know and getting somewhere close to what we expect; that's called exploration. And choosing something we are not sure of and the possibility of learning more and more is called exploitation.

In this chapter, we also saw various practical applications of reinforcement learning such as self-driving cars, a drone autonomous taxi, AlphaGo, and so on.

Furthermore, we learned about reinforcement learning frameworks OpenAI Gym and BURLAP. We set up the development environment and wrote our first program on both frameworks. In the upcoming chapters, we will use these frameworks extensively and focus on practical examples.

The next chapter is very important in order to understand the reinforcement learning paradigm. In the next chapter, we will discuss MDP; it defines the reinforcement learning problem and we will discuss the solutions of that problem. Moreover, we will cover the practical implementation of MDP and you will also learn how to create object-oriented MDP.

2

Markov Decision Process

In this chapter, we are going to see how to do planning in uncertain domains. People who are aware of decision theory will understand that **Markov Decision Process (MDP)** is an extension of it; the only difference is that it is focused on making a long-term plan of action. We will start with the basics of MDP and we will learn all about states, actions, transitions, and rewards. We will look into a practical example of building an MDP domain using BURLAP. We will further implement object-oriented MDP's domain. We will also learn how all the MDP's components tie into the Bellman equation. Then, we will explore what it means to have an optimal plan for an MDP. We will also learn about Markov chains. We will finish by looking at some of the major weaknesses of this approach and see how they can be addressed.

Introduction to MDP

An MDP is a discrete time-state transition system. MDP is actually a reinforcement learning task and it satisfies all the requirements of a Markov property. Furthermore, finite MDPs or finite MDPs having the finite actions and state fulfill the requirement of a Markov property. Finite MDPs are mainly important in reinforcement learning.

An MDP can be described formally with four components:

- A set of possible world states: S
- A set of possible actions: $A(s)$ or A
- Model: $T(s, a, s') \sim Probability(s' \mid s, a)$
- A real-valued reward function: $R(s) \sim R(s, a) \sim R(s, a, s')$

To understand this framework, we will use the GridWorld example, as depicted in the following figure:

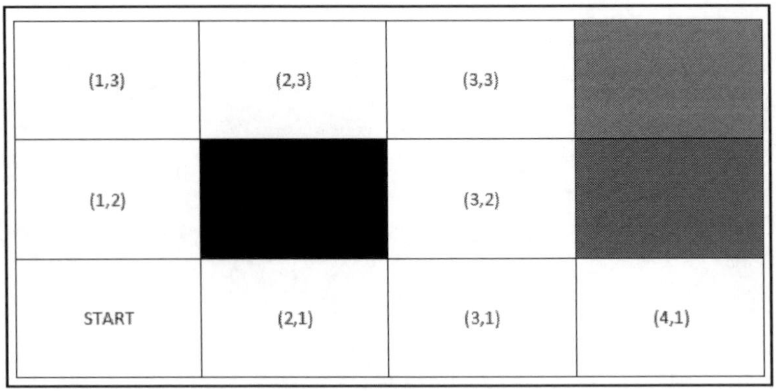

Figure 2.01: GridWorld

State

MDP has a set of states; it represents all the states that one can be in. In the GridWorld example, it has *12* states and we can represent them in X and Y coordinates; say, the start state is *(1,1)* or the goal state is *(4,4)*. Actually it doesn't matter whether we call these as *1, 2, 3 ...... 12* or *A,B,C ... L*. The point is that there are states that represent something and we should know which state we happen to be in. We can represent state as *s*.

Action

Next are actions--things that you can do in a particular state. Actions are the things I am allowed to execute when I am in a given state. What will be the actions in the GridWorld? In the GridWorld, we can take four types of actions: *UP, DOWN, LEFT,* and *RIGHT*. The point is that your action set will represent all the things that the agent, robot, or person we are trying to model is allowed to do. Now, in its generalized form, you can think of the set of actions one can take as the function state *A(s)*. However, most of the time, people just treat it as set of actions or actions that are allowed on the particular state and represent it as *a*.

Model

The third part of our framework is the model, sometime called **transition model**. It describes the rules of the games that apply, or is rather the physics of the world. It's basically a function of three variables: state, action, and another state. It produces the probability that you end up transitioning *s'* given that you were in state *s* and you took action *a*. Here, *s'* is the state where you end up and *s* and *a* are the given state and action, respectively. In our GridWorld example, we are at the start state. The probability of going up is *0.8*, the probability of going right is *0.1*, and the probability that we end up where we started is *0.1*. If we sum up all the probabilities, it becomes *1*, and that's the way it works. The model is really an important thing and the reason for its importance is that it describes the rules of the game. It tells us what will happen if we do something in a particular place. It captures everything we can know about the transition:

$$T(s, a, s') \sim Probability(s' | s, a)$$

These processes are called Markov, because they have what is known as the Markov property. That is, given the current state and action, the next state is independent of all preceding actions and states. The current state captures all that is relevant about the world in order to predict what the next state will be.

The effects of an action taken in a state depend only on that state and not on the prior history.

Reward

Next is the reward. It is a scalar value that you get from being in a state. There are three different definitions of rewards (*R*); sometimes it will be very useful to think about them in different ways.

R(s) means we get a reward when entering into the state. *R(s, a)* means we get a reward when being in a state and taking an action. *R(s, a, s')* means we get a reward when being in a state, taking an action, and ending up in a new state. These are all mathematically equivalent but it is easier to think about one form or another:

$$R(s) \sim R(s, a) \sim R(s, a, s')$$

The preceding four components define a problem; now, we'll look into the solution. The solution to the MDP is called policy.

Policy

A plan or a result of classical planning can be either an ordered list of actions or a partially ordered set of actions meant to be executed without reference to the state of the environment. When we looked at conditional planning, we considered building plans with branches in them that observed something about the state of the world and acted differently depending on the observation. In an MDP, we can assume that it takes only one step to go from any one state to another. Hence, in order to be prepared, it is typical to compute a whole policy rather than a simple plan.

 A policy is a mapping from states to actions. It says, no matter what state you happen to find yourself in, here is the action that it's best to take now. Because of the Markov property, we'll find that the choice of action needs to depend only on the current state (possibly the current time as well) and not on any of the previous states.

A policy is a function that takes state and returns an action. In other words, for any given state you are in, it tells you the action you should take:

$$\pi(s) \to a$$

MDP - more about rewards

Generally, in a reinforcement learning problem, the actions of the agent will give not only the immediate rewards but also the next state of the environment. The agent actually gets the immediate reward and the next state, and then agent needs to decide on further actions. Furthermore, the agent normally determines how it should take the future value into account; it's called **model of long-run optimality**.

The agent also has to learn from the delayed rewards; it sometimes takes a long sequence of actions to retrieve an irrelevant reward and, after some time, it reaches a state with a high reward. The agent should also learn which of its actions give it a high reward based on the past history. This will help decide future actions.

Let's take an example of a chess game. I played a long game of chess and it took *100* moves and at the end I lost the game. However, I actually lost the game on the 8th move; I made a mistake and reversed two moves because it was a new opening that I was just learning. From that point on, I played a beautiful game, but the truth is that the other player had an advantage that I never overcame. I lost the game, not because I played poorly but because I made one bad move and that move happened very early. This is the notion of a late reward. I played this long game of chess and maybe I played well and screwed up in the end.

Or maybe I played a mediocre game but I had a couple of brilliant moves and that's why I won. Or maybe I played very well in the beginning and poorly at the end. Or the other way round! The truth is that you don't really know; all you know is that you take a bunch of actions and you get the reward signal back from the environment such as *I won the game* or *I lost the game*. Then we have a problem: of all the actions I took, what was the action that led me to ultimately win or lose or get whatever reward I got?

In this particular case, we are in some state, take some action, and get some reward for the action we took. We get a sequence of state and action tuples and ultimately we have to figure out what action we took for the given state we were in. It helps to determine the ultimate sequence of rewards that we saw. This problem is called **temporal credit assignment**.

Now, we will look into the GridWorld example from `Chapter 1`, *Reinforcement Learning*. Think about how we learn to get from the start state to the goal (+1) or failure (-1) depending on the kind of reward we see.

In the GridWorld example, the only change is in the rewards we receive for all states other then the goal (green) and failure (red) state. Let's say we give the reward for all the states as +2, and goal and failure have rewards of +1 and -1. Just to remind you of the rule, the game continues until we reach the goal or failure state:

$$R(s) = +2$$

As the reward is +2, which is very high, and the target is to get the maximum rewards, in this case we will never get to the goal or failure state because the game ends as soon as it has reached to these states and that's the end of our treasure gathering:

+ (1,3)	+ (2,3)	← (3,3)	+1
+ (1,2)		← (3,2)	-1
+ Start	+ (2,1)	+ (3,1)	↓ (4,1)

Figure 2.2: GridWorld R(s)=+2

Refer to *Figure 2.2*; it displays what action the agent will choose when the reward is +2. Let's start with state **(3,3)**; what action should we take here? We should never go right because it's ends the game and we want to continue getting rewards. We should take left (←) to that state. So, we never reach the goal state. Now, consider we are in the state **(3,2)**. What action should be take here? We don't want to go to failure state because it ends the game and we don't want to go up because it has a chances that we take right from there. Instead we, should take left (←); in this case, we will be in the same state because we cannot go into the block state. In state **(4,1)**, we should not go up because it will end up the game. We would prefer to go down (↓) and, as this is the boundary state, it means we would be in the same state as we were. All other states with **+** don't matter because there is no chance to end the game and we continue getting the rewards.

As seen in the previous example, because the reward is positive and we just accumulate the rewards, we always avoid the goal and failure states. It doesn't matter that they have a **+1** or **-1** reward.

Now take another example as shown in *Figure 2.03*, where we the reward is -2 for all the states except goal and failure where reward is **+1** and **-1**:

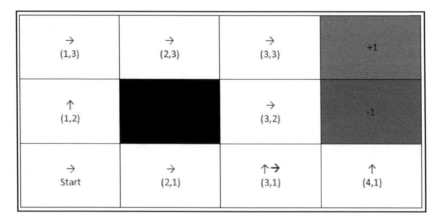

Figure 2.3: GridWorld R(s)=-2

Refer to *Figure 2.3*; it displays all the actions the agent can choose when the reward is -2. Now, our target should be to exit the game as early as possible, because traversing each state will give us a -2 reward. Let's start with state **(3,3)**; we would definitely go to the right (→) to get **+1** and end the game. Now, let's think about **(4,1)**. What action should we take? Should we go around and jump into the **+1**? That will take three steps of -2 reward each. It will become *-6* and at the end we will get *+1* reward, which makes it *-5*. The best we can do is go up (↑) and end the game. Now, consider the state **(3,2)**; we will go right (→) to end the game. For state **(3,1)**, we have both options to go right or to go up and end the game.

Here the reward is so strongly negative that we just need to end the game quickly. We try to take the shortest path to end the game no matter whether we finish at the goal or failure state.

Now, take one more example, where the reward is *-0.04*:

$$R(s) = -0.04$$

What will having this small negative reward encourage you to do? It's making us think about each step taken and a little bit of punishment. The best way to finish is to get to the goal state and get a +1 reward after the penalty of *-0.04* for each step. That means a small negative reward everywhere encourages you to end the game.

→ (1,3)	→ (2,3)	→ (3,3)	+1
↑ (1,2)	⬛	↑ (3,2)	-1
↑ Start	← (2,1)	← (3,1)	← (4,1)

Figure 2.04: GridWorld R(s) = -0.04

From the start state, it actually goes towards goal state and it's the same policy we saw before. Here, the interesting state is **(3,1)** where we can go straight up to the goal instead of going the long way round. But by taking the long way, we are picking up little bit of negative rewards for a while (*-0.24*) though we avoid going to the state that gives *-1*.

After looking into different reward values $R(s) = +2$, $R(s) = -2$ and $R(s) = -0.04$, it seems that minor changes in the reward matter. When the reward function's value differs, we see that some of the decisions are actually different.

Another way to think about a reward that it has main knowledge as it keeps the history of good and bad moves, our agent will only act and take a decision based on the history of rewards. If we want to design the MDP to capture some world, then we have to think carefully about how we set the rewards in order to get the behavior that we wish. No matter what you do, you have to inject the domain knowledge somehow; otherwise, there is no learning to do and, in this case, the reward is basically telling you how important it is to get to the end.

Optimal policy

What is our criterion for finding a good policy? In the simplest case, we'll try to find the policy that maximizes, for each state, the expected reward for executing that policy in the state. This is a particularly easy problem because it completely decomposes into a set of decision problems--for each state, find the single action that maximizes the expected reward:

$$E\ [r_t \mid \pi, s_t]$$

We've been assuming infinite horizons. When we think about the last GridWorld as per *Figure 2.04*, the game doesn't end until we reach an observing state. We have two observing states: goal and failure. This implies that the we live forever and we have an infinite time horizon to work with. If we don't have an infinite horizon to work with, we might end up with something different. In the GridWorld example where we have a reward of -0.04 and we find the optimal policy, imagine we were at **(3,1)** state. Rather than going up, it makes sense to go the long way round because we get some negative reward, but it's a small negative reward compared to the positive reward where we end up. This only makes sense if we will live long enough and we can afford to take the long route. What would happen if we have only three time steps left and then game would end no matter where we end up? Then it's clearly better to go ahead and quickly get to the **+1**, even though there is some chance to falling into **-1**, as opposed to trying to loiter on the long route where it's guaranteed that we will never reach **+1**.

Whether to take a risk or not depends on the reward and on whether we have infinite time to get to the observing state or not. If you don't have an infinite horizon but a finite horizon, then two things happen. One is that the policy might change because the GridWorld might have reached to an end because we are in a finite horizon.

Secondly and more importantly, the policy will change even though we were in the same state. Let say we are in the **(3,1)** state and we don't have infinite amount of time but we still have *100* million time steps. Then it still makes sense to take the longer route. But if I change this *100* million to two, three or four, then the policy will change even though we are in the same state.

We discussed the notion of policy that maps states to actions. In terms of Markov properties, it doesn't matter where we were; it only matters where we are now and always takes the same action. However, this is only true in an infinite horizon case:

$$\pi(s) \rightarrow a$$

If we are in the finite horizon case and it's counting down every time we take a step, suddenly, depending upon the time stamps left, we might take a different action:

$$\pi(s, t) \rightarrow a$$

It is important to understand that without the infinite horizon assumption, we lose the notion of stationary in our policy.

We have implicitly discussed not only the reward we get in the single state but also the rewards we get through sequences of states that we take.

Let say we have two sequences of states and we put them in the utility functions $U(S_0\ S_1\ S_2\ S_3\ .....)$ and $U(S_0\ S'_1\ S'_2\ S'_3\ .....)$:

$$If\ U(S_0\ S_1\ S_2\ S_3\ .....) > U(S_0\ S'_1\ S'_2\ S'_3\ .....)$$

Since S_0 is common in both the series, it also turns out as follows:

$$then\ U(S_1\ S_2\ S_3\ .....) > U(S'_1\ S'_2\ S'_3\ .....)$$

These are two different sequences and, in the beginning we were comparing them with S_0 in front of both the sequences. It means that S_0 following by all the S and S_0 following by all S primes, then we have the same preference when S_0 is missing and it is called stationary of preferences. Another way to look at it is as follows: if we prefer one sequence of states today over another sequence of states, then we will prefer that sequence of states over the same sequence tomorrow.

If we believe that the utility of one sequence of states is greater than the utility of another sequence of states, both today and tomorrow, then it actually forces us to do some variation such as adding sequence of states or adding rewards of the sequence of states.

The utility that we receive by visiting the sequence of states is simply a sum of rewards that we receive for visiting those states:

$$U(S_0\ S_1\ S_2\ S_3\ .....) = \sum_{t=0}^{\infty} R(s_t)$$

Now, the previous equation has a problem that it goes to infinity, like in our earlier example when reward was +2 the game never end.

Now, consider the following two sequences of states and the reward we receive; in the first one, we receive a reward of **+10**, and in the second one, some instances of reward are **+10** and some are **+20**. This goes on forever:

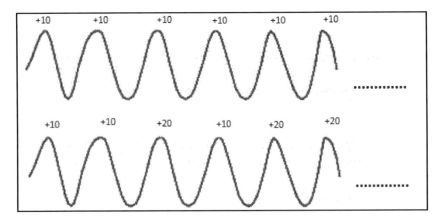

Figure 2.05 Sequence of states

Which is better? The answer is neither. Some people say that the bottom one is better because in the bottom we are getting **+20** rewards in some occasions. What is the utility of the top one? *10+10+10+10+10+10 .... = ∞*. And what is the utility of the bottom one? *10+10+20+10+20+20 .... = ∞*.

The utility of both of them is ∞. Is one of them is bigger than the other? Neither is bigger then other, because both of them are equal to ∞. The reason they are equal to ∞ is that all we do is accumulate rewards and we are always getting positive rewards no matter what we do. This is the existential dilemma of immortality. If we live forever and we can always get to a better place, then it really doesn't matter what we do.

If we look at the bottom sequence of states, because we are getting more rewards occasionally, it seems like the right intuition to have. But it's just not built into this particular scheme. It turns out that there is very easy way we can build this into utility scheme by making one tiny change.

All I have done is replaced the equation on top with an alternate version of the equation. I multiply γ with the rewards of states; here γ is between 0 and 1. So, it's exponentially implodes:

$$U(S_0\ S_1\ S_2\ S_3\ .....) = \sum_{t=0}^{\infty} \gamma^t\ R(st)\ 0 < \gamma < 1\ //Case\ 1$$

We will rewrite the previous equation and bound it with the largest reward we will ever see, in the following way:

$$U(S_0\ S_1\ S_2\ S_3\ .....) = \sum_{t=0}^{\infty} \gamma^t\ RMAX\ 0 < \gamma < 1\ //Case\ 2$$

What does it look like? This is a geometric series and is exactly equal to:

$$Rmax\ /\ (1\text{-}\gamma)$$

In the previous equation, when γ is close to 1, we divide by something very tiny, which is like multiplying it by something really big. So, it's magnifying the reward, but it's not infinity until γ gets all the way up to 1, and that's the same case we were in before. That's the reason we wrote that γ is between 0 and 1, 0 inclusive but strictly less then 1. If we include 1 also then it is exactly like the first case because 1 to a power is always 1. So, this is actually a generalization of the sort of infinite sum of rewards. This is called discounted rewards, discounted series, or discounted sum, and it allows us to go to infinite distances in finite times. The difference between case 1 and case 2 is that, by doing the discount, we get to add the infinite sequence and still get something finite. The intuition here is that since γ is less then 1, eventually as we raise it to a power, it becomes 0. This is like having a finite horizon but that horizon is always the same finite distance away no matter where you are in time, which means its effectively infinite.

The discount factor gamma is a number between *0* and *1*, which has to be strictly less than *1*. Usually it's somewhere near *0.9* or *0.99*.

This model has a very convenient property that the optimal policy is stationary. It's independent of how long the agent has run or will run in the future (since nobody knows that exactly). Once you've survived to live another day, in this model, the expected length of your life is the same as it was on the previous step, and so your behavior is the same as well.

More about policy

After going through the utilities and discounted reward, we can now write down what the optimal policy is. The optimal policy is simply π^*, the one that maximizes our long-term expected reward. We have an expected value of the sum of the discounted rewards at time *t*, given π:

$$\pi^* = argmax\pi \; E \; [\textstyle\sum_{t=0}^{\infty} \gamma^t \; R(S_t) \mid \pi \;]$$

These are the sequences of states we are going to see in a world where we follow π. And it's an expectation because things are non-deterministic. The policy that maximizes the value of that expression gives the highest expected reward.

We know what the optimal policy is, except that it's not very clear what to do with it. All we have really done is written down what we knew it was we were trying to solve. However, it turns out that we have defined the utility in such a way that it's going to help us to solve it. The utility of the particular state depends on the policy I am following and that's simply going to be the expected set of states that I am going to see from that point on given I am following the policy:

$$U\pi(s) = E \; [\textstyle\sum_{t=0}^{\infty} \gamma^t \; R(S_t) \mid \pi, \; s_0{=}s \;]$$

The difference in this equation compared with the previous one is that the utility of the policy out of state is what will happen if we start running from that state and we follow that policy. How good is it to be in some state? Well, it's exactly as good to be in that state as what we expect to see from that point on, given that we are following a specific policy where we started in that state.

Another important point is that the reward for entering a state is not the same thing as the utility for that state. Reward gives us immediate feedback, but utility gives us long-term feedback. The reward for a state is the actual value that we get for being in that state. Utility is both the reward we get for that state and all the rewards that we are going to get from that point on. Let's say I want to go to a college for a master's degree but it costs me $10,000. If I spend $10,000, at the end I get a degree. The point is that there is an immediate negative reward of $10,000. But at the end of the day, I get something positive out of it. It not just prevents you from taking short-term positive things if that is going to lead to long-term negative things, it also allows you to take short-term negative if it will lead to long-term positives. Utility is really about accounting for all delayed rewards. Given the following mathematical expression of delayed rewards, we will be able to start dealing with the credit assignment problem:

$$R(s) \neq U\pi(s) = E\left[\sum_{t=0}^{\infty} \gamma^t R(S_t) \mid \pi, s0{=}s\right]$$

Bellman equation

Now that we have the utility and π^*, we can actually do an even better job of writing out π^*:

$$\pi^*(s) = argmaxa \sum s' \, T(s, a, s') \, U\pi^*(s')$$

So, the optimal policy of a state is actually to look over all the actions and sum up the next state's transaction probability so that the probability ends up in the state s'. Now we have the utility of s' following the optimal policy. The preceding equation says that the optimal policy is one that, for every state, returns the action that maximizes my expected utility.

Now, this is rather circular, so it's basically a recursion. We will go through the exercise later in this chapter where we figured out the geometric series by effectively doing recursion. Now, I will write one more equation and we'll be one step closer to actually seeing it. Of course, if we are in the infinite horizon with a discounted state, even though we are one step closer, we won't actually be any closer:

$$U^{\pi^*}(s) = R(s) + \gamma \, max_a \sum_{s'} T(s, a, s') \, U^{\pi^*}(s')$$

The true utility of the state s then is the reward that I get for being in the state; plus, I am now going to discount all of the reward that I get from that point on.

Once we go to our new state s', we are going to look at the utility of that state. It's sort of modular recursion. We are going to look at overall actions and which action gives us the highest value of the state; it's kind of like the π^* expression. Once we figure that out, we know what actions we are going to take in state s' and we are going to discount that because it just ups the gamma factor in all the rewards in the future. Then, we are going to add it to our immediate reward.

In some sense, all I have done is kept substituting pieces back into one another. So, the true utility of being in a state is the reward you get in that state plus the discount of all the rewards you are going to get at that point, which, of course, is defined as the utility you are going to get for the states that you see; but each one of those is defined similarly. So, the utility you will get for s'' will also be further discounted, but since it's multiplied by gamma, that will be gamma squared. Then s''' will be gamma cubed, so that's just unrolling this notion of utility.

This is a very important equation, called the Bellman equation. This equation was invented by a Bellman, and in some scenes it turns out to be the key equation for solving MDPs and reinforcement learning. It is the fundamental recursive equation that defines the true value of being in some particular state. It accounts for everything that we care about in MDPs. The utilities themselves deal with the policy that we want, the gammas are discounted, and all the rewards are here. The transaction matrix is here representing the actions or all the actions we are going to take. So basically, the whole MDP is referenced inside of this and allows us, by determining utilities, to always know what's the best action to take. What's the one that maximizes the utility? If we can figure out the answer of the Bellman equation, the utilities of all the states, as perforce know what the optimal policy is. It becomes very easy.

Bellman was a very smart guy who took all the neat stuff of MDPs and put it in a single equation. Let's try to solve this equation, since it is clearly the key equation, the most important equation we are going to solve:

$$U\pi^*(s) = R(s) + \gamma \, maxa \, \Sigma s' \, T(s, a, s') \, U\pi^*(s')$$

How are we going to make that work? We wrote this down as the utility of s. How many s' are there? We have N states, which means this isn't really one equation. How many equations are there? N equations. How many unknowns are there in the Bellman equation? The R's are known, the T's are known, so the only things missing are the Us. There are N equations in N unknowns. If the equation is linear, then we know how to solve N equations in N unknowns.

We will further look into the solutions of the Bellman equation in `Chapter 3`, *Dynamic Programming*, in the *Value iteration* and *Policy iteration* section.

A practical example of building an MDP domain

In this section, we will do a practical MDP, which is used by many planning and learning BURLAP algorithms. We will cover how we can implement an MDP in BURLAP. Also, we will look into interaction with MDP and its visualization.

GridWorld

GridWorld is a 2D environment. It can be used by an agent to move in any direction (south, west, north, or east), one unit at a time, provided that there are no walls in the way. The following image is an example; an agent's position is highlighted with a gray circle whereas the walls of the environment are painted black. Mainly, the agent's goal in a GridWorld is to navigate to some location. However, there are many variants and we will look into GridWorld as an MDP.

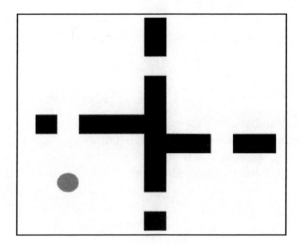

Figure 2.06: Example of GridWorld

In the GridWorld example in consideration, the set of states given are the likely places of the agent. The actions are west, north, east, and south. Considering that the agent will move in GridWorld in the anticipated direction with high probability (*0.8*) and in any other direction with a lower probability (*0.2*), we will define the transition dynamics to be stochastic. This can be stochastically imagined as a robot model that possesses slightly unreliable driving skills. The transition dynamics will also encode the walls of our GridWorld. This is done by specifying the particular movements that would lead into a wall, resulting in returning to the same state. We will also cover the reward function in this chapter.

Terminal states

The concept of terminal states comes in handy in various problems. We call it terminal state when the agent reaches a state and all further actions of the agent cease. It is used to define goal-directed tasks where the action of the agent stops when the agent reaches failure, goal conditions, and so on.

In out GridWorld example, we will specify the top-right corner to be a terminal state.

Java interfaces for MDP definitions

Familiarity with Java interfaces and data structures helps in defining your own MDP in BURLAP. This can further be used with BURLAP's planning and learning algorithm. We will also be implementing the interface to define our GridWorld. This is a **Unified Modeling Language (UML)** diagram for the aforementioned elements:

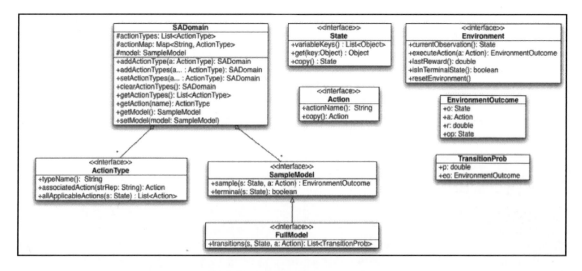

Figure 2.07: Java classes/interfaces of an MDP in BURLAP

Single-agent domain

Single-agent domain is also called `SADomain`. The data structure actually stores all information about the MDP that we define and passes this information to different learning and planning algorithms.

State

`State` is an interface and we implement it to define the MDP state space using a state variable. The instance of this object will define the state space from the single agent.

Action

`Action` is also an interface and we use this interface to define all the actions of the agent that it can perform. If our MDP action sets are unparameterized and discrete, then we can consider using `SimpleAction` and define the complete action in string format.

Action type

Action type is another interface; it uses a factory design pattern and is used to generate our agent actions. Furthermore, this interface provides an option to define the preconditions for actions. This means that we can define the preconditions for some specific set of states and not for all states. It also has a functionality that allows us to define the characterizations of agent actions that are allowed in the specific state. If the actions are unparameterizations, then those actions are allowed in all the states.

SampleModel

`SimpleModel` is also an interface and it helps us to define the MDP model. This interface is required to implement the method to provide sampling of transitions. It provides all the possible next states and the reward from a previous state on the specific action taken. Please note that some planning algorithms need more details, but on the other hand, to get more details, we need to provide more information. For example, some planning algorithms need the complete set of possible transitions with occurrence probabilities. If we are using this level of planning algorithms, then we have to implement the `FullModel` interface, which is an extension of `SampleModel`.

Environment

`Environment` is also an interface. MDP specifies the real nature of the environment; moreover, it requires an agent that will interact with the real environment, either for executing a policy or through learning. Environment is a certain state of the world where the agent will perform all its actions. We can get the environment where the agent can interact by implementing this interface. If we define the MDP by ourselves, then we do not need to implement this interface. We need to use the `SimulatedEnvironment` class and `SampleModel` with `SADomain` and we can simulate the complete environment by ourselves.

EnvironmentOutcome

A tuple that contains a previous state or observation also captures the action taken in that MDP specific state and a reward received, and even the next observation or state from where the environment transitioned. When an action is taken, it returns an environment instance from `SampleModel`.

TransitionProb

Also a tuple, it contains a double and an `EnvironmentOutcome` object; it specifies the probability of the specified transition by `EnvironmentOutcome`. When querying transition probability, it typically contains a list of objects returned by the `FullModel` instance.

Defining a GridWorld state

In order to define a GridWorld state, we will define how states look. We first create a class that will generate our `SADomain`; this will keep all the constants from various, very important values. Then we will use these constants when we define our state.

Now, let's start creating the `GridWorldExample` class, which implements `DomainGenerator`. Actually, `DomainGenerator` is an interface that is mostly used in BURLAP programs; it has a method for generating an object of `Domain`:

```
package project;

//We will import all the required java libraries
import java.util.List;
import java.awt.*;
import java.awt.geom.Ellipse2D;
import java.util.ArrayList;
import java.awt.geom.Rectangle2D;

//Now we will import all the BURLAP libraries, there are lot of them to
implement and it ease all our development

//This library is related to implement SA Domain
import burlap.mdp.singleagent.SADomain;

//This library is related to implement single agent simulated environment
import burlap.mdp.singleagent.environment.SimulatedEnvironment;

//This library is related to implement single agent model
import burlap.mdp.singleagent.model.FactoredModel;

//This library is related to implement state painter
import burlap.visualizer.StatePainter;

//This library is related to implement domain generator
import burlap.mdp.auxiliary.DomainGenerator;

//This library is related to implement transition probabilities
import burlap.mdp.core.StateTransitionProb;
```

```
//This library is related to implement state render layer
import burlap.visualizer.StateRenderLayer;

//This library is related to implement visualization
import burlap.visualizer.Visualizer;

//This library is related to implement terminal function
import burlap.mdp.core.TerminalFunction;

//This library is related to implement actions
import burlap.mdp.core.action.Action;

//This library is related to implement universal action type
import burlap.mdp.core.action.UniversalActionType;

//This library is related to implement states
import burlap.mdp.core.state.State;

//This library is related to implement reward function
import burlap.mdp.singleagent.model.RewardFunction;

//This library is related to implement full state model on single agent
import burlap.mdp.singleagent.model.statemodel.FullStateModel;

//This library is related to implement visual explorer
import burlap.shell.visual.VisualExplorer;

//This library is related to implement state painter
import burlap.visualizer.StatePainter;

public class GridWorldExample implements DomainGenerator {

  public static final String VARIABLE_A = "a";
  public static final String VARIABLE_B = "b";

  public static final String AGENT_ACTIONS_EAST = "east";
  public static final String AGENT_ACTIONS_NORTH = "north";
  public static final String AGENT_ACTIONS_SOUTH = "south";
  public static final String AGENT_ACTIONS_WEST = "west";


 public SADomain generateDomain() {
    return null;
    //For now leave it as it is, we will later use it
 }

}
```

Now, class with constants defined, let us now create a class that describes all the GridWorld states (we put all these states in a different file). Our class has to implement the State interface. Then, we will implement MutableState as well; it is actually an extension of the State interface. Let's implement it in the following code:

```
//We will import all the required java libraries
import java.util.Arrays;
import java.util.List;

//Now we will import all the BURLAP libraries, there are lot of them to
implement and it ease all our development

//This library is related to implement Deep copy state
import burlap.mdp.core.state.annotations.DeepCopyState;

//This library is related to implement mutable states
import burlap.mdp.core.state.MutableState;

//This library is related to implement state utilities
import burlap.mdp.core.state.StateUtilities;

//This library is related to implement exception handling
import burlap.mdp.core.state.UnknownKeyException;

import static project.GridWorldExample.VARIABLE_A;
import static project.GridWorldExample.VARIABLE_B;

public class GridStateEX implements MutableState{

@Override
    public MutableState set(Object keyVariable, Object objValue) {
        return this;
    }

    @Override
    public List<Object> keyVariable() {
        return null;
    }

    @Override
    public Object get(Object keyVariable) {
        return null;
    }

    @Override
    public GridStateEX copy() {
        return null;
```

```
        }

    }
```

As you can see in the earlier code, the GridWorld state will be completely defined by our agent's a and b location. Now, let's see the constructors and the data member in our class:

```
    public int a;
    public int b;

    public GridStateEX() {
    }

    public GridStateEX(int a, int b) {
      this.a = a;
      this.b = b;
    }
```

As you can see in the code, MutableState objects are not possible to modify or access as these are state variables and after defining them we cannot do these operations. The only way to access and modify these variables is when some client code exactly knows the type of state object.

Now, we need to define a class constant for the key variables:

```
    private final static List<Object> keys =
  Arrays.<Object>asList(VARIABLE_A, VARIABLE_B);
```

You need to note that we are using strings for the name of the variable and constants were already defined in the GridWorldExample domain generator.

Now let's implement the variableKeys, set, and get methods, which is done mostly as you would expect:

```
    @Override
    public MutableState set(Object variableKey, Object value) {
        if(variableKey.equals(VARIABLE_A)){
            this.a = StateUtilities.stringOrNumber(value).intValue();
        }
        else if(variableKey.equals(VARIABLE_B)){
            this.b = StateUtilities.stringOrNumber(value).intValue();
        }
        else{
            throw new UnknownKeyException(variableKey);
        }
        return this;
    }
```

```
@Override
public List<Object> variableKeys() {
    return keys;
}


@Override
public Object get(Object variableKey) {
    if(variableKey.equals(VARIABLE_A)){
        return a;
    }
    else if(variableKey.equals(VARIABLE_B)){
        return b;
    }
    throw new UnknownKeyException(variableKey);
}
```

Now we need to consider two things. Firstly, if the client code passes a variable that is not an a or b key, then we need to through an exception, UnKnownKeyException. Secondly, in the set method, we pass the variable value and process though the StateUtility method. This method accepts Object as input. If the object is of type string, then it returns the number instance of the number that represents string. If the object is of type number, then it simply returns it and casts as a number.

Now, we need to implement the copy method. This method should return the state object, which is simply a copy of this state:

```
@Override
public GridStateEX copy() {
    return new GridStateEX(a, b);
}
```

As the state data fields are just simple Java primitives, the copy will return a deep copy. Apparently, modifications in the copy state data members will not have any effect on the values of the state:

```
@DeepCopyState
public class GridStateEX implements MutableState{
    ...
}
```

Now, we are almost done with our GridWorld state. Let's add a `toString` method; it will be a meaningful string representing our state. To implement it, we simply use the method of `StateUtilities`:

```
@Override
public String toString() {
    return StateUtilities.stateToString(this);
}
```

Finally, we've completed defining the GridWorld state.

Defining a GridWorld model

Now, we are ready to define the GridWorld and we will also define the actions that generate rewards and transitions. To start up, we define the 11x11 GridWorld and it's divided into four rooms:

```
protected int [][] map_GridWorld = new int[][][]{
        {0,0,0,0,0,1,0,0,0,0,0},
        {0,0,0,0,0,0,0,0,0,0,0},
        {0,0,0,0,0,1,0,0,0,0,0},
        {0,0,0,0,0,1,0,0,0,0,0},
        {0,0,0,0,0,1,0,0,0,0,0},
        {1,0,1,1,1,1,1,1,0,1,1},
        {0,0,0,0,1,0,0,0,0,0,0},
        {0,0,0,0,1,0,0,0,0,0,0},
        {0,0,0,0,0,0,0,0,0,0,0},
        {0,0,0,0,1,0,0,0,0,0,0},
        {0,0,0,0,1,0,0,0,0,0,0},
};
```

We are going to use the `FactoredModel`, which is required to define the GridWorld model.

A `FactoredModel` divides its responsibilities into three components. `SampleStateModel` is the state transition, `RewardFunction` actually gets the rewards for the state `TerminalFunction` and `transitions` defines the terminal states of the MDP:

```
protected class GridWorldExampleStateModel implements FullStateModel{

    // We will implement it below

}
```

Now, we will define our domain and we have north, east, west, and south actions. The probability of 0.8 is defined so that the agent can go to the intended direction with 0.8 probability and 0.2 is the probability that it will take a random action:

```
protected double [][] transitionExampleProbs;

public GridWorldExampleStateModel() {

    this.transitionExampleProbs = new double[4][4];

    for(int i = 0; i < 4; i++){
        for(int j = 0; j < 4; j++){
            double p = i != j ? 0.2/3 : 0.8;
            transitionExampleProbs[i][j] = p;
        }

    }

}
```

Agent action in the GridWorld domain represents the `string` name (it should be implemented as an `int` value, but we did this here because of simplicity). This is the reason we need to write a method that converts an action name into an `int` value that will be used in the direction transition matrix:

```
protected int actionDir(Action a){
    int adir = -1;
    if(a.actionName().equals(AGENT_ACTIONS_NORTH)){
        adir = 0;
    }
    else if(a.actionName().equals(AGENT_ACTIONS_SOUTH)){
        adir = 1;
    }
    else if(a.actionName().equals(AGENT_ACTIONS_EAST)){
        adir = 2;
    }
    else if(a.actionName().equals(AGENT_ACTIONS_WEST)){
        adir = 3;
    }
    return adir;
}
```

Now, we need to define all possible outcomes from a state transition; we want to query the possible outcome when the agent is moving in some specific direction. We will implement this functionality in a method:

```
protected int [] moveExampleResult(int curA, int curB, int
exampleDirection){

    //first thing we will change in a and b from direction
    //using 3: west; 2:east; 1: south; 0: north;
    int adelta = 0;
    int bdelta = 0;
    if(exampleDirection == 0){
        adelta = 1;
    }
    else if(exampleDirection == 1){
        bdelta = -1;
    }
    else if(exampleDirection == 2){
        adelta = 1;
    }
    else{
        adelta = -1;
    }

    int na = curA + adelta;
    int nb = curB + bdelta;

    int _width = GridWorldExample.this.map_GridWorld.length;
    int _height = GridWorldExample.this.map_GridWorld[0].length;

    //Now we need to verify that it is a valid new position
    if(na < 0 || na >= _width || nb < 0 || nb >= _height ||
            GridWorldExample.this.map_GridWorld[na][nb] == 1){
        na = curA;
        nb = curB;
    }


    return new int[]{na,nb};

}
```

The previous method returns an array with two elements; the first element is the new position a of an agent and the other element is the y position of an agent. The basic functionality is just to add and subtract the value depending on the agent action direction. Furthermore, we also verify in the map that the agent position moves towards the wall; then, there is no value change in the position.

Now, we will implement this functionality in our code:

```
@Override
public State sample(State s, Action act) {

    s = s.copy();
    GridStateEX gsExample = (GridStateEX)s;
    int curA = gsExample.a;
    int curB = gsExample.b;

    int adirExample = actionDir(act);

    //sample direction with random roll
    double random = Math.random();
    double _sumProb = 0.;
    int _dir = 0;
    for(int i = 0; i < 4; i++){
        _sumProb += this.transitionExampleProbs[adirExample][i];
        if(random < _sumProb){
            _dir = i;
            break; //found direction
        }
    }

    //get resulting position
    int [] _newPos = this.moveExampleResult(curA, curB, _dir);

    //set the new position
    gsExample.a = _newPos[0];
    gsExample.b = _newPos[1];

    //return the modified state
    return gsExample;
}
```

We make a copy of the input state, modify it in the code, and return in the end. Then we retrieve the agent a and b positions by typecasting the state into our GridStateEX.

Now we are going to code the transition method:

```
@Override
public List<StateTransitionProb> stateTransitions(State st, Action act) {

    //get agent current position
    GridStateEX gsExample = (GridStateEX) st;

    int curA = gsExample.a;
    int curB = gsExample.b;
```

```
        int _adir = actionDir(act);

    List<StateTransitionProb> tpsExample = new
  ArrayList<StateTransitionProb>(4);
    StateTransitionProb _noChange = null;
    for(int i = 0; i < 4; i++){

        int [] newPosExample = this.moveExampleResult(curA, curB, i);
        if(newPosExample[0] != curA || newPosExample[1] != curB){
      //We will write the possible new outcome
      GridStateEX _ns = gsExample.copy();
            _ns.a = newPosExample[0];
            _ns.b = newPosExample[1];

            //Now create the object of transition probability and add this
  to our possible outcomes
            tpsExample.add(new StateTransitionProb(_ns,
                this.transitionExampleProbs[_adir][i]));
        }
        else{
      //Check if it is a block state, it means the possible direction is
  not changed.
            if(_noChange != null){
                _noChange.p += this.transitionExampleProbs[_adir][i];
            }
            else{
                //In case no block state then move the transition
                _noChange = new StateTransitionProb(st.copy(),
                  this.transitionExampleProbs[_adir][i]);
                tpsExample.add(_noChange);
            }
        }

    }


    return tpsExample;
  }
```

The previous method is very similar to our sample method. The only difference is that instead of random moves towards a specific direction, we iterate through all the possible states. For all of them, we copy the input state, change the position based on the `moveResult` method, and finally put it into `StateTransitionProb`. It is actually determined from the transition matrix.

We performed some extra steps to do bookkeeping in the preceding method. If the agent hits the wall, then the position will not change. If wall is in multiple directions, then all those directions result in no movement from the agent.

As we've just completed the state transition model, let's write the code for TerminalFunction and RewardFunction. We first write TerminalFunction:

```
public static class TFExample implements TerminalFunction {

    int goalA;
    int goalB;

    public TFExample(int goalA, int goalB){
        this.goalA = goalA;
        this.goalB = goalB;
    }

    @Override
    public boolean isTerminal(State st) {

        //get location of agent in next state
        int _ax = (Integer)st.get(VARIABLE_A);
        int _ay = (Integer)st.get(VARIABLE_B);

        //check if this is the goal state
        if(_ax == this.goalA && _ay == this.goalB){
            return true;
        }

        return false;
    }

}
```

Now, we will implement the reward function. Similar to the previous example, it returns a reward of +100 if it is a goal state; otherwise, it returns −1:

```
public static class RFExample implements RewardFunction {

    int goalA;
    int goalB;

    public RFExample(int goalA, int goalB){
        this.goalA = goalA;
        this.goalB = goalB;
    }
```

```
@Override
public double reward(State st, Action act, State sprimeExample) {

    int _ax = (Integer)st.get(VARIABLE_A);
    int _ay = (Integer)st.get(VARIABLE_B);

    //check if it is a goal state
    if(_ax == this.goalA && _ay == this.goalB){
        return 100.;
    }

    return -1;
}


}
```

Consider that the reward function is using _sprime instead of the s argument. The _sprime argument means the state where the agent transitioned; on the other hand, s means the state the agent just left.

Now we are almost done with our domain. We add the following two members into out GridWorldExample method to allow the clients to set up the goal state:

```
protected int _goala = 10;
protected int _goalb = 10;
```

Add the method as follows:

```
public void setGoalLocation(int _goala, int _goalb){
    this._goala = _goala;
    this._goalb = _goalb;
}
```

Complete the implementation of the method generateDomain:

```
@Override
public SADomain generateDomain() {

    SADomain domainExample = new SADomain();


    domainExample.addActionTypes(
            new UniversalActionType(AGENT_ACTIONS_NORTH),
            new UniversalActionType(AGENT_ACTIONS_SOUTH),
            new UniversalActionType(AGENT_ACTIONS_EAST),
            new UniversalActionType(AGENT_ACTIONS_WEST));
```

```
        GridWorldExampleStateModel _smodelExample = new
GridWorldExampleStateModel();
        RewardFunction _rf = new RFExample(this._goala, this._goalb);
        TerminalFunction _tf = new TFExample(this._goala, this._goalb);

        domainExample.setModel(new FactoredModel(_smodelExample, _rf, _tf));

        return domainExample;
    }
```

The GridWorld environment is ready and we've created all the major elements of the MDP; now, we can use the environment with BURLAP libraries. Lastly, we also need the visualization API to see GridWorld and be able to perform next actions.

Creating the state visualizer

Now it's time to create a visualizer. The way provided in BURLAP is to use state visualization. We need to implement `StatePainter` (one or more), which will be added to `StateRenderLayer`.

In our GridWorld example, we will use two objects of `StatePainter`, one for drawing the agent location and another for drawing the walls in GridWorld.

This will be the inner class in `GridWorldExample`:

```
public class WallPainterExample implements StatePainter {

    public void paint(Graphics2D _g2, State st, float _cWidth, float
      _cHeight) {

        //we display the wall in black
        _g2.setColor(Color.BLACK);

        //seting floats for the height and weight of our domain
        float _fWidth = GridWorldExample.this.map_GridWorld.length;
        float _fHeight = GridWorldExample.this.map_GridWorld[0].length;

        //check the single cell width
        //the complete map will be painted on the whole canvas.

        float _width = _cWidth / _fWidth;
        float _height = _cHeight / _fHeight;

        for(int i = 0; i < GridWorldExample.this.map_GridWorld.length;
          i++){
```

```
                for(int j = 0; j <
                  GridWorldExample.this.map_GridWorld[0].length; j++){

                    //Check if it is a wall
                    if(GridWorldExample.this.map_GridWorld[i][j] == 1){

                        //left coordinate of cell on our canvas
                        float _rx = i*_width;

                        float _ry = _cHeight - _height - j*_height;

                        //Now paint into the ractangle
                        _g2.fill(new Rectangle2D.Float(_rx, _ry, _width,
                          _height));

                    }
                }
            }
        }
    }

    public class AgentPainterExample implements StatePainter {

        @Override
        public void paint(Graphics2D _g2, State st,
                            float _cWidth, float _cHeight) {

            //agent will be filled in gray
            _g2.setColor(Color.GRAY);

            //set up floats for the width and height of our domain
            float _fWidth = GridWorldExample.this.map_GridWorld.length;
            float _fHeight = GridWorldExample.this.map_GridWorld[0].length;

            //determine the width of a single cell on our canvas
            //such that the whole map can be painted
            float _width = _cWidth / _fWidth;
            float _height = _cHeight / _fHeight;

            int _ax = (Integer)st.get(VARIABLE_A);
            int _ay = (Integer)st.get(VARIABLE_B);

            //left coordinate of cell on our canvas
            float _rx = _ax*_width;

            //top coordinate of cell on our canvas
            //coordinate system adjustment because the java canvas
            //origin is in the top left instead of the bottom right
```

```
        float _ry = _cHeight - _height - _ay*_height;

        //paint the rectangle
        _g2.fill(new Ellipse2D.Float(_rx, _ry, _width, _height));

    }
}

public StateRenderLayer getStateRenderLayer(){
    StateRenderLayer rl = new StateRenderLayer();
    rl.addStatePainter(new GridWorldExample.WallPainterExample());
    rl.addStatePainter(new GridWorldExample.AgentPainterExample());
    return rl;

}

public Visualizer getVisualizer(){
    return new Visualizer(this.getStateRenderLayer());
}
```

In the previous code from `AgentPainter`, we received the actual location of the agent through the x and y variables. Based on these positions, we will draw a circle.

Now, we will add some more methods for our class `GridWorldExample` to package the objects and visualize it.

Testing it out

Now that we've made all the pieces of our domain, let's test it out! A good way to test out a domain is to create a `VisualExplorer` that let's you act as the agent and see the state of the world through a `Visualizer`. Add the following main method to `GridWorldClassExample`:

```
public static void main(String [] args){

    GridWorldExample _gen = new GridWorldExample();
    _gen.setGoalLocation(10, 10);
    SADomain _domain = _gen.generateDomain();
    State _initialState = new GridStateEX(0, 0);
    SimulatedEnvironment _env = new SimulatedEnvironment(_domain,
      _initialState);

    Visualizer _v = _gen.getVisualizer();
    VisualExplorer _exp = new VisualExplorer(_domain, _env, _v);
```

```
        _exp.addKeyAction("w", AGENT_ACTIONS_NORTH, "");
        _exp.addKeyAction("s", AGENT_ACTIONS_SOUTH, "");
        _exp.addKeyAction("d", AGENT_ACTIONS_EAST, "");
        _exp.addKeyAction("a", AGENT_ACTIONS_WEST, "");

        _exp.initGUI();

    }
```

Now, we are ready to compile and run the program:

```
mvn compile
```

To run the code, use the following command:

```
mvn exec:java -Dexec.mainClass="project.GridWorldExample"
```

When you run the `GridWorldExample` class, the visual explorer should pop up, which will look like this:

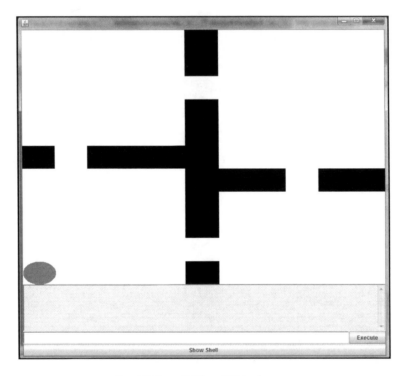

Figure 2.08: Output of building an MDP domain program

Markov chain

To build up some intuitions about how MDPs work, let's look at a simpler structure called Markov chain. A Markov chain is like an MDP with no actions and a fixed probabilistic transition function from state to state.

Let's take an example of a three-state Markov chain:

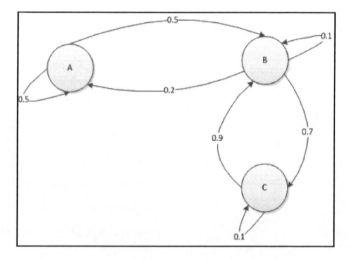

Figure 2.09: Markov chain, three states with probability

The transition probabilities are shown on the arcs between the states. Note that the probabilities on all outgoing arcs of each state sum up to **1**.

Markov chains don't always have reward values associated with them, but we're going to add rewards to ours. We'll make states **A** and **C** have an immediate reward of **0**, and state **B** have immediate reward of **10**:

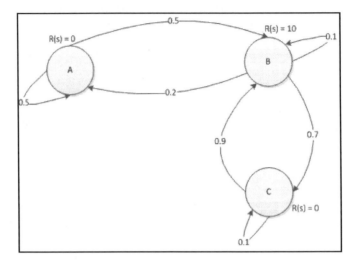

Figure 2.10: Markov chain with probability and rewards

Now, we can define the infinite horizon expected discounted reward as a function of the starting state. We'll abbreviate this as the value of a state:

$$V(s)$$

So, how much total reward do we expect to get if we start from state *s*? Well, we know that we'll immediately get a reward of *R(s)*:

$$V(s) = R(s)$$

But then, we'll get some reward in the future too. That reward is not worth as much to us as the reward in the present, so we multiply by the discount factor, gamma:

$$V(s)=R(s)+\gamma()$$

Now, we consider what the future might be like. We'll compute the expected long-term value of the next state by summing over all possible next states *s'*, the product of the probability of making a transition from *s* to *s'*, and the infinite horizon expected discounted reward or value of *s'*:

$$V(s)=R(s) + \gamma\Sigma_{s'}\, P(s'|s)\, V(s')$$

Since we know R and P (those are given in the specification of the Markov chain), we'd like to compute V. If n is the number of states in the domain, then we have a set of n equations in n unknowns (the values of each state). Luckily, they're easy to solve.

So, here are the equations for the values of states in our example, assuming a discount factor of 0.9:

$$\gamma=0.9$$

$$V(A)= 0+0 .9(0.5\ V(A)+0.5\ V(B))$$

$$V(B)=10+ 0.9(0.2\ V(A)+0.1\ V(B)+0.7\ V(C))$$

$$V(C)= 0+ 0.9(0 .9\ V(B)+0.1\ V(C))$$

Now, if we solve for the values of the states, we see that $V(A)$ is 40.5, $V(B)$ is 49.5, and $V(C)$ is 49.1. This seems at least intuitively plausible. State 1 is worth the least, because it's kind of hard to get from there to state two. State two is worth the most; it has a large reward and it usually goes to state three, which usually comes back again for another large reward. State three is close to state two in value because it usually takes only one step to get from three back to two:

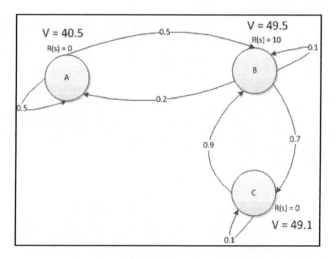

Figure 2.11: Markov chain with values of the states

If we set gamma to zero, then the values of the nodes would be the same as their rewards. If gamma were small but non-zero, then the values would be smaller than they are in this case and their differences would be more pronounced.

Building an object-oriented MDP domain

Let's consider the following decision problem shown in *Figure 2.12*. From the initial state **S0** we have a choice of three actions **a**, **b** and **c**. The immediate reward associated with each of these actions is zero but these three actions take us to different states with different possible rewards available from these states. Action a takes us to state **S1**, from which only action is to loop at each step back into state **S1** with reward of **P1**. If we take action **b** at the initial state, then we will spend the rest of the time alternating between state **S2** and **S4**. We will gain a reward of **P2** each time we move from **S2** to **S4** and we will receive the reward **P3** on the return trip. If we take an action **c** from the initial state we will move into state **S3** from which only next action is **S5** that has no reward. After that, we repeatedly loop in state **S5** with a reward of **P4** at each step:

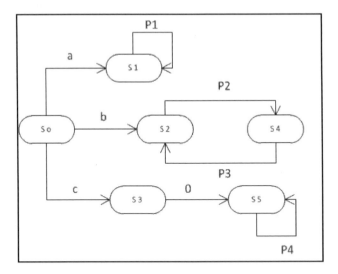

Figure 2.12: MDP state diagram

Now, the effective discount factor for this scenario is γ.

Given the parameters **P1**, **P2**, **P3**, and **P4**, our problem is to determine for which values of gamma we prefer the initial action **a**, **b**, and **c**. We will solve this problem by setting up a MDP encapsulating this state diagram in BURLAP.

Burlap uses the object-oriented paradigm to represent MDP. Here is the brief overview of how MDPs can be represented and created using the library.

An MDP as a whole is represented in BURLAP by a `Domain` object. Domains can be created directly but it is often useful to use one of several classes in BURLAP library, specifically to generate certain types of MDPs. These classes are implementations of the `DomainGenerator` interface:

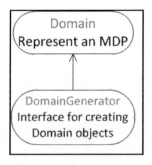

Figure 2.13: Domain

Let's begin the process of building our object oriented MDP to represent the state diagram, as demonstrated in *Figure 2.12*. Our first step is to define the set of states for our MDP:

```
package projects;

//We will import all the required libraries

//This library is for implementing run time exceptions
import javax.management.RuntimeErrorException;

//Now we will import all the BURLAP libraries, there are lot of them to
implement and it ease all our development


import burlap.mdp.auxiliary.DomainGenerator;
import burlap.mdp.auxiliary.common.SinglePFTF;
import burlap.mdp.core.StateTransitionProb;
import burlap.mdp.core.TerminalFunction;
import burlap.mdp.core.action.Action;
import burlap.mdp.core.action.UniversalActionType;
import burlap.mdp.core.oo.OODomain;
```

```
import burlap.mdp.core.oo.propositional.PropositionalFunction;
import burlap.mdp.core.oo.state.OOState;
import burlap.mdp.core.oo.state.ObjectInstance;
import burlap.mdp.core.oo.state.generic.GenericOOState;
import burlap.mdp.core.state.State;
import burlap.mdp.singleagent.common.SingleGoalPFRF;
import burlap.mdp.singleagent.environment.SimulatedEnvironment;
import burlap.mdp.singleagent.model.FactoredModel;
import burlap.mdp.singleagent.model.RewardFunction;
import burlap.mdp.singleagent.model.statemodel.FullStateModel;
import burlap.mdp.singleagent.oo.OOSADomain;
import burlap.shell.visual.VisualExplorer;
import burlap.visualizer.*;


//This library is related to implement Domain
import burlap.domain.singleagent.graphdefined.GraphDefinedDomain;

import burlap.mdp.singleagent.oo.OOSADomain;


//This library is related to implement Value Iterations
import
burlap.behavior.singleagent.planning.stochastic.valueiteration.ValueIterati
on;

public class OOMDPFirst
{

    DomainGenerator domain_generator;
    OOSADomain var_domain_;
    int var_StatesNum_;
    public OOMDPFirst()
    {
        this.var_StatesNum_ = 6;
    }
}
```

Notice that I am importing several packages at the beginning of the program. The class I build, OOMDPFirst currently has two fields, a Domain and a DomainGenerator. In my constructor for OOMDPFirst, I am instantiating a new GraphDefinedDomain and assigning it to the OOMDPFirst DomainGenerator field domain_generator. I then use a method from the GraphDefinedDomain object to generate an appropriate domain object, which is then assigned to the OOMDPFirst domain field.

Now that we have created the set of states, let's designate one of the states in our domain to be the initial state for the MDP. At the moment, we haven't defined any transitions between states. Let's added `initState`; field which has the type of the BURLAP object state. Now initialize this field in our constructor:

```
State var_initial_state;
```

Now, let's add actions to the domain as well. To add actions to the domain objects we generate, we can use the method built into the `GraphDefinedDomain` class, `setTransition`. This method is use to define both the set of actions and the transition function for the MDP. The first argument is `int` giving the ID of the state `S` we are transitioning from. The second argument is also `int`, giving the ID the action we are defining. The third argument is `int` giving the ID of the state `T` we are transitioning into. The forth argument is the `double`, giving the probability of transitioning to a state `T` upon taking this action:

```
public OOMDPFirst(double var_parameter1_, double var_parameter2_,
    double var_parameter3_, double var_parameter4_)
    {

        this.var_StatesNum_ = 6;
        this.domain_generator = new GraphDefinedDomain(var_StatesNum_);
        // actions from initial state 0
        ((GraphDefinedDomain) this.domain_generator).setTransition(0,
            0, 1, 1.);
        ((GraphDefinedDomain) this.domain_generator).setTransition(0,
            1, 2, 1.);
        ((GraphDefinedDomain) this.domain_generator).setTransition(0,
            2, 3, 1.);
        // actions from initial state 1
        ((GraphDefinedDomain) this.domain_generator).setTransition(1,
            0, 1, 1.);
        // actions from initial state 2
        ((GraphDefinedDomain) this.domain_generator).setTransition(2,
            0, 4, 1.);
        // actions from initial state 4
        ((GraphDefinedDomain) this.domain_generator).setTransition(4,
            0, 2, 1.);
        // actions from initial state 3
        ((GraphDefinedDomain) this.domain_generator).setTransition(3,
            0, 5, 1.);
        // actions from initial state 5
        ((GraphDefinedDomain) this.domain_generator).setTransition(5,
            0, 5, 1.);
    }
```

Notice that I am casting `this.dg`, which is our `DomainGenerator` object to a `GraphDefinedDomain` before calling `setTransition`. This is needed because `setTransition` is not defined for the `DomainGenerator` class. Another point to notice is that we are defining all of these actions before we call `this.domain_generator.generateDomain` call. We are calling the `setTransition` function first because it tells the `GraphDefinedDomain` object to include these transitions.

The next element of the MDP that we need to include is the `RewardFuction`. BURLAP comes with an interface which we can use to implement a custom `RewardFuction` in our code. First, we need to import the `RewardFuction` we did earlier then we add the `RewardFuction` member to our `OOMDPFirst` class. Now, within the `OOMDPFirst` class, let's make an static class that will implement the `RewardFuction` interface. I am going to call it `RewardFourParam`, since the rewards will be based on the four parameters `P1`, `P2`, `P3`, and `P4` we have in our state diagram. `P1` through `P4` will be member doubles of the `RewardFourParam` and the constructor for the `RewardFourParam` will just initialize these members based on the inputs. We can go ahead and add a line to the end of the constructor for `OOMDPFirst`. It assigns a new `FourParmRF` object to the `OOMDPFirst` new `._varReward_func` member:

```
RewardFunction _varReward_func;
_varReward_func = new RewardFourParam(var_parameter1_, var_parameter2_,
var_parameter3_, var_parameter4_);
```

Now, in order to implement the reward function interface we need to override the reward method. This should map the reward scheme from our state diagram.

The reward method takes a state, a grounded action, and another state. It actually represents the state before the action, the action taken, and the state entered after the action. The method needs to return `double`. Here, I used the static `getNodeId` method of the `GraphDefinedDomain` class to retrieve the ID of the state the agent is in before acting. Then based on the state ID, return the appropriate reward. In state zero and three, the reward is zero. In state one, the reward is `P1`. Then in state two, it is `P2`. In state four, the reward is `P3`, and in state five, the reward is `P4`:

```
public static class RewardFourParam implements RewardFunction
{
    double var_parameter1_;
    double var_parameter2_;
    double var_parameter3_;
    double var_parameter4_;
public RewardFourParam(double var_parameter1_, double
  var_parameter2_, double var_parameter3_, double var_parameter4_)
{
```

```java
            this.var_parameter1_ = var_parameter1_;
            this.var_parameter2_ = var_parameter2_;
            this.var_parameter3_ = var_parameter3_;
            this.var_parameter4_ = var_parameter4_;
    }
        @Override
    public double reward(State st, Action a, State sprime)
        {
            int _var__var_SID=6;
            double r;
            if(_var__var_SID == 0 || _var__var_SID ==3)
            {
                r=0;
            }
            else if(_var__var_SID == 1)
            {
                r=this.var_parameter1_;
            }
            else if(_var__var_SID == 2)
            {
                r=this.var_parameter2_;
            }
            else if(_var__var_SID == 4)
            {
                r=this.var_parameter3_;
            }
            else if(_var__var_SID == 5)
            {
                r=this.var_parameter4_;
            }
            else
            {
        throw new RuntimeErrorException(null, "Unknown State
"+_var__var_SID);
            }
            return r;
        }
    }
```

Finally, to complete the definition of our MDP, we need to specify the states in which the agent's action terminates. For this particular problem, the MDPs we are building won't have any terminal states. The `NullTermination` class implements the terminal function interface in such a way that no state is considered terminal. So, let's use the `NullTermination` class. `TerminalFuction` is already imported with the core package. To import `NullTermination`, we need to add the import statement, as follows:

```
import burlap.mdp.core.TerminalFunction;
```

Then, we need to add the `TerminalFuction` member to the `FirstOOMDP` class and set it to be a new `NullTermination` object in the `FirstOOMDP` constructor:

```
TerminalFunction tf;
//set it in the FirstOOMDP constructor
this.tf = new NullTermination();
```

Now that we've finished defining the MDP in BURLAP, we can use a planning or reinforcement algorithm provided by BURLAP to solve this MDP. We will solve it in the next chapter.

Summary

This is a good time to stop and ask ourselves what we have learned. The first thing we learned is the MDP; we learned all about states, actions, transitions, rewards, and discount.

I just want to point out that there are some people who think that the discount is a part of the definition of the problem and there are some people who think that it's more of a parameter to your algorithm. So, I tend to think of the discount as something you're allowed to fiddle with, as opposed to it being a fundamental part of the problem.

In any case, the important thing here is that there is some underlying process you care about that is supposed to represent the world--states, rewards, actions, and transitions--and capture that fairly well. The discount is, in some sense, an important part of the problem, because it tells you how much you want to care about the future versus the past. However, it's reasonable to think of it as something you might want to change outside of the kind of underlying physics of the world.

In some sense, the states, actions, and transitions represent the physical world and the rewards and discount represent the kind of task description. However, it would be great if we could decide to define states differently, and doing that would impact both your actions and the transition function and so on. However, the basic idea is right: there's some underlying process we're trying to capture and I think it's exactly right to say that states, actions, and transitions sort of capture it, while rewards and discounts capture more of the nature of the task you're trying to do in that underlying world.

In that context, we also discussed two really important concepts: policies and value functions (utilities). How do utilities differ from rewards? The utilities factor in the long-term aspects, and the rewards just tell us at each moment. Utilities are like a group of rewards. We discussed how we can assign a value to an infinite sequence of rewards, but it helps if we use discounting to do that so that we don't get infinitely large sums. This allowed us to deal with infinite sequences but treat them as if their value is finite, thus solving the immortality problem. All these things were tied up together in the Bellman equation itself, which is an awesome equation.

In this chapter, we also covered some practical examples such as building the MDP domain using BURLAP. Furthermore, we looked at how to implement object-oriented MDPs as well.

In the next chapter, we will look at how to solve the Bellman equation. We will further look into two approaches, value iteration and policy iteration. We will learn how to implement these algorithms using BURLAP. Furthermore, we will learn how to evaluate a policy. We will discuss Bellman equations and see the relationships between their different components.

3

Dynamic Programming

There are different methods of optimizing a reinforcement learning problem. In this chapter, we will be focusing on dynamic programming. Dynamic programming is a powerful technique for optimization and comprises breaking the problem into smaller subproblems that are not independent. This is very useful for breaking big problems into smaller problems. It is useful in mathematics (fields such as operations research and economics) and computer science (where the algorithm's complexity can be substantially improved through methods such as **memoization**). In this context, programming actually means planning, as dynamic programming consists of forming a table of solutions.

Dynamic programming, like the divide-and-conquer method, solves problems by combining solutions to subproblems. Divide-and-conquer algorithms partition the problem into independent subproblems, solve the subproblems recursively, and then combine their solutions to solve the original problem. In contrast, dynamic programming is applicable when subproblems are not independent, that is, when subproblems share subproblems. In this context, a divide-and-conquer algorithm does more work than necessary, repeatedly solving common subproblems. A dynamic programming algorithm solves every subproblem just once and then saves its answer in a table, thereby avoiding the work of recomputing the answer every time the subproblem is encountered.

Learning and planning

We know MDP; now we need to understand what it needs to learn in that context. The idea of being able to take a MDP model, which consists of a transaction function, **T**, and a reward function, **R**; it goes through some code and a policy comes out. We know that a policy is like *PI*. It maps states to actions. The whole activity is called **planning**:

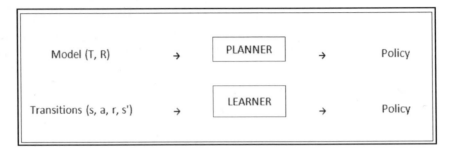

Figure 3.01: Learning and planning

Now we are going to look into a different setup here. We are still interested in spitting out the policy and figuring out how to behave to maximize rewards. However, a learner is going to do something different. Instead of taking a model as input, it's going to take a transition. It's going to take samples of being in some state, taking some action, observing a reward, and observing the state that is at the other end of that transaction. Using that information, we are going to learn a policy instead of computing it; we call this **learning**:

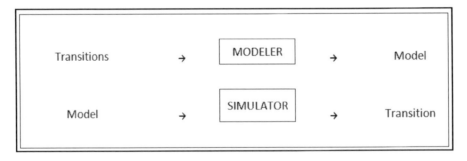

Figure 3.02: Subprocesses of planning and learning

We've discussed planning and learning; there are two other subprocesses or subcomponents that might be useful to think about. One is the notion of a **MODELER**; what the **MODELER** can do is takes a **Transition** and build a **Model** out of it. Second is the **SIMULATOR** and it is a kind of inverse, where it take a **Model** and generates a **Transition**. Now what we can do is combine *Figure 3.01* and *Figure 3.02*; so we have a **MODELER** that takes **Transitions** and turns it to a **Model**, and once we have a **Model**, we already know from *Figure 3.01* how we can use the **PLANNER** to turn the **Model** into a **Policy**.

Figure 3.03: Model-based reinforcement learning

Are there any algorithms for the planner? Yes, it is value iteration and policy iteration. So, we can run either of these planning algorithms; they take the **Model** and return the **Policy**. What do we call this approach or overall system that turns **Transition** into **Policy**? It's called **model-based reinforcement learning**. Let's contrast this with a kind of opposite idea. That is, we can map a **Model** through a **SIMULATOR** into a **Transition**. And then we have the ability to do reinforcement learning; we can use those **Transition** into **Policy**:

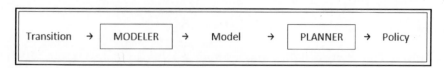

Figure 3.04: Model-free planner or RL-based planner

We start off with a model and then we pretend that we don't have a model. We are just in a learning situation by turning the model into transitions merely by simulating them. Then the learner interacts with the simulator and spits out a policy. We called this a **model-free planner** or **RL-based planner**. Just to point out, one of the most successful applications of reinforcement learning is Jerry Tassara's backgammon playing program, which used an RL-based planner. Backgammon is a board game, so we have a complete model of it, but we don't really know how to plan it. It's a very complex, very large state space. So, he actually used a simulator of backgammon to generate transitions and then used the reinforcement learning approach, **Temporal Difference (TD)**, to create a policy for that. Thus, his TD, **TD-Gammon** system, followed exactly this RL-based planner. We will learn about TD in the next chapter.

Evaluating a policy

We want our learning algorithms to return optimal policies. But to do that, we need to understand what we mean by optimal. We've already discussed policy in the context of MDPs, but I thought it might be worth revisiting just to see that there are different choices we can make. And the choices that we make have implications about what it means to be optimal. Let's say we have some particular policy that we're going to follow. By following that policy from some initial state, we're going to have a sequence of states, actions, and rewards. But there are actually multiple possible sequences of state, actions, and rewards because the domains are stochastic. So let's say that we've got some particular policy we want to evaluate and it generates the following first sequence of states with **0.6** probability, and second sequence of states with **0.1** probability, and third sequence of states with **0.3** probability:

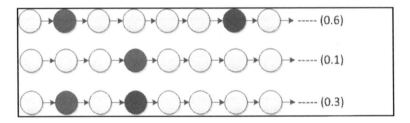

Figure 3.05: Evaluating a policy

How do we turn all those possibilities into a single number so that we can say that this policy is good and it has this value, but the other one is a smaller value, so should I like this one? What was a sequence of sequences, or a set of sequences of states, and turn them into a single number?

These are the four steps we need to evaluate a policy:

1. State the transition to immediate rewards or R.
2. Truncate according to the horizon or T.
3. Summarize sequences or *Return*.
4. Summarize over sequences or weighted average.

So the first step is actually a reward function. We need to add all the rewards of a particular sequence to get one number. The second step is truncating the sequence to a finite horizon (that is, in the preceding example, $T = 5$ means we only consider the states between *1* to *5* and cut it off after just five states). In the third step, we need to take that list of truncated numbers, and for each of the sequences, turn it into a single number for that sequence. This is also called *Return*:

$$Return = \sum T_{i=1} \gamma i\, R_i$$

Now you can imagine having a discount factor of *0.8*. This gives us a way of summing up the numbers that have been generated by these states and getting a single number for each sequence. Finally, the fourth step: we have to take those multiple numbers, one number for each of the sequences, and turn them into a single number that summarizes all of them. So, we just take the weighted average. Now we should be able to reduce this entire sequence to a single number. Let's consider the following parameters:

- $\gamma = 0.8$
- Reward at green is *+1*
- Reward at red is *-0.2*
- All other states' reward is *0*
- *T=5*

The first step is to put the rewards for all the states; as this is the finite horizon with *T=5*, we break the sequence and consider only the first five states:

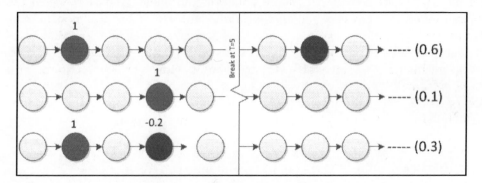

Figure 3.06: Evaluate the policy break at T=5

Now that we have done the truncating, we just need to summarize each of the sequences to get the value of $Return = \sum_{i=1}^{T} \gamma^i R_i$. Please note that the discounted value is γ^i and here i is the index number:

1st sequence = (0.8)1 (1) = 0.8

2nd sequence = (0.8)3 (1) = 0.512

3rd sequence = (0.8)1 (1) + (0.8)4 (-0.2) = 0.718

Now we need to calculate the weighted average; that is, for each sequence, we need to multiply the results of each sequence with the probability and then add them together:

= (0.8 * 0.6) + (0.512 * 0.1) + (0.718 * 0.3)

= 0.48 + 0.0512 + 0.215

= 0.7466

We reduce the entire sequence to a single number, that is, *0.75*.

Value iteration

Is the Bellman equation linear? No, because this equation contains max and that is problematic. This max operation makes the equation non-linear. So it's looking really good for a moment there. We have got N equations and N unknowns and we know how to solve that, but the max operation makes it a very weird non-linearity. And there's kind of no nice way to deal with this. So, we have got N equations and N unknowns, and they are non-linear. This means we can't solve it the way we want to. However, we can do something fairly similar, something that actually allows us to solve this equation. Here's the algorithm that, sort of works. It's really simple. We just start with some arbitrary utilities, but then we update them based on their neighbors. And then we simply repeat:

1. Start with arbitrary utilities.
2. Update the utilities based on the neighbors.
3. Repeat until convergence.

What does this based on neighbors mean? It actually means we are going to update the utility for a state based on all the states that it can reach. So, let's write down the equation that tells us how to update them and it will be clear:

$$U_{t+1}(s) = R(s) + \gamma \, max_a \, \Sigma_{s'} \, T(s, a, s') \, U_t(s')$$

We are going to have a bunch of utilities since we are looping through this. Let's just say every time we loop through is time t. So, I am going to update all of my utilities to make them better, and it turns out that I can do so by simply updating at every iteration. I estimate the utility of some state S by simply recalculating it to be the actual reward that I get for entering state S plus the discount utility that I expect given the original estimates of my utility. I am going to update the utility of S by looking at the utilities of all the other states, including itself and weigh those based on my probability of getting there given that I took an action. What action am I going to take? Well, the one that maximizes my expected utility. So, it's sort of figuring out what to do in a state assuming that the expected utility is the right answer for the future.

Why is this going to work? It just started out as arbitrary utilities. The next little step about updating utilities based on neighbors makes some sense because effectively a neighbor is any state that you can reach, which is determined by the transition function. But all I am doing is reaching states that are also made up of arbitrary values. Why should that help me? Well, because of $R(s)$. This is the actual truth. The actual reward I get for entering into a state is a true value. So, effectively I'll be propagating out the true value, or true reward, or the true immediate reward that I get for entering the state. Through all of the states I am going to see and propagate this information back and forth, until ultimately I converge. We start off with an arbitrary value and it seems like it could be really wrong. So do we like adding truth to wrong? Yes, but then the next time around I have been adding truth twice to wrong, and then more truth to wrong, and more truth to wrong. Eventually, I am adding more and more and more truth, and it will overwhelm the original wrong. It helps that the wrong is being discounted. I mean there's an actual proof you can look up but in the end I think, I tend to think this as a kind of simple contraction proof that effectively at every step you have to be moving towards the answer. Because you have added in more of the reality, more of the truth. The utility of the state is just all of the rewards that you are going to see. So, at every time step, you have added the reward that you are going to see, and then all the rewards that you are going to see after that. And so you have gotten the better estimate of the sequence of rewards you are like to see from the state. And if that gets better for any of the states, then eventually that betterness will propagate out to all the other states. That will just keep happening and you will keep getting closer and closer for the true utility of states until you eventually run out of closeness.

Does this also help that gamma is less than one? Yes, it does. The basic idea here is that you start out with some noise, but at every step, you are getting some truth, and the truth gets added, and then in the next iteration, more truth gets added and so on. So, as you have some estimate of some particular state S, you get to update it based on truth. It's an actual reward and you bring in more truth from the other utilities, as well. As the particular utility gets better, that closeness to the true utility is then spread to all the states that can reach it. Because gamma is less than one, you basically get to overwhelm the past in this case which is original arbitrary utilities. And so you keep iterating through this, the latest truth becomes more important than the past less truth. We're always getting closer and closer and closer to the truth. This is an easy way to find the true value of states and you can do it by iterating; it's called **value iteration**. It works remarkably well. So, it doesn't give the answer but it gets us something closer and closer to the answer. And eventually it will converge. We will get so close to the convergence it doesn't matter. And once we have the true utility, we know how to define the optimal policy in terms of utilities. So, if I give you the utilities, and you are in some state, then the optimal policy is just look at all the states you might get to. Figure out the expectation that you are going to get for a given action. Pick whichever one is maximum and it's done. So, solving for the utilities are the true value of a state. Is effectively the same thing as solving for the optimal policy. Now it seems like you know what we are doing, we can look into our GridWorld example. We have *Bellman Equation* and the *Utilities Equation*. These are just what we have written down earlier:

$$U\pi^*(s) = R(s) + \gamma \, maxa \, \Sigma s' \, T(s, a, s') \, U\pi^*(s') \, [Bellman \, Equation]$$

$$Ut+1(s) = R(s) + \gamma \, maxa \, \Sigma s' \, T(s, a, s') \, Ut(s') \, [Utilities \, Equation]$$

Now I want to figure out how value iteration would work from the first iteration and the second iteration for this particular state in *Figure 3.07* that I marked with x? And the information given as follows:

$\gamma = 1/2$

$R(s) = -0.4$ for all the states except the Goal and Failure states

$V0(s) = 0$ for all the states except for Goal and Failure states

$V1(x) = ?$ $V2(x) = ?$

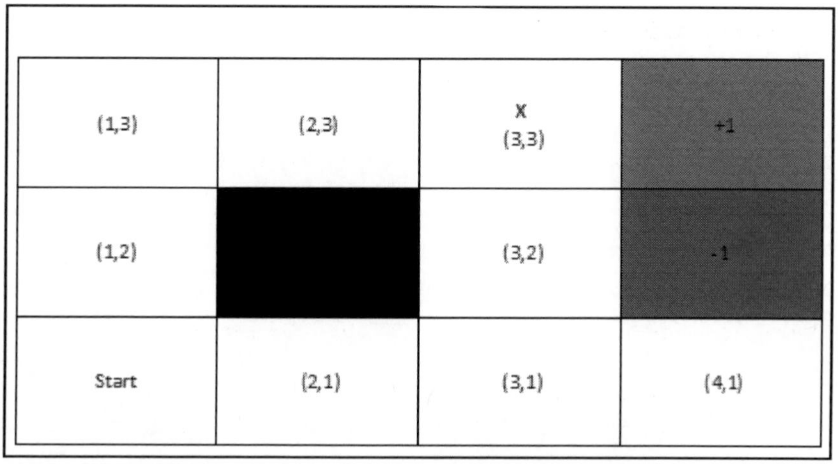

(1,3)	(2,3)	X (3,3)	+1
(1,2)		(3,2)	-1
Start	(2,1)	(3,1)	(4,1)

Figure 3.07: Finding policy in GridWorld

We are at state **x** that is **(3, 3)** as mentioned in *Figure 3.07*. According to the equation of utilities, the reward at *x*, which means *-0.04*, plus gamma which is *1/2*. Now we need to do the actions. There are three possible states we could go in. One is back to **x** that is **(2, 3)** and has a value of zero. Another is the underneath of **x** that is **(3, 2)** and also has a value zero. And the last one with probability of *0.8* that has a value of **+1** which is the goal state:

$$U1(x) = -0.04 + 1/2 \ [0+0+0.8(1)]$$

$$= -0.04 + 0.4$$

$$= 0.36$$

To do the same thing for U_2, we are going to need the U_1 values for a bunch of other states. So, we know that now the utility at **(3, 3)** is *0.36*. What was U_1 for the state **(3,2)**? As we want to avoid falling into the failure state, so that the best thing or the optimal policy for this state as we see in the previous sections, we should go up, which will get us *-0.04*. And all other states utility is *0* as mentioned in the question except the goal and failure state that has the utility of **+1** and **-1**:

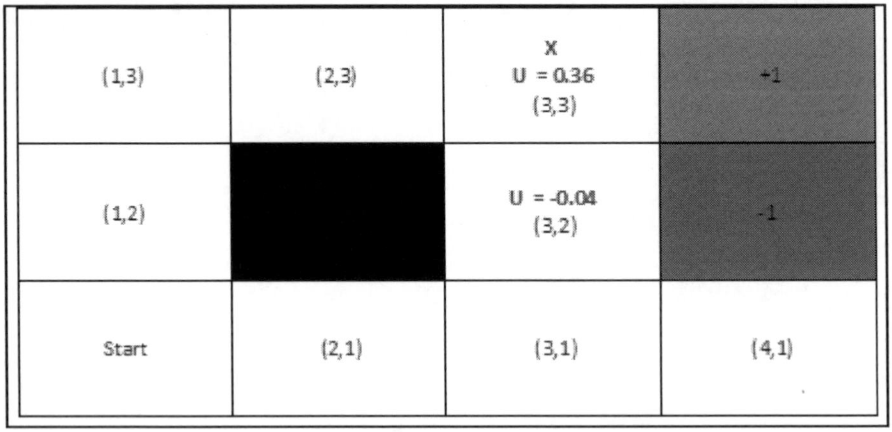

(1,3)	(2,3)	X U = 0.36 (3,3)	+1
(1,2)	⬛	U = -0.04 (3,2)	-1
Start	(2,1)	(3,1)	(4,1)

Figure 3.08: Finding policy U_2 in GridWorld

Now we will find a policy for $U_2(s)$ as follows:

$$U_2(s) = -0.04 + 1/2 \, [(0.36)(0.1) + (-0.04)(0.1) + (1)(0.8)]$$

$$= -0.04 + 0.416$$

$$= 0.376$$

Now you can notice that next time around the utility for the *x* state is bigger than zero. In fact, it will keep getting bigger and bigger than zero. As we can see, it went from *0.36* to *0.376*. Do you realize that the reason that the value iteration works is because eventually value propagates out from its neighbors. The first time we calculate *0.36* without really worrying about anything around it because the utilities are all zero, and in fact, based on the initial utilities even for the state **(3, 2)** we can go to block state instead of going to the up state. But after sometime, this state becomes a true representation of its utility and, in fact, gets higher and higher. You also notice that after another time step we are going to start looking at the value of state **(3, 1)** as well.

So, eventually we are going to figure out the utilities or the values for all the states. Goal state **+1** going to propagate out towards the other states. Where the failure state **-1** will propagate out less because we are going to try to avoid falling into the failure state. Now it propagating out is the true values of these states. But what's a policy? A policy is a mapping from state to action. It is not a mapping from states to utilities. So, if we have *U*, we can figure out π, but *U* is actually much more information than we need to figure out *pi*. If we have a *U* that is not the correct utility, but say, has the ordering of the correct actions, then we are actually doing pretty well. It doesn't matter whether we have the wrong utilities. We don't care about having the correct utilities, even though by having the correct utilities, we have the right policy. All we actually care about is getting the right policy, and order matters there rather than absolute value. Given utilities, we can find π, given π there's an infinite number of utilities that are consistent with it. So, what you end up wanting to do is get a utility that's good enough to get you to π. Which is one reason why you don't have to worry about getting the absolute convergence in value iteration. But it gives us a hint that something we might do that's a little bit better with the policies that might go faster in practice.

Value iteration implementation using BURLAP

Now it's time to do some code to understand the concept of value iteration. We will use BURLAP to implement this example. We start up we need to implement the class for value iteration, we name it as `MDPValueIteration`. This class will extend `MDPSolver` and it also implements two interface: `QProvider` and `Planner`. We are implementing `QProvider` because we need to implement the method `planFromState`. We implement `Planner` interface because we need to figure out the Q-value using the value iteration. One thing to note is that `QProvider` interface extends another interface called `QFunction`, and `QFunction` interface extends the another interface called named `ValueFuction`. We need to import all these interfaces and we are going to use it in our class `MDPValueIteration`:

```
import burlap.behavior.policy.GreedyQPolicy;
import burlap.behavior.policy.Policy;
import burlap.behavior.policy.PolicyUtils;
import burlap.behavior.singleagent.Episode;
import burlap.behavior.singleagent.MDPSolver;
import burlap.behavior.singleagent.auxiliary.EpisodeSequenceVisualizer;
import burlap.behavior.singleagent.auxiliary.StateReachability;
import burlap.domain.singleagent.gridworld.GridWorldDomain;
import burlap.domain.singleagent.gridworld.GridWorldTerminalFunction;
import burlap.domain.singleagent.gridworld.GridWorldVisualizer;
import burlap.domain.singleagent.gridworld.state.GridAgent;
import burlap.domain.singleagent.gridworld.state.GridWorldState;
import burlap.mdp.core.action.Action;
```

```java
import burlap.mdp.core.state.State;
import burlap.mdp.singleagent.SADomain;
import burlap.mdp.singleagent.model.FullModel;
import burlap.mdp.singleagent.model.TransitionProb;
import burlap.behavior.singleagent.planning.Planner;
import burlap.behavior.valuefunction.ConstantValueFunction;
import burlap.behavior.valuefunction.QProvider;
import burlap.behavior.valuefunction.QValue;
import burlap.behavior.valuefunction.ValueFunction;
import burlap.statehashing.HashableState;
import burlap.statehashing.HashableStateFactory;
import burlap.statehashing.simple.SimpleHashableStateFactory;
import burlap.visualizer.Visualizer;
import java.util.*;

public class MDPValueIteration extends MDPSolver implements QProvider,
Planner
{
 @Override
public double value(State st)
{
 return 0.0;
}
 @Override
public List<QValue> qValues(State st)
{
 // It is auto generate method
return null;
}
 @Override
public double qValue(State st, Action act)
{
 // It is auto generate method
return 0.0;
}
 @Override
public Policy planFromState(State asinitState)
{
 // It is auto generate method
}
 @Override
public void resetSolver()
{
 // It is auto generate method
}

}
```

As MDPSolver is a subclass, the instance will create the data members automatically that represent the domain and a task (it includes the discount factor represented as alpha, HashableStateFactory represented as hsf, and the domain represented as SADomain). Moreover, the major thing that value iteration needs to store is the estimation of the value function. The value function is eventually a representation between state to real value. As we are aware that HashMap provides fast access, we are using HashableStateFactory. It will enable us to give a HashableState object from the states. We also initialize all the variables and because we want it to run faster, we provide a value that is very close to the optimal value function. We also provide a parameter that clearly states until when it executes and when it will terminate. Now let's take up the following code as per the previous explanation:

```
protected Map<HashableState, Double> mdpValueFunction;
protected ValueFunction vinit;
protected int numIterations;

public MDPValueIteration(SADomain saDomain, double alpha,
   HashableStateFactory hsf, ValueFunction initializeVF, int
numIterations)
  {
  this.solverInit(saDomain, alpha, hsf);
  this.vinit = initializeVF;
  this.numIterations = numIterations;
  this.mdpValueFunction = new HashMap <HashableState, Double> ();
  }
```

As our super class MDPSolver will keep the our members for HashableStateFactory, discount factor, and domain, we need to initialize them using the solverInit method. One more important component value iteration (VI) is needed. We did not provide this parameter to the constructor that is the full state space. The reason we did not provide it upfront that it is a MDP and for state space it will be infinite because for any given input only the finite set of state space is reachable. We need to provide the algorithm that defines our state space. But for the sake of clarity, we provide the set of all possible states from any given state ourselves, and this operation is performed only when the planning details are requested from the unseen state. Now let's define all these in the code:

```
public void performReachabilityFrom(State sState)
  {
  Set<HashableState> hashStates =
    StateReachability.getReachableHashedStates(sState, this.domain,
    this.hashingFactory);

//initialize the value function for all states
  for(HashableState hash: hashStates)
  {
```

```
   if (!this.mdpValueFunction.containsKey(hash))
   {
      this.mdpValueFunction.put(hash, this.vinit.value(hash.s()));
   }
  }
 }
```

Let me explain the previous code. The first thing we did is to use the BURLAP API, `StateReachability`, to determine all the reachable states, and then we just iterate the list. For all the `HashableState` that we never had an entry to initialize it to the value, it is coming from the `ValueFunction`. You can note that the value function is just `hash.s()`. So our states are actually sets of `HashableState` objects.

Now we need to implement the q_Value and we've already defined the method for getting q_Value of the states. So, we will implement the methods as a Bellman equation:

```
@Override
public List<QValue> qValues(State st) {
 List<Action> app_Actions = this.applicableActions(st);
 List<QValue> qValue_state = new ArrayList<QValue>(app_Actions.size());
 for(Action act : app_Actions){
    qValue_state.add(new QValue(st, act, this.qValue(st, act)));
 }
 return qValue_state;
}


@Override
public double qValue(State st, Action act) {
if(this.model.terminal(st)){
 return 0.;
 }

//We need to check the possible outcomes
 List<TransitionProb> tran_prob = ((FullModel)this.model).transitions(st,
act);

//We need to aggregate all the possible outcome
 double aggregate_q = 0.;
 for(TransitionProb tran_probability : tran_prob){

//Now we need to check the reward for the transition
 double reward = tran_probability.eo.r;

//We also need to determine the value of the next state
 double valueP=this.mdpValueFunction.get
    (this.hashingFactory.hashState(tran_probability.eo.op));
```

```
//now add the contribution weighted using discounting and
//transition probability for the next state
aggregate_q += tran_probability.p * (reward + this.gamma * valueP);
}
return aggregate_q;
}
```

One thing to note is the `q_Value` method returns a value of `QValue`. We will explain the Q-function in the next chapter, so for now, no need to worry about it. You may be thinking where these model data members come from. Let me explain it here. As we extend the class `MDPSolver` and we call the method `solverInit`, it then automatically opens the model that includes the domain and a model data member. This is the most effective and convenient way, because we also allow a client to change that model to something else whenever it comes out of the domain object. It is called the `setModel` method. Note the model cast to the `SampleModel` interface. To implement dynamic programming, we require a `Full_Model`, and we think that the model is of the same type, so we typecast to it and call the `Full_Model` transition method. Now we have everything to do the planning and it's time to do the implementation of the method `planFromState`. When we want to run the planning from the initial state, we call this method. In this method, we need to check if the planning is already running on that state. If it is running, then we will not do anything assuming that we already have the complete value for it. But if the planning is not running, then we need to find all the reachable states and run a value iteration for the provided number of iterations. Just to revise for you, running a value iteration in an iterative manner for the complete state space and the value of each state is re-estimated as per the Bellman equation. At the end of the `planFromState`, we need to return a suitable policy instance to implement the planning results. Let's say the value iteration is converged. The optimal policy is the highest Q-value. So, we will return a `GreedyQPolicy` instance:

```
@Override
public GreedyQPolicy planFromState(State initState) {

    HashableState hashedInitState =
        this.hashingFactory.hashState(initState);
    if(this.mdpValueFunction.containsKey(hashedInitState)){

//doing planning here
    return new GreedyQPolicy(this);
    }

//In case this state is new then we need to find all the reachable state
from this state
    this.performReachabilityFrom(initState);

//We need to do the iterations over the complete state space
```

```
  for(int i = 0; i < this.numIterations; i++){

//Each state to iterate
 for(HashableState sh : this.mdpValueFunction.keySet()){

//value update as per bellman equation
 this.mdpValueFunction.put(sh, QProvider.Helper.maxQ(this, sh.s()));
 }
 }
 return new GreedyQPolicy(this);
 }
```

Now we are almost done. We just need to implement the resetSolver method in the MDPSolver, which resets all of the data if no planning calls had been made. For the implementation of value iteration, just clear the value function:

```
@Override
public void resetSolver() {
   this.mdpValueFunction.clear();
}
```

To test the code, we need to use the planning algorithm with the GridWorld as we implemented in the earlier chapters. Or we can also implement the main method as per the following code to test the value iteration implementation with GridWorld. It also evaluates a single roll out of the resulting policy and we can see the results graphically as well:

```
public static void main(String [] args){

 GridWorldDomain grid_world_domain = new GridWorldDomain(11, 11);
 grid_world_domain.setTf(new GridWorldTerminalFunction(10, 10));
 grid_world_domain.setMapToFourRooms();

//set the value to 80% to go to intended direction
 grid_world_domain.setProbSucceedTransitionDynamics(0.8);
 SADomain sa_Domain = grid_world_domain.generateDomain();

//get initial state with agent in 0,0
 State st = new GridWorldState(new GridAgent(0, 0));

//set a discount factor to 0.99 discount factor, a value function that
initializes
 //the states to 0, and will run for about 30 iterations
 //over the state space
 MDPValueIteration value_Iteration = new MDPValueIteration(sa_Domain, 0.99,
new
    SimpleHashableStateFactory(), new ConstantValueFunction(0.0), 30);
```

```
//run planning from our initial state
 Policy policy = value_Iteration.planFromState(st);

//evaluate the policy with one roll out visualize the trajectory
Episode episode = PolicyUtils.rollout(policy, st, sa_Domain.getModel());
Visualizer v =
GridWorldVisualizer.getVisualizer(grid_world_domain.getMap());
  new EpisodeSequenceVisualizer(v, sa_Domain, Arrays.asList(episode));

}
```

Now we are ready to compile and run the program:

```
mvn compile
mvn exec:java -Dexec.mainClass="project.MDPValueIteration"
```

Output of the value iteration

Here's the output of our `MDPValueIteration` program as shown in *Figure 3.09*.

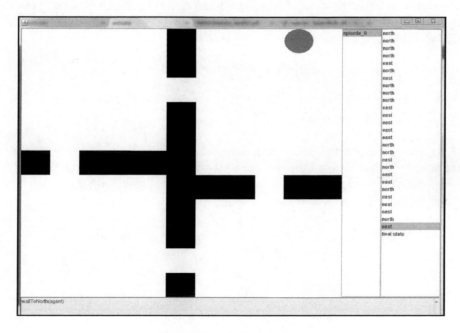

Figure 3.09: Output of the value iteration

Policy iteration

Now let's see whether we can do something that might be faster and just as good as what we have been doing with value iterations. We are going to emphasize the fact that we care about policies, not values. Now it's true that given the true utilities we can find a policy, but maybe we don't have to find the true utilities in order to find the optimal policy. So, here is the algorithm; it's going to look a lot like value iteration:

1. Start with π_0 <--- *Guess*.
2. Evaluate the given π_t calculate $U_t = U^{\pi}_t$.
3. Improve $\pi_{t+1} = argmax_a \sum T(s, a, s') U_t(s')$.

We are going to start with some initial policy; let's call it π. That's just going to be a guess, so it's going to be an arbitrary setting of actions that you should take in different states. Then we are going to evaluate how good that policy is, and the way we are going to evaluate it at time T is by calculating its utility. I call it U sub t, which is equal to the utility we get by following a policy. So, given a policy, we are able to evaluate it by figuring out what the utility of that policy is. Then we are actually going to improve that policy in a way similar to what we did with value iteration. We are going to update our policy, Time t plus 1, to be the policy that takes the action that maximizes the expected utility based on what we just calculated for π_t.

Notice that this will allow us to change π over time because:

- If we discover that in some state where there is a very good action
- That state gets you to some really nice place

it gives you a really big reward. This continues and you do fairly well. Well, then all other states that can reach that state might end up taking a different action than they did before, because now the best action would be to move towards that state. So, step 2 and 3 can actually lead to some improvement of the policy over time. But the key thing we have to figure out here is exactly how to compute U_t. Well, the good news is that we know how to do it, and it's actually pretty easy. It boils down to our favorite domain equation:

$$U_t(s) = R(s) + \gamma \sum_{s'} T(s, \pi_t(s), s') U_t(s')$$

It's similar to the Bellman equation, but note that max is gone. Instead of max, there's a policy in the transition function. A choice of action is being determined by the policy, and that's actually the only difference between now and what we were doing before. Rather than having this max over actions, we already know what action we are going to take. It's determined by the policy we are currently following. It isn't just as hard as solving with max. What was the problem that we were solving before with the max? The Bellman equation, and we were solving a bunch of equations! How many of them? We were solving N equations. And how many of them are unknowns? We have N unknowns. What's the difference between domain, N equations and N unknowns and Bellman, N equations with N unknowns? N is the same and there is no max. And what was it that made solving so hard before? The max made the equation non-linear. It is now gone and this is a set of linear equations. It's just a bunch of sums and π is effectively a constant.

So, we have N equations and N unknowns, but it's a linear equation. Now that we have in linear equations and unknowns, we can actually compute this in a reasonable amount of time. It appears so. Is it still more expensive than doing value iteration? Yes, but here we don't have to do as many iterations as we were doing before. So once we have evaluated it, which we know how to do, and we've improved it, we just keep doing that until the policy doesn't change. This does look a lot like value iteration, doesn't it? It seems like making bigger jumps somehow in the policy space instead of the value space. Hence we call it policy iteration.

This inversion can still be very painful if we don't worry about being highly efficient. We know it's roughly N cubed, and if there are a lot of states, this can be kind of painful. But it turns out that there's a little trick we can do: a little step evaluate iteration here for a while to get an estimate. Then we can, kind of, cycle through. So, there are all kinds of clever things we might want to do, but at a high level, without worrying about anything, you know the details of the constants, it is a general process of moving through policy space. By picking a specific policy, we are able to turn a non-linear equation into a linear equation. Taking advantage of this often turns out to be very helpful.

Bellman equations

In the last chapter, we learn about Bellman equations, that the value of a state is the max over of:

- All the actions
- The reward that you get for taking that action on this state
- Plus the discounted value of the state

you end up in weighted by the probability.

Here's the Bellman equation for a quick reference:

$$U(s) = R(s) + \gamma \, max_a \, \Sigma s' \, T(s, a, s') \, U(s')$$

Now, I am going to change it a little bit, as follows:

$$V(s) = max_a \, (R(s, a) + \gamma \, \Sigma s' \, T(s, a, s') \, V(s'))$$

What's the difference in both the equations? First of all, the parenthesis just lets us group things. Then I use *V* for value instead of utility. And I write rewards as *R(s, a)* instead of *R(s)*. As we learned in the previous chapter, *R(s)*, *R(s,a)*, and *R(s, a, s')* all are mathematically equivalent. It's just the notational difference and it really leads you to the same stuff:

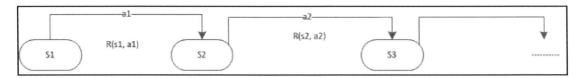

Figure 3.10: State diagram

The Bellman equation is supposed to represent the sequence of rewards received by an agent that's hopping around the world. It starts off in state **s1**, takes an action **a1**, and gets a reward **R(s1, a1)**. Then it lands at state **s2**. From there, it takes an action **a2** and receives a reward of **R(s2, a2)**. It ends up in state **s3**. This process continues forever.

We write the value of the sequence for *Figure 3.10* as per our equation:

$$V(s1) = maxa_1(R(s1, a1) + \gamma \Sigma s2 \, T(s1, a1, s2) \, maxa_2(R(s2, a2) + \gamma \Sigma s3 \, T(s2, a2, s3).......\,)$$

We start off with state s_1, and notice that eventually we get to some new state, in this case, s_2. This value can also be represented by the value function, so that is what gives us this recursive form. The value of the next state can be plugged in to represent the infinite rest of the sequence, as depicted here:

$$V(s1) = maxa_1(R(s1, a1) + \gamma \Sigma s2 T(s1, a1, s2)$$

$$V(s2)\ maxa_2(R(s2, a2) + \gamma \Sigma s3 T(s2, a2, s3)\ V(s3)\ \dots\dots)$$

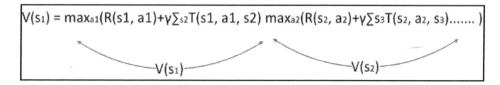

Figure 3.11: Recursive equation

We are going to generalize this Bellman equation to Bellman equations. We are going to do so by noting that in the previous derivation we capture the $V(s)$ and the whole V consists of sub V in it. You have an infinite number of these things going on forever and ever. So there are actually a number of other ways we can group this infinite sequence:

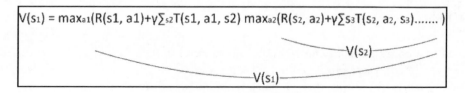

Figure 3.12: Recursive equation called as Q(s, a)

The expression after the max, starting from R, and then moving forward repeats again as $V(S_2)$. So we can actually make a new equation that depends on the substructure repeated. Let me write that out:

$$Q(s, a) = R(s, a) + \gamma \Sigma s'\ T(s, a, s')\ max_{a'}\ Q(s', a')$$

$$Q(a) = R(s, a) + \gamma \Sigma s'\ T(s, a, s')\ max_{a'}\ Q(a')$$

I will call it $Q(s, a)$ and I will say it's equal to $R(s, a)$ plus the discount factor times the sum over the next possible state, so the probability of getting there, times $max\ a'$, our next max, of and then there's that repeating structure again. So, we can just plug in Q of s prime for that. This gives us another Bellman equation that, instead of starting at the S point, starts after the action has started.

So here's a summary of what we just discussed. We actually have these two different forms of the Bellman equation. One is *V*, which we can think of as standing for value and the other is *Q*, which we can think of as standing for quality. But mostly, they're just letters from the end of the alphabet that we made up names for. Likewise, we had *U* for utility; so these are *V* for value and *Q* for quality. Anyway, the point is that these are just expressions that represent different pieces of overall sequence of states, rewards, and actions:

$$V(s) = max_a \, (R(s, a) + \gamma \, \Sigma s' \, T(s, a, s') \, V(s'))$$

$$Q(s, a) = R(s, a) + \gamma \, \Sigma s' \, T(s, a, s') \, max_{a'} \, Q(s', a')$$

Why are we bothering to create this quality function when the value function worked just fine? In some sense, because they are both equally good. But in fact what's going to turn out to be the case is that this Q form of the Bellman equation is going to be much more useful in the context of reinforcement learning. The reason for this is that we will be able to take expectations of infinite quantity using experienced data. And we don't actually need to have direct access to the reward function or the transition function to do that. Whereas if we are going to try to learn *V* values, the only way to connect one *V* value to the next *V* value is by knowing the transitions and rewards. So this is going to be really helpful in the context of reinforcement learning, where we don't know the transitions and rewards in advance. We have got the *V* function telling us what happens when we are at a state. We also have a Q-function to tell us what would happen when we are at an action. There should be at least one more thing when you're at the infinite state and getting a reward and that's *R*. We write it as *C(s, a)*; here *C* is just a representation and we called it continuation. The idea was introduced in a paper by Tom Dietrich. In it he showed that sometimes if the reward function is really complicated, it can help to derive or re-express the Bellman equation in the following form where the reward gets left off and we only observe the reward later in the flow:

$$C(s, a) = \gamma \, \Sigma_{s'} \, T(s, a, s') \, max_{a'} \, R(s', a') + C(s', a')$$

We have gotten into a state, we took an action, and then we sort of got our self reward. Now I want to know what's going to happen next. So I'm going to get the discount sorted towards the future. What's the future? Well, the future is, I have to get to the next state. That summation over *S* prime is my expectation on where I'm going to end up next. It refers to *s* and *a*, which are passed in, on the left side of the equation. Then I'm going to actually take the best action, and I will see the reward that I got for taking the action in the state I ended up in. That puts me in the same place I was in before and so I can continue with the rest of the sequence.

The relationship between Bellman equations

All these different Bellman equations, since they come from that same infinite sequence, can be related to each other like "by blood":

$$V(s) = max_a \ (R(s, a) + \gamma \sum_{s'} T(s, a, s') \ V(s'))$$

$$Q(s, a) = R(s, a) + \gamma \sum_{s'} T(s, a, s') \ max_{a'} \ Q(s', a')$$

$$C(s, a) = \gamma \sum_{s'} T(s, a, s') \ max_{a'} \ R(s', a') + C(s', a')$$

So what we will fill in the following table? how do we express the V function in terms of the Q-function? How do we express the V function in terms of the C function? Each row here shows how we express that function in terms of the other three:

	V	Q	C
V	$V(s) = V(s)$	$V(s) =$	$V(s) =$
Q	$Q(s, a) =$	$Q(s, a) = Q(s)$	$Q(s, a) =$
C	$C(s, a) =$	$C(s, a) =$	$C(s, a) = C(s)$

The one that I am going to do is really easy: writing V in terms of Q. If we think about the equation, the value is immediately a max over actions. So it's just the max of over actions of $Q(S,a)$. One way of saying that is the true value of a state is just, we are going to take the best action. It's the value of each of the actions you could take in the state, the best of which is the one we are actually going to take. $V(s) = max_a \ Q(s, a)$ Now we will write for V in terms of C and there is a similar argument to make for C. You had a state followed by an action, and that gives you Q. But in C, you have sort of the state followed by an action, and a reward. So C is happening after the reward, right. It should be the reward that you get plus C. $V(s) = max_a \ R(s, a) + C(s, a)$ So one of the things that's interesting, already, if we have C and we want V, we still need to know the reward function. But if we want V and we know Q, we don't need any other special knowledge about the way the model works. The Q-values kind of encapsulate all that we need in terms of, at least for computing, V. Now we need to write for Q in terms of V, here V in terms of Q and C is easier because it's the future. V is like the first thing before the future comes along. And Q and C captures the next set of things in the sequence. The equation start with $R(s, a)$ and then after that, once we have the rewards, it's just, discounted value where we are going to end up next. So what's the end of this thing? V of S prime. So the trick there, is to realize that we don't have to go backwards in time. We just have to unroll the infinite sequence until we get to a point where we can express it in terms of V:

$$Q(s, a) = R(s, a) + \gamma \sum_{s'} T(s, a, s') \ V(s')$$

Now we need to write for Q in terms of C. I just substitute what I write about V and it can be expressed in terms of C and by substituting the bit for the V that we did in Q. $Q(s, a) = R(s, a) + C(s, a)$. The next box is C in terms of V; we again start as we did before to substitute the V in the C equation:

$$C(s, a) = \gamma \, \Sigma s' \, T(s, a, s') \, V(s')$$

The continuation for being in some state and taking some action is the discounted next state value, which we already have in this case (we have V). Now the last box, that is, C in terms of Q. There's a similar argument there. Just write the same C equation and then replace this part with $Q(s, a)$:

$$C(s, a) = \gamma \, \Sigma_{s'} \, T(s, a, s') \, max_a \, Q(s', a')$$

Now, I put all the derived equations into the table and it looks like this:

	V	Q	C
V	$V(s) = V(s)$	$V(s) = max_a \, Q(s, a)$	$V(s) = max_a \, R(s, a) + C(s, a)$
Q	$Q(s, a) = R(s, a) + \gamma \, \Sigma s' \, T(s, a, s') \, V(s')$	$Q(s, a) = Q(s)$	$Q(s, a) = R(s, a) + C(s, a)$
C	$C(s, a) = \gamma \, \Sigma s' \, T(s, a, s') \, V(s')$	$C(s, a) = \gamma \, \Sigma_{s'} \, T(s, a, s') \, max_a \, Q(s', a')$	$C(s, a) = C(s)$

Summary

In this chapter, we covered in detail how dynamic programming is used in reinforcement learning, and then we solved the Bellman equation using value iteration and policy iteration. So, are any of these polynomials time algorithms? Considering the way we have been discussing them, no. But you can map these to linear programs and turn them into polynomial problems. So yes, these problems can be solved that way.

In the next chapter, we will discuss a very important topic--temporal difference learning.

4

Temporal Difference Learning

Temporal Difference (TD) learning is one of the most commonly used approaches for policy evaluation. It is a central part of solving reinforcement learning tasks. To derive optimal control, policies have to be evaluated. This task requires value function approximation. At this point, TD methods find application. The use of eligibility traces for backpropagation of updates as well as bootstrapping of the prediction for every update state make these methods very powerful. This chapter gives an understanding of the TD algorithms as presented by R Sutton in his paper. We will look into TD learning and practical implementations of TD algorithms.

Introducing TD learning

To introduce TD learning, it helps to have a little bit of context about reinforcement learning in a more general way. So we can see how the different methods for doing reinforcement learning fit together. Think about reinforcement learning this way:

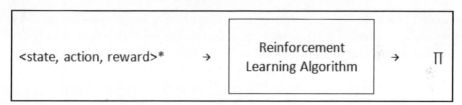

Figure 4.1: Reinforcement learning policy

We discussed the **<state, action, reward>** sequence earlier. So, let's say I am in a state and I take an action. I get a reward back and end up in a new state. I take a new action again and get a new reward, and this just continues. I put a state, action, and reward inside a bracket and put a star over it to indicate that this is some sequence: state, action, reward. That's what comes as input to a reinforcement learning algorithm. What the reinforcement learning algorithm produces as output is a policy.

There are three main families of reinforcement learning algorithms. The one that's most like what we've discussed so far is the **model-based reinforcement learning algorithm**. A model-based reinforcement learning algorithm takes the **state, action, and reward** that it gets and sends them to a **Model Learner**, which learns the transitions and rewards. Once you've learned those **Transaction/Reward**, you can put them through an **MDP Solver**, which can be used to spit out a **Q***, an optimal value function. Once you have the optimal value function, just by taking the **argmax** of the state that you are in, you can choose which action to take in any given state; that gives you the policy. So, it's still mapping the **state, action, reward** sequence to policies, but it's doing so by creating all these intermediate values in between:

Figure 4.2: Model-based reinforcement learning

Let me just add one more thing, which is the **Model Learner**. It takes the history that it's seeing. It also takes the current estimate of **Transaction/Rewards** to produce a new estimate of the transition rewards. So this, kind of, represents the learning piece of the sequence.

Now the second class of reinforcement learning algorithms that's important is referred to as **value-function-based learning**, or sometimes **model-free reinforcement learning**. The beginning and the end of it are still the same. We're taking sequences of **state, action, reward** and producing a policy; we even have this **Q*** in between that we generate the policy from using the **argmax**. But now, instead of feeding back the transitions and rewards, we're actually feeding back **Q***, and we have a direct value update equation that takes the **state, action, reward** that it just experienced, the current estimate of **Q***. Actually, it's kind of more **Q** than **Q***, and uses that to generate a new **Q**, which is then used to generate a policy.

So, instead of explicitly building a model and using it, it just somehow directly learns the **Q** values from state, actions and rewards:

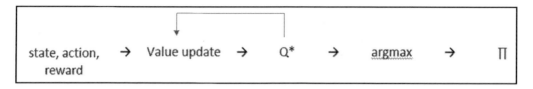

Figure 4.3: Value-function-based reinforcement learning

Then, the third class of reinforcement learning algorithms comes from the fact that you can sometimes take the policy itself and feed it back to a policy update that directly modifies the policy based on the state action rewards you receive. So, in some sense, this is much more direct, but the learning problem is very difficult because the kind of feedback you get about the policy isn't very useful for directly modifying the policy:

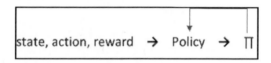

Figure 4.4: Policy search

You can see in *Figure 4.5* that, in some sense, all of these three approaches get simpler as we go down to the policy search, and we can also say that the learning is more direct. And as we go up, the learning problems become more supervised, in the sense that we can imagine learning to predict next states and next rewards from previous states and previous rewards to learning **Transaction/Reward** pretty directly. It's basically a supervised learning problem. We get to see what the output is supposed to be. In value-function-based reinforcement learning, we don't quite get to see what the output is supposed to be, but we do get values that we can imagine propagating backwards.

In policy search, we get very little useful feedback in terms of how to change our policy to make it better:

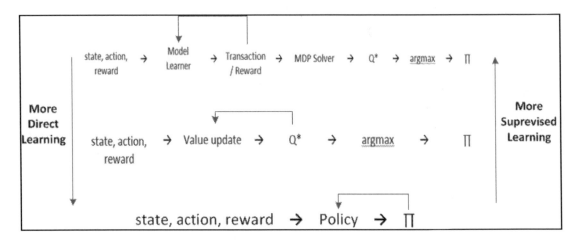

Figure 4.5: All three learning approaches

Different problems have different trade-offs as to whether or not one of these is the best thing to do. A lot of research has been focused on value-function-based, because in some ways it strikes a nice balance between keeping the computations and learning updates relatively simple. But there are plenty of cases where we'd rather do model-based or policy search.

TD lambda

The algorithm we're going to look at now is originally by Sutton, called **TD lambda** (λ). This algorithm is about learning to make predictions that take place over time.

A concrete way of looking at this is how we can form a sequence of states; state zero goes to state one, state one goes to state two and state two goes to a final state. Each time there is a transition, there is some reward associated with it. We are going to try to predict the expected sum of discounted rewards from that:

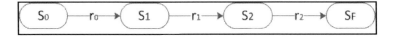

Figure 4.6: A concrete example

This is going to be a really important subroutine for trying to do reinforcement learning, because we are going to use the notion that we can predict future rewards to try to better choose actions to generate high rewards.

So, for the kinds of prediction problems that we are going to be learning with TD methods, it's helpful to have a concrete example to *ground out* some of these terms. Let's take up *Figure 4.7* as a Markov chain:

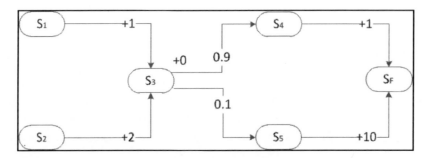

Figure 4.7: Example of a Markov chain

As per the previous figure, there are states S_1, S_2, S_3, S_4, S_5, and S_F (the final state). I have labeled each of the transitions with the reward obtained when we make a transition from that to the next. Note that the transition out of S3 actually is a stochastic transition, with 90 percent probability of going to S_4 and 10 percent probability of going to S_5.

What we learn here is a value function, as follows:

$$V(S) = 0, \ if \ S = SF$$
$$= E\,[\,r + \gamma\,V(S')\,], \ for \ all \ other \ states$$

A function that maps the state to some number, where that number is set to *0* for the final state, and for every other state it is the expected value of the reward plus the discounted value of the state that we end up in, which is averaged across all the different states we might end up in.

Now we are going to compute *V(S3)* given the preceding Markov chain. Just to make things a little bit nicer and more friendly, we assume $\gamma = 1$, so you don't have to multiply by funny numbers.

Let's work this out. It is actually pretty straightforward. The first insight is that we want to go backwards. The reason is that we already know what the answer for the final state is, and we can go back one step and use that to figure out what the states before are, and so on and so forth.

The value of S_F would be zero, that's given. Then what would be the value of S_4? S_4 is the reward we get for leaving that state and taking the action plus gamma times the state we are going to end up in:

$$V(S_4) = 1 + \gamma * 0$$
$$V(S_4) = 1$$

Then for S_5, we can do the same thing:

$$V(S_5) = 10 + \gamma * 0$$
$$V(S_5) = 10$$

The question was asked about S_3. Let's do S_3; it would be the reward that we get, which is 0 as mentioned in *Figure 4.6* plus gamma times the value of the state that we end up in. Well, if we end up in state S_4, that would be 1, but if we end up in state S_5, then it would be 10. As mentioned, 90 percent of the times we end up at state S_4 and 10 percent of times we end up at S_5:

$$V(S_3) = 0 + (\gamma * 1 * 0.9) + (\gamma * 10 * 0.1)$$
$$V(S_3) = 0 + (1 * 1 * 0.9) + (\gamma * 10 * 0.1)$$
$$V(S_3) = 0.9 + 1$$
$$V(S_3) = 1.9$$

In the same way, we will calculate the value of S_1 and S_2:

$$V(S_1) = 1 + (\gamma * 1.9)$$
$$V(S_1) = 1 + (1 * 1.9)$$
$$V(S_1) = 1 + 1.9$$
$$V(S_1) = 2.9$$

$$V(S_2) = 2 + (\gamma * 1.9)$$
$$V(S_2) = 2 + (1 * 1.9)$$
$$V(S_2) = 2 + 1.9$$
$$V(S_2) = 3.9$$

Estimating from data

Now let's think about how we can get the same values from data instead of knowing in advance the model of *Figure 4.7*, the particular Markov chain. So let's imagine we are going to do a series of simulations starting from S_1. It's going to hop around. It's going to go S_1 to S_3, then to either S_4 or S_5, then to S_F, and then stop. So let's imagine we have done that and these are the episodes:

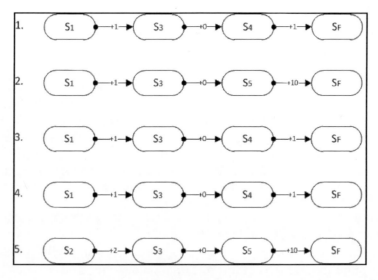

Figure 4.8: Episodes of states

These are the sequences that come out of it. So, the first time we run it, it goes from S_1 to S_3 to S_4 to S_F. The next time it goes S_1 to S_3 to S_5 to S_F, then it goes S_1 to S_3 to S_4 to S_F, and so on. What we are interested in is how to actually estimate the value of state 1 after the first three episodes or first four episodes. The fifth episode doesn't involve S_1, so presumably we shouldn't include it for now.

We can look at episode 1 and see what the value for S_1 turned out to be. Because gamma is equal to 1, we just add up the numbers on the arrows. So the value of S_1 in episode one is 2. The value to S_1 in episode 2 is *11*, and the value to S_1 in episode 3 is 2 again. Now if we want to know an appropriate estimate after three episodes, we just average these three numbers. After three episodes it will be like this:

$$V(S_1) = (2 + 11 + 2)/3$$
$$= 15/3$$
$$= 5$$

And after four episodes:

$$V(S1) = (2 + 11 + 2 + 2)/4$$
$$= 17/4$$
$$= 4.25$$

We can incrementally compute an estimate for the value of a state given the previous estimate. After three episodes, how do we get four? After four, how do we get five? After five, how do we get six? And then after ten thousand how do we get ten thousand one?

When we go from episode 3 to episode 4, the value of S_1 drops from 5 to 4.25. That's a big jump. We calculate the value of S_1 in the last section, and the value of S_1 is 2.9. So in principle, with an infinite amount of data, that's what we should get. We should get 2.9 as our estimate, but in this particular case, we are actually a little bit higher. Now the question is, why? Because we haven't seen enough data yet. In the second episode we saw *11* once. So it looks as if *11* happens a third of the time for three episodes instead of a tenth of the time as per the given probability in *Figure 4.7*. We have an over-representation of the higher reward. So our estimate ends up being skewed high. In the limit, it should all start to work out and we'll get one-tenth plus eleven. But in this case, we get a higher reward than expected.

Now we are going to derive a piece of the TD equation just by working through this example, again in a slightly different way. We said that the value estimate for S_1 after three episodes was 5. Then we ran another episode, number four, starting from that state S_1 with value +2. Can we figure out just from this information what the new estimate's going to be?

$$V_3(S_1) \quad R4(S_1) \qquad V_4(S_1)$$
$$5 \qquad\quad 2 \qquad \rightarrow \qquad ?$$

Let's work through this step by step. We have everything indexed by time, so we know that 5 is an estimate of the last three episodes. We should be able to weight the first one with 3 and the other with 1; that will give the right answer. What do we mean here by weighting? Since 5 is the average of the first three episodes, *15* is the total from the first three episodes, right? We have seen it three times:

$$V_3(S_1) \qquad R4(S_1) \qquad V_4(S_1)$$
$$5 \qquad\qquad 2 \qquad \rightarrow \qquad ?$$
$$(3*5) \quad + \quad (2*1)/4 \quad = \quad 4.25$$

In fact, that's exactly how we did it earlier as well. Now let's generalize this concept to make an equation:

$$V_{T-1}(S_1) \quad R_T(S_1) \quad \rightarrow \quad V_T(S_1)$$

So we should be able to do the same kind of calculation with these quantities symbolically:

$$V_T(S_1) = [(T\text{-}1)\, V_{T\text{-}1}(S_1) + R_T(S_1)]/T$$

Now let's do a little bit of algebra on this equation. First I am just going to divide the previous equation with T and split it into two pieces of the sum. Then I can regroup the things as follows:

$$V_T(S_1) = (T\text{-}1/T)\, V_{T\text{-}1}(S_1) + (1/T)\, R_T(S_1)$$

Learning rate

I introduced the additional learning rate (α) parameter, we can call it alpha:

$$V_T(S) = V_{T\text{-}1}(S) + \alpha_T\, [R_T(S) - V_{T\text{-}1}(S)]\ where\ \alpha = 1/T$$

However, there's an interesting thing that popped out of this particular way of rewriting. In the previous equation, we are looking at a kind of TD that our update to the value is going to equal the difference between the reward that we got at this step and the estimate that we had at the previous step; this difference is actually going to drive the learning. So if the difference is zero, then things don't change. If the difference is big and positive, then the learning rate goes up; if it's big and negative then it goes down. As we get more and more episodes, this learning parameter becomes smaller and smaller, so we make smaller and smaller changes. $R_T(S) - V_{T\text{-}1}(S)$ can look like an error. Moving less and less and less as time goes on is just what we are supposed to do at the learning rate.

 Learning rate, sometimes called step size, is actually for determining when the newly obtained information will override the previous information. It it is zero or close to zero, it means the agent did not learn anything yet. On the other hand, if it is one or close to one, it means that the agent is very close to being well trained for this environment.

Properties of learning rate

There is a very general property that can be stated about learning algorithms. Suppose we have a learning update rule like this:

$$V_T(S) = V_{T-1}(S) + \alpha_T [R_T(S) - V_{T-1}(S)] \text{ where } \alpha = 1/T$$

In the previous equation, the value at time T is equal to the value at time $T-1$ plus some learning rate times the difference between the new estimate and the previous estimate:

$$Lim_{T \to \infty} V_T(S) = V(S)$$

It's actually learning the right thing, but there are conditions that we have to put on the learning rate sequence. The learning rate sequence must have the property that if we sum up all the learning rates, it sums up to infinity. However, the square of the learning rate is less then infinity:

$$\Sigma_T \alpha_T = \infty$$
$$\Sigma_T \alpha_T^2 < \infty$$

At the first approximation, the learning rates have to be big enough so that you can move to the true value, no matter where you start. But they can't be so big that they don't damp out the noise and actually do a proper job of averaging. So, if you just accept that these two conditions should be true, that gives you a way of choosing different kinds of learning rate sequences.

Overview of TD(1)

Now we are in a position to actually state the TD(1) update rule. Here is the structure of the TD(1) update rule:

```
Episode T
    For all S, e (S)=0 at start of episode, V_T (S) = V_T-1 (S)
        r_t
    After S_t-1 →S_t : (Step t)
        e (S_t-1) = (S_t-1) + 1
    For all S,
        V_T (S) = V_T (S) + α_T [r_t + γV_T-1 (S_t) - V_T-1 (S_t-1)]  e (S)
        e (S) = γ e (S)
```

Each time we start a new episode, we are going to initialize the eligibility $e(s)$ for all the states to zero. So we just start them off as ineligible at the start of the episode. We start off our estimate for the value function for this episode to be initialized to whatever it was at the end of the previous episode:

$$V_T(S) = V_{T-1}(S)$$

Then, each time, we take a step within the episode, a step from some S_{t-1} to some state S_t to get a reward r_t. First, we update the eligibility of the state that we just left:

$$e(S_{t-1}) = (S_{t-1}) + 1$$

Then go through all the states. Compute one quantity that is the same for all states; this is the TD. It is the reward plus the discounted value of the state that we just got to minus the state that we just left. We're going to use the values that we got from the previous iteration or previous episode. That's going to be our TD $(\alpha_T [r_t + \gamma V_{T-1}(S_t) - V_{T-1}(S_{t-1}))$. We're going to apply that TD to all states, proportional to the eligibility of those states and of course the learning rate:

$$V_T(S) = V_T(S) + \alpha_T [r_t + \gamma V_{T-1}(S_t) - V_{T-1}(S_{t-1})] e(S)$$

Then we decrease, or decay, the eligibility for those states. And then we're going to the next step:

$$e(S) = \gamma \, e(S)$$

So, the value at state S is going to be updated based on TD quantity $(\alpha_T [r_t + \gamma V_{T-1}(S_t) - V_{T-1}(S_{t-1}))$, which is the same for everybody.

Let's go through a tiny little example and then see the magic of it; see that it actually produces the same outcome that we would have gotten with the update rule discussed previously.

An example of TD(1)

Let's walk through the pseudocode to see how the value updates work.

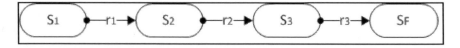

Figure 4.9: Example of TD(1)

We start off at the beginning of an episode. We say that the eligibility for all the states is zero:

$$e(S_1) = 0$$
$$e(S_2) = 0$$
$$e(S_3) = 0$$

And the new value function is whatever the value function was at the end of the previous episode. So we just make a note of that. What we're going to do for this example is just keep track of the changes. So ultimately, this is all going to get added to whatever the previous value was:

$$V_T(S) = V_{T-1}(S)$$

Now we make a transition, and the first transition we make is from S_1 to S_2 with reward r_1. What does that do to the eligibility? Well, for S_1, it sets the eligibility to *1*:

$$e(S_1) = 1$$
$$e(S_2) = 0$$
$$e(S_3) = 0$$

Then we are going to loop through all the states, and we're going to apply the same little update to all of them. The update has this form: whatever the current learning rate is times the reward that we just experienced (r_1) plus gamma times whatever the previous iteration value was for the state that we landed in minus the previous iteration's value of the state that we just left. This quantity is actually going to get added to all the states, but the amount to be added to all the states is proportional to the eligibility for that state. And since, at the moment, states S_2 and S_3 are ineligible (they have their eligibility set to *0*), nothing's really happening there; we're only making an update with respect to state S_1:

$$\alpha_T \left[r_1 + \gamma \, V_{T-1}(S_2) - V_{T-1}(S_1) \right]$$

So these are the changes that we've made so far to the new value function for S_1, S_2, and S_3:

$$\Delta V(S_1) = \alpha_T [r_1 + \gamma V_{T-1}(S_2) - V_{T-1}(S_1)] + 0 + 0$$
$$\Delta V(S_2) = 0$$
$$\Delta V(S_3) = 0$$

Next we have to decay the eligibility for all the states. So the *0s* decay to *0*, and the *1* decays down to gamma:

$$e(S_1) = \gamma$$
$$e(S_2) = 0$$
$$e(S_3) = 0$$

Now we take the next step, which is from S_2 to S_3 with reward r_2.

First, we have to update the eligibility of the state that we just left, so the S_2 eligibility is up to *1*:

$$e(S_1) = \gamma$$
$$e(S_2) = 1$$
$$e(S_3) = 0$$

What's the new quantity? It's r_2 plus gamma times the value of the state that we just got to minus the state we just left:

$$\alpha_T [r_2 + \gamma V_{T-1}(S_3) - V_{T-1}(S_2)]$$

So this update is now independent of the state we are actually changing. We are going to apply that everywhere. But we are going to apply it proportionally to the eligibility. So the eligibilities are at the moment γ, *1*, and *0*. We just have to add this into the other things. And in particular, we're multiplying by the eligibility:

$$\Delta V(S_1) = \alpha [r_1 + \gamma V_{T-1}(S_2) - V_{T-1}(S_1)] + \gamma \alpha_T [r_2 + \gamma V_{T-1}(S_3) - V_{T-1}(S_2)] + 0$$
$$\Delta V(S_2) = 0 + \alpha [r_2 + \gamma V_{T-1}(S_3) - V_{T-1}(S_2)]$$
$$\Delta V(S_3) = 0$$

We need to do some simplification:

$$\Delta V(S_1) = \alpha \ [r_{1+} \gamma \ r_2 + \gamma^2 \ V_{T-1}(S_3) - V_{T-1}(S_1)]$$
$$\Delta V(S_2) = \alpha \ [r_2 + \gamma \ V_{T-1}(S_3) - V_{T-1}(S_2)]$$
$$\Delta V(S_3) = 0$$

It compacts really nicely and so we have something that's of a similar form as we had before. So the last thing we do after we've done all those value updates is update the eligibilities and we're ready for the next step:

$$e(S_1) = \gamma^2$$
$$e(S_2) = \gamma$$
$$e(S_3) = 0$$

The next step takes us from S_3 to S_F. We get reward r_3 when that happens. First, we update the eligibility for that state:

$$e(S_1) = \gamma^2$$
$$e(S_2) = \gamma$$
$$e(S_3) = 1$$

Now we compute the quantity that we are going to add to all the state updates. This gives us r_3 plus gamma times the previous value of the state that we just ended up in minus the state we came from:

$$\alpha_T \ [r3 + \gamma \ V_{T-1}(S_F) - V_{T-1}(S_3)]$$

This update is going to get applied to all the states, proportional to their eligibility. So, we can do that same thing again; just add this quantity into all these things and simplify:

$$\Delta V(S_1) = \alpha \ [r_{1+} \gamma \ r_2 + \gamma^2 \ r_{3+} \gamma^3 \ V_{T-1}(S_F) - V_{T-1}(S_1)]$$
$$\Delta V(S_2) = \alpha \ [r_{2+} \gamma \ r_3 + \gamma^2 \ V_{T-1}(S_F) - V_{T-1}(S_2)]$$
$$\Delta V(S_3) = \alpha \ [r_{2+} \gamma \ V_{T-1}(S_3) - V_{T-1}(S_3)]$$

We can now state a claim that just follows very clearly from the example. That is, this TD(1) update actually does the same thing as the outcome-based update, which is to say, we wait to see what all the rewards and the discounted rewards are on the entire trajectory. Then we just update our prediction for the state that they started from with those rewards. So, at least in the case where there are no repeated states, we visit a state more than once along a trajectory. Everything beautifully cancels and what you get is exactly the same update. The TD(1) update is exactly the same update as waiting for the outcomes and updating based on that.

> TD(1) is the same as outcome-based updates (if there are no repeated states).

So if we were doing outcome-based updates, then basically, we are just looking at all the rewards that we see, the values that we kind of expected along the way. It's exactly what we have learned before.

But if we have a repeated state, then we are basically ignoring anything we learned along the way during the episode. So outcome-based updates learn nothing during the episode. If we sequence up there, instead of being S_1, S_2, S_3 and S_F, it would have been S_1, S_2, S_3, S_1, and S_F. Then we would have seen the rewards as r_1, r_2, r_3, and some other reward. Let's call it r_1 prime. We would be pretending as if we didn't already know something about state 1, because we also saw it go from state 1 to state 2 and saw a particular reward r_1.

So what this TD(1) update lets you do is, when you see S_1 again and sort of back up its value. You have captured the fact that last time you were in S_1, you actually went to S_2 and saw reward r_1. So it's like outcome-based updates, now with extra learning or inside-the-episode learning.

Why TD(1) is wrong

Now that we have discussed how we can compute these outcome-based estimates with TD(1) estimates, I am going to tell you that it's not exactly what we want. I am going to explain why TD(1) is wrong sometimes.

TD(1) is not using all the data; it's using just individual runs. So, when a rare thing happens on a run, we could end up with an estimate that's quite far off and it may stay that way for a long time. Whereas the maximum likelihood estimate seemed to push you in the direction of using the data that you have got to the best of your ability. So what this is pointing out is that maybe we don't want to do TD(1).

There are some nice things about TD(1), however; we can shape up some of these other issues and come up with something even better.

Overview of TD(0)

Here is a rule that we are going to call the TD(0) rule, which gives it a different name from TD(1). Eventually we are going to connect TD(0) and TD(1) together. And the rule looks like this. Not so unfamiliar!

$$V_T(S_{T-1}) = V_T(S_{T-1}) + \alpha_T [r_t + \gamma V_T(S_t) - V_T(S_{t-1})]$$

The way we are going to compute our value estimate for the state that we just left when we made a transition at episode T is the previous value plus we are going to move a little bit in the direction with our learning rate toward the reward that we observed plus the discounted estimated value of the state that we ended up in minus the estimated value of this state that we just left:

```
Episode T
    For all S, at start of episode, V_T (S)  = V_T-1 (S)
            r_t
    After  S_t-1 → S_t  : (Step t)
    For all S = S_t-1,
       V_T (S)  = V_T (S)  + α_T [r_t  + γV_T-1 (S_t)  -  V_T-1 (S_t-1)]
```

What would we expect this outcome to look like on average? If we are in some state S_{t-1} and we make a transition, we don't know what state we are going to end up in. However, there are some probabilities here. If we take its expectation, it's going to look like this:

$$V_T(S_{T-1}) = E_{St}[r + \gamma V_T(S_t)]$$

If we repeat this update over and over again, what we are really doing is sampling different possible S_t values. So we are taking an expectation over what we get as the next state of the reward plus the discounted estimated value of that next state.

Here's the idea: if we repeat this update rule on the finite data that we have got over and over again, then we are actually taking an average with respect to how often we have seen each of those transitions. It really is computing the maximum likelihood estimate. That finite data thing is important because if we had infinite data, then everything would work. In the infinite data case, this is also true, but TD(1) also does the right thing in infinite data. Everything gets averaged out and it will do the right thing.

However, here we have got a finite set of data so far. The issue is that if we run our update rule over that data over and over again, we are going to get the effect of having a maximum likelihood model. That's not true of the outcome-based model. In the data that we just saw, where there was one transition from S_2 to anything else, we can run over that over and over again. But the estimate is not going to change; it's always going to be exactly that. We can contrast this with the outcome-based idea, where we are not doing this sort of bootstrapping. We are not using the estimate that we have gotten at some other state. We actually use the reward sequence. As a result of that, if we have seen a reward sequence only once, as in the case of S_2, repeating that update doesn't change anything.

Whereas in TD(0), we are using the intermediate estimates that we have computed and refined on all the intermediate nodes. To improve our estimates, we have to apply the intermediate computation into all the states that we have encountered. It's actually kind of connecting the values of states to the other values of the states, which is what we want. And this is literally using the experience that it saw and ignoring the fact that there are intermediate states.

TD lambda rule

We have talked about two different algorithms, TD(0) and TD(1). There is a larger algorithm that includes both of these as special cases. It's going to have the property that when lambda is set to *0*, we get TD(0), and when lambda is set to *1*, we get TD(1). We also get update rules for all sorts of in-between values of lambda.

Both TD(0) and TD(1) have updates based on differences between temporally successive predictions. One algorithm, TD(λ), covers both!

Here's the algorithm of TD(λ):

```
Episode T
    For all S, e (S)= 0 at start of episode, V_T (S) = V_T-1 (S)
            r_t
    After S_t-1 →S_t : (Step t)
      e (S_t-1) = (S_t-1) + 1
    For all S,
      V_T (S) = V_T (S) + α_T [r_t + γV_T-1 (S_t) - V_T-1 (S_t-1)]   e (S)
      e (S) = λ γ e (S)
```

You notice that it's exactly similar to the TD(1) algorithm, except that in the last line we add λ:

$$e(S) = \lambda \, \gamma \, e(S)$$

Here's the trick: if you give a value of λ to 1, then it becomes TD(1), and if you put the value of λ as 0, then it becomes a TD(0) algorithm.

What we are going to look at next is how to think about this rule. This generalized TD lambda rule makes some sense so that it is kind of converting it into quantities that we can understand.

K-step estimator

It turns out that if we want to understand TD lambda, a really useful way of studying it is by studying not TD lambda (opposite to TD lambda). So in particular, we are going to look at k-step estimators for a moment, and then we are going to relate that back to TD lambda.

Here's what a k-step estimator is:

$$E_1 \, V(S_t) = V(S_t) + \alpha_T [r_{t+1} + \gamma \, V(S_{t+1}) - V(S_t)]$$
$$E_2 \, V(S_t) = V(S_t) + \alpha_T [r_{t+1} + \gamma \, r_{t+2} + \gamma^2 \, V(S_{t+2}) - V(S_t)]$$
$$E_3 \, V(S_t) = V(S_t) + \alpha_T [r_{t+1} + \gamma \, r_{t+2} + \gamma^2 \, r_{t+3} + \gamma^3 \, V(S_{t+3}) - V(S_t)]$$
$$E_K \, V(S_t) = V(S_t) + \alpha_T [r_{t+1} + ...+ \gamma^{k-1} \, r_{t+k} + \gamma^k \, V(S_{t+k}) - V(S_t)]$$
$$E_\infty \, V(S_t) = V(S_t) + \alpha_T [r_{t+1} + ...+ \gamma^{\infty-1} \, r_{t+\infty} + \gamma^\infty \, V(S_{t+\infty}) - V(S_t)]$$

Let's say, we're trying to estimate the value of a state, S_t. So it's a state that we are just leaving as a function of what happens next. Let's look at this first estimator. It says that we are going to estimate the value of a state that we're leaving by moving it a little bit in the direction of the immediate reward plus the discounted estimated value of the state that we landed in. We are going to just move a little bit in that direction. Do you recognize the first estimator? It is TD(0). It's just like a one-step look-ahead sort of thing. That is why we are calling it TD(0). That's the way to think about if there's a one-step estimator. In that, we will use the immediate reward that we got plus the value of the state we land in.

Let's contrast this with a two-step estimator. We call it **E2** or **Estimator 2**, where we estimate the value of a state we're leaving. We're going to move a little bit in the direction of the immediate reward that we received plus the discounted reward that we receive next, plus the double discounted value of the state that we landed in two steps from now. So, instead of considering where we were before, we did an estimate by taking one reward. And we estimated the rest of the sequence using our current estimates. Here we're taking two rewards and using that as our immediate estimate plus our estimate of the future taken as the state that we reach two steps from now.

So we used two steps--two real steps followed by this kind of look-ahead thing. We can do that for three steps right here. We can also do that for k, where we're estimating the value of a state by k rewards summed up here, and then we estimate the value of the future by looking at the state we end up in k-steps from now and discounting that by k-steps.

In fact, if we continue doing this arbitrarily, we eventually get to infinity, where we get the sum of rewards and it keeps going on till infinity. We look at the state that we end up at infinity, which of course, isn't a real thing. But it's okay, because we discounted by gamma to infinity, which is zero. So this piece actually drops out, and we just end up with an infinite sum of rewards.

Now, the last estimator E_5 should look familiar. It is TD(1). So now we have got TD(0) on one hand as a one-step estimator and TD(1) on the other hand as an infinity step estimator. We have got these other things in between that we don't really have or possibly even need a name for.

So what we need to do next is relate these quantities to TD lambda, which we're going to show is a weighted combination of all these estimators.

Relationship between k-step estimators and TD lambda

Here's how we relate the k-step estimators that we just discussed with TD lambda. We will be using a weighted combination of all the estimators for any one of these TD lambda algorithms. The weights are going to look like this:

$$E_1 \, 1 - \lambda$$
$$E_2 \, \lambda(1 - \lambda)$$
$$E_3 \, \lambda^2(1 - \lambda)$$
$$E_K \, \lambda^{k-1}(1 - \lambda)$$
$$E_\infty \, \lambda^\infty$$

It's 1 minus lambda for the one-step estimator, lambda times 1 minus lambda for the two-step estimator, lambda squared times one minus lambda for the three-step estimator, lambda raised to *K-1* times one minus lambda for the k-step estimator, and then all the way down to lambda raised to infinity. Of course, that literally doesn't get any weight.

When we change the value of a state *V(S)*, we are going to change it with respect to all the different estimators. All the different estimators are going to give us their own preferences as to what we should be moving the value toward. And we are just going to take a convex combination, a weighted combination of all of them each time we do an update for the value of a state.

So there are a couple things that we should probably check. One, make sure that the estimator's weights sum up to *1*:

$$\sum_{k=1}^{\infty} \lambda^{k-1}(1 - \lambda)$$

Now suppose we put the value of λ as *0* and *1*:

		$\lambda = 0 \left[\mathrm{TD}(0)\right]$	$\lambda = 1 \left[\mathrm{TD}(1)\right]$
E_1	$1 - \lambda$	1	0
E_2	$\lambda(1 - \lambda)$	0	0
E_3	$\lambda^2(1 - \lambda)$	0	0
E_K	$\lambda^K(1 - \lambda)$	0	0
E_∞	λ^∞	0	1

If lambda is *0*, we get a weight of *1* on the first estimator and zero on all the rest, When lambda is *1*, we get *0* for all these except for the last one. So, when the value of lambda is *0*, it is actually equal to *TD(0)*, and when the value of lambda is *1*, it is equal to *TD(1)*.

The important thing to note is any instance of in-between values of lambda, such as a *0.5* or *0.3*. We get weights on all of these estimators.

Summary

This chapter was all about TD learning. We started off with different ways to solve reinforcement learning problems. There were three ways to think about it: model-based learning, value-based learning, and policy-based learning. TD methods fall under value-based learning. Then, we actually derived the kind of incremental way of building up estimates of the values, and we called it outcome-based. All that really means is you look at the outcomes of what you experience from different trajectories and episodes through the space, and you use that to build up your estimate of the values of various states.

We can treat reinforcement learning as a kind of supervised learning. The major difference is reinforcement learning takes some time for trial and error and learns from the environment, and we have to wait for some time and see what happened; then use that as a training example. But we can't really wait for time to end, because it's kind of too late to use any of the information there. So what we want are incremental methods that can actually do updates along the way. That would be equivalent to waiting until the end but actually gives us results sooner.

Then we went through the learning rate. In order for us to be sure that we are going to learn something, that learning rate had to have certain properties. These are the two properties we learned: $\sum \alpha_T = \infty$ and $\sum \alpha_T^2 < \infty$. We want a learning rate sequence that would allow us to move the value to wherever it needs to go to converge.

In the next chapter, we will look into Monte Carlo methods in reinforcement learning. Monte Carlo methods allow learning optimal behavior directly from interaction with the environment. It requires only experience or sample sequences of states, actions, and rewards from actual or simulated interaction with an environment. It is also easy and efficient to focus Monte Carlo methods on a small subset of a state. We will go through Monte Carlo methods with practical examples implemented in Python.

5
Monte Carlo Methods

In this chapter, we will discuss Monte Carlo approaches. The idea behind Monte Carlo is simple; it uses randomness to solve problems. Monte Carlo methods learn directly from episodes of experience. It is model-free and no knowledge of MDP transitions or rewards is needed.

We will discuss in detail the Monte Carlo methods and Monte Carlo for control. We will also implement an example of using GridWorld and the *Blackjack* game in Python.

Monte Carlo methods

In 1930, a Monte Carlo method was used for the first time by Enrico Fermi, who was a student of neutron diffusion. But Fermi did not publish anything about it; the modern version of Monte Carlo was named by Stanislaw Ulam in 1946 in honor of his uncle who often borrowed money from relatives to gamble in Monte Carlo Casino (Monaco). Ulam came up with this idea while recovering from surgery and playing solitaire. He tried to estimate the probability of winning given the initial state.

 Any method that can solve a problem by generating a random number and observing the fraction of numbers that obey some property is called the **Monte Carlo** method.

The main idea behind this is very simple: using randomness to solve problems. For example, we use a Monte Carlo tree search to find the best possible moves in AI. **DeepMind AlphaGo** used a Monte Carlo tree search combined with deep reinforcement learning and a convolutional network to defeat Lee Sedol, the *Go* world champion. We will discuss this later in the chapter.

The following are advantages of Monte Carlo methods in dynamic programming techniques:

1. Directly from interaction with the environment, Monte Carlo allows us to learn optimal behavior.
2. It can only be used on a small subset of states.
3. Monte Carlo can be used with simulations.

Let's consider the example of GridWorld as explained in Chapter 1, *Reinforcement Learning*. We will apply a Monte Carlo method to a GridWorld scenario. As usual, the agent starts at state (1, 1) and follows an internal policy. The rewards are received at each step and saved into a history of all states visited.

The agent starts from a state called start state and follows its internal policy. At each step, it records the reward obtained and saves a history of all the states visited until it reaches a terminal state. The agent is able to execute actions, in this case up, down, left, and right. Here, the green square represents the goal, the red square represents failure, and the black square is the space where you cannot enter. It acts as a wall. If you reach the green square (goal), your world is over and you begin from the start state again. The same holds for the red square. This means the agent cannot go through the red square to get to the green square.

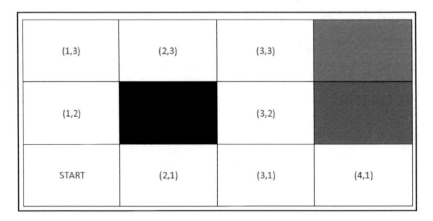

Figure 5.1: GridWorld 3x4

As discussed earlier, an episode is the sequence of all states from the starting to the terminal state. Now let's suppose that our agent recorded the following three episodes:

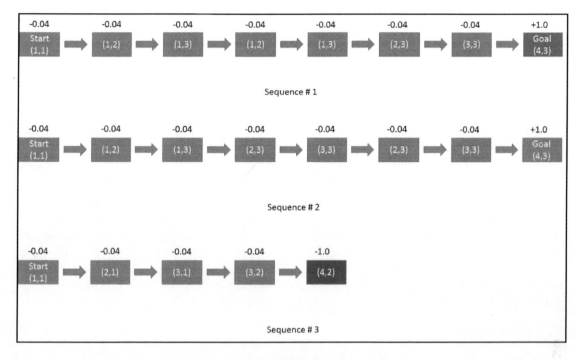

Figure 5.2: Episodes of GridWorld

A visit is actually an agent's occurrence in a state. It is very important because it defines the two approaches of Monte Carlo.

- **First visit Monte Carlo**: Defined as the average of returns following the first visit to *s* in a set of episodes.

- **Every visit Monte Carlo**: This is defined as the average of returns following all the visits to *s* in a set of episodes. It extends more naturally to function approximation and eligibility traces.

What does return mean? It is the sum of discounted rewards. We've already discussed this in the Bellman equation and utility of state in Chapter 2, *Markov Decision Process*, and Chapter 3, *Dynamic programming*, respectively:

$$Return(s) = \sum_{t=0}^{\infty} \gamma t \, R(St)$$

First visit Monte Carlo

We will further discuss Monte Carlo with the following example:

```
Initialize:
    π ← policy to be evaluated
    V ← an arbitrary state-value function
    Returns(s) ← an empty list, for all s ∈ S

Repeat forever:
    Generate an episode using π
    For each state s appearing in the episode:
        G ← return following the first occurrence of s
        Append G to Returns(s)
        V (s) ← average(Returns(s))
```

Both first visit Monte Carlo, and every visit Monte Carlo converge to $v\pi(s)$ as the number of visits (or first visits) to s goes up to infinity. This is easy to see for the case of first visit Monte Carlo. In this case, each return is an independent, identically distributed estimate of $v_\pi(s)$ with a finite variance.

For example, we have the discount factor γ, the reward function $R(s)$, and S_t, which is the state reached at time t. We can calculate the return for state $(1,1)$ of the first episode, with $\gamma = 0.9$:

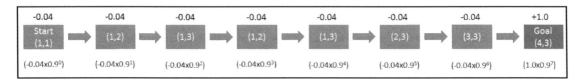

Figure 5.3: Episode 1 of GridWorld

The return for the first episode is as follows:

$$= (-004x0.9^0) + (-004x0.9^1) + (-004x0.9^2) + (-004x0.9^3) + (-004x0.9^4) + (-004x0.9^5) + (-004x0.9^6) + (1.0x0.9^7)$$
$$= 0.27$$

As we follow the same steps and procedures, the results are similar in the second episode. But for the third episode, the return is different: -0.79. After three episodes, the results are 0.27, 0.27, -0.79. Now, how can we use the estimates of utility return? We need to use the core equation of the Monte Carlo method, which will give us the utility of a state which follows policy π:

$$U^{\pi}(s) = E\,[\,\sum_{t=0}^{\infty} \gamma^t\, R(S_t)\,]$$

You can see only one difference if you compare the previous equation that is used in calculating the return. We take the expectation of the return to obtain the function utility; that is the only difference. Now, to find the state utility, we need to calculate the state expectation. In the example we used, after three episodes, the utility of state *(1, 1)* will be as follows:

(0.27 + 0.27 - 0.79) / 3 = -0.08.

The previous estimations in the last three episodes are incorrect. We need to see more episodes to get the true value.

Now let's roll a dice (six-sided); it gives any one of the numbers from *1* to *6* with equal probability. If we sum *1+2+3+4+5+6* and divide by 6, then we get *3.5*. Now we will implement the same thing in Python:

```python
#We will import all the scientific libraries using _numPy package
import numpy as _numP

# Trowing a _varDice_rand for N intervals and evaluating the anticipation

_varDice_rand = _numP.random.randint(low=1, high=7, size=3)
print("Anticipation (throughing 3 intervals): " +
   str(_numP.mean(_varDice_rand)))

_varDice_rand = _numP.random.randint(low=1, high=7, size=10)
print("Anticipation (throughing 10 intervals): " +
   str(_numP.mean(_varDice_rand)))

_varDice_rand = _numP.random.randint(low=1, high=7, size=100)
print("Anticipation (throughing 100 intervals): " +
   str(_numP.mean(_varDice_rand)))

_varDice_rand = _numP.random.randint(low=1, high=7, size=1000)
print("Anticipation (throughing 1000 intervals): " +
   str(_numP.mean(_varDice_rand)))

_varDice_rand = _numP.random.randint(low=1, high=7, size=100000)
print("Anticipation (throughing 100000 intervals): " +
   str(_numP.mean(_varDice_rand)))
```

The output is as follows:

```
Anticipation (throughing 3 intervals): 4.0
Anticipation (throughing  10 intervals): 2.9
Anticipation (throughing 100 intervals): 3.47
Anticipation (throughing  1000 intervals): 3.481
Anticipation (throughing  100000 intervals): 3.49948
```

As you can see, the true value of the expectation converges to *3.5*. In a Monte Carlo algorithm, we do exactly the same thing but we want the utility function for all the states based on each episode return.

Now we will implement the algorithm in Python. We will write a module, gridworld.py, which contains GridWorld; we use it to create a GridWorld of any size and add the terminal states and obstacles. The agent can move in the GridWorld, which is following a specific policy. Now we will create a *4x3* GridWorld via the following code:

```python
#We will import all the scientific libraries using numpy package

import numpy as _numP_

#We will import Grid World package

from gridworld import GridWorld

#Now we define our environment 3 by 4 Grid World

environment = GridWorld(3, 4)

# Now we will Define state matrix
# And adding the obstacle at the position (1,1)
# Finally adding the termina states

var_matrix_state_ = _numP_.zeros((3,4))
var_matrix_state_[0, 3] = 1
var_matrix_state_[1, 3] = 1
var_matrix_state_[1, 1] = -1

# Now we will define our matrix for reward
# And set the reqard as -0.04 for all states

var_matrix_reward_ = _numP_.full((3,4), -0.04)
var_matrix_reward_[0, 3] = 1
var_matrix_reward_[1, 3] = -1

# Here we will define our matrix for transition
```

```
# and also define the actions probabilities

var_matrix_transition = _numP_.array([[0.8, 0.1, 0.0, 0.1],
                                       [0.1, 0.8, 0.1, 0.0],
                                       [0.0, 0.1, 0.8, 0.1],
                                       [0.1, 0.0, 0.1, 0.8]])

# It's time to define the matrix for policy
# 1=RIGHT, 0=UP, 3=LEFT, 2=DOWN, -1=NoAction NaN=Obstacle



var_matrix_policy = _numP_.array([[1, 1, 1, -1],
                                  [0, _numP_.NaN, 0, -1],
                                  [0, 3, 3, 3]])

# Set the matrices

environment.setStateMatrix(var_matrix_state_)
environment.setRewardMatrix(var_matrix_reward_)
environment.setTransitionMatrix(var_matrix_transition)
```

You can see the previous code and notice that it's a very small program; we've defined the complete GridWorld with all the required properties. Here, take note that the optimal policy is *-0.04*. Now we will reset the environment and the agent will move from the starting position. We'll use the render method to display our GridWorld:

```
#We reset the Grid World environment
var_obser_ = environment.reset()


#Render method will display our Grid World
environment.render()
```

Once we run the program, the output is as follows:

```
- - - *
- # - *
O - - -
```

In the previous program, we used the following markings:

- Free position is marked as –
- Obstacle is marked as #
- Terminal state is marked as *

Now we will write a loop that runs the episodes:

```
for _ in range(1000):

    var_actions_ = var_matrix_policy[var_obser_[0], var_obser_[1]]

    var_obser_, var_rewards_, var_done_ = environment.step(var_actions_)

    print("")

    print("Total actions_: " + str(var_actions_))

    print("Total Rewards: " + str(var_rewards_))

    print("Complete: " + str(var_done_))

    environment.render()

    if var_done_:

        break
```

As per the matrix transitions and the policies, the output should be as follows:

```
- O - * - - O * - - - O
- - - - - - - - - - - -
- # - * - # - * - # - *


- - - * - - - * O - - *
O - - - - - - - - - - -
- # - * O # - * - # - *
```

As we've already implemented the Monte Carlo method, now it's time to introduce the learning rate (discount factor) to *0.999*, the policy as π_*, and also the model transition we implemented earlier. The current model transition will work *80* percent of the time correctly. Now we will implement it in the following code:

```
def fuc_return_get(par_list_state_, par_gamma_df):

    var_count_ = 0

    var_value_return = 0


    for var_visit in par_list_state_:
```

```
        var_rewards_ = var_visit[1]

        var_value_return += var_rewards_ * _numP_.power(par_gamma_df,
    var_count_)

        var_count_ += 1

    return var_value_return
```

The function `fuc_return_get()` takes two inputs: a list of states in the form of a tuple (which is actually the position and reward), and the discount factor. The output is the list of actions.

Now we are going to use this `fuc_return_get()` function in the loop so that we can get the estimate of utilities for each episode. This is the major part of the code; that's why I am putting many comments to make it more understandable:

```
# Define the empty matrix utility
var_matrix_utility_ = _numP_.zeros((3,4))

# Now we initialize it
var_matrix_mean_running = _numP_.full((3,4), 1.0e-10)
par_gamma_df = 0.999 #discount factor
var_epoch_tot = 50000
var_epoch_print = 1000

for var_epoch_ in range(var_epoch_tot):
  #now new episode start from here
    var_list_episode = list()


    #First Observation will be Reset and return
    observation = environment.reset(exploring_starts=True)

    for _ in range(1000):
    # Now we will take the action from the matrix action
        var_actions_ = var_matrix_policy[var_obser_[0], var_obser_[1]]

        # Now the agent will move one step and notice the observation and
reward from the environment
        var_obser_, var_rewards_, var_done_ =
environment.step(var_actions_)

        # Include that visit into the list of episode
        var_list_episode.append((var_obser_, var_rewards_))
        if var_done_: break
```

```
    # Here the episode is completed, now we will estimate the utilities
    var_count_ = 0

    # We will check here that is this the first visit in the state
    var_matrix_checkup = _numP_.zeros((3,4))

    # Now we are going to implement the First visit Monte Carlo method
    # And for all the states it is store it in the list of episodes and
check if it is first visit and estimate the returns.

    for var_visit_ in var_list_episode:
        var_obser_ = var_visit_[0]
        var_row_ = var_obser_[0]
        var_col_ = var_obser_[1]
        var_rewards_ = var_visit_[1]

        if(var_matrix_checkup[var_row_, var_col_] == 0):
            return_value = fuc_return_get(var_list_episode[var_count_:],
par_gamma_df)
            var_matrix_mean_running[var_row_, var_col_] += 1
            var_matrix_utility_[var_row_, var_col_] += return_value
            var_matrix_checkup[var_row_, var_col_] = 1
        var_count_ += 1

    if(var_epoch_ % var_epoch_print == 0):
        print("Matrix utility later " + str(var_epoch_+1) + " no of
iterations:")
        print(var_matrix_utility_ / var_matrix_mean_running)

#Finally we will check the mstrix utility received
print("Matrix utility later " + str(var_epoch_tot) + " no of iterations:")
print(var_matrix_utility_ / var_matrix_mean_running)
```

Now we run the code and it displays the utility matrix for every 1,000 iterations:

```
Matrix utility later 1 no of iterations:
[[ 0.59184009 0.71385957 0.75461418 1.0 ]
 [ 0.55124825 0.0 0.87712296 0.0 ]
 [ 0.510697 0.0 0.0 0.0 ]]

Matrix utility later 1001 no of iterations:
[[ 0.81379324 0.87288388 0.92520101 1.0 ]
 [ 0.76332603 0.0 0.73812382 -1.0 ]
 [ 0.70553067 0.65729802 0.0 0.0 ]]

Matrix utility later 2001 no of iterations:
[[ 0.81020502 0.87129531 0.92286107 1.0 ]
 [ 0.75980199 0.0 0.71287269 -1.0 ]
```

```
[ 0.70275487 0.65583747 0.0 0.0 ]]
```

. . .

```
Matrix utility later 50000 no of iterations:
[[ 0.80764909 0.8650596 0.91610018 1.0 ]
 [ 0.7563441 0.0 0.65231439 -1.0 ]
 [ 0.69873614 0.6478315 0.0 0.0 ]]
```

You can see that the utilities are getting more and more accurate, and in a finite way, it all converges to true values.

If you see both the matrices of utilities, you will notice that they are mostly similar, but there are two major differences. The estimation for unity is zero for *(3, 1)* and *(4, 1)*. This is one of the advantages of a Monte Carlo method, but on the other hand, it is also considered one of the limitations. In the policy we used, the agent always starts from the bottom-left corner and the transition probabilities are responsible for the wrong estimations. The agent starts from state *(1, 1)* and then it never reaches that state, so it is never able to estimate the correct utility for the corresponding states. As I mentioned earlier, there is a disadvantage but there is also an advantage. Let's say our GridWorld is very big. Then it saves our time to only estimate the utilities of the specific state in which we are more interested, so it actually saves resources and time and our focus is only on the specific subspace.

Maybe some of you wonder why we are estimating the utility for each state. What is the reason for this? The reason is that we want to explore the states from the start and continuously explore making the agent to all possible states. This is the basic principle of reinforcement learning, to learn from exploration.

To start exploring, we just need to use this code:

```
observation = environment.reset(exploring_starts=True)
```

At the beginning of all new episodes, the agent will start from a random position. Now we will run the script again and get the following output:

```
Matrix utility later 1 no of iterations:
[[ 0.87712296 0.918041 0.959 1. ]
 [ 0.83624584 0.0 0.0 0.0 ]
 [ 0.0 0.0 0.0 0.0 ]]

Matrix utility later 1001 no of iterations:
[[ 0.81345829 0.8568502 0.91298468 1.0 ]
 [ 0.76971062 0.0 0.64240071 -1.0 ]
 [ 0.71048183 0.65156625 0.62423942 0.3622782 ]]
```

```
Matrix utility later 2001 no of iterations:
[[ 0.80248079 0.85321 0.90835335 1.0 ]
 [ 0.75558086 0.0 0.64510648 -1.0 ]
 [ 0.69689178 0.64712344 0.6096939 0.34484468]]


   . . .


Matrix utility later 50000 no of iterations:
[[ 0.8077211 0.86449595 0.91575904 1.0 ]
 [ 0.75630573 0.0 0.65417382 -1.0 ]
 [ 0.6989143 0.64707444 0.60495949 0.36857044]]
```

Now, as you can see in the results, we got the correct values even for states *(3, 1)* and *(4, 1)*. So far we just assumed that we had a policy and we were using that policy to estimate the utility. Now the question is: what do we do if we do not have a policy? In that case, there is another method called model-free Monte Carlo estimation.

Example – Blackjack

Blackjack is a very popular game played throughout the world in casinos. It is also called the twenty one game. This is a very simple and thrilling game. We'll discuss this game because we want to implement the game features in our code and later we will implement Monte Carlo methods.

Objective of the game

All the participants try to reach as close as possible to *21* but they are not allowed to go over *21*.

Card scoring/values

This varies from game to game, but most of the time the ace is equal to *1* or *11*, the face cards are of value *10*, and other cards have the value mentioned on them.

The deal

Once all the players have completed their bets, the dealer will start giving one card to each player and one card to himself as well. In the next round, the cards are face up for each player, and for the dealer, the second card is face down.

So, all the players and dealer receive two cards. For each player, both the cards are face up, and for the dealer, one card is face up and one card is face down.

Naturals

Let's say a player has an ace and a second card of value *10* (picture card or a ten-number card); then it sums up to *21*. This is called a *Blackjack* or natural. In this case, the dealer immediately pays one and half times the total bet amount. If the dealer has a *Blackjack*, then he/she takes all the money of the bet from the player. If the dealer and the player both are in the same situation, then it's a tie.

The gameplay

At each turn, the player has to decide whether he needs another card or not; we call it **hit** or **stand**. The decision of when to stop is actually avoiding not going above *21*. If the player asks for more cards and goes above *21*, then he loses the game; this situation is called **burst**. If the player asks for another card, it means he is actually getting close to *21*.

Applying the Monte Carlo approach

Blackjack gameplay is formulated as a finite and episodic MDP. Each game is an episode, the reward is +1 for winning the game, -1 for losing the game, and 0 for a tie. Within the game, the rewards are zero and do not apply any discount as $\gamma = 1$. The actions for players are either to stick or to hit and the state depends on the dealer card or player card. The card bank (from where the cards are drawn) is an infinite set of decks, so keeping track of the cards is of no use.

If the player has one ace counted as *11* and is not bust, then we can say that the ace is usable. The player will make a decision based on three scenarios. First, his current sum is *12 - 21*. Second, the dealer has one ace card. And third, the player has a usable ace. These three scenarios make up a total of *200* states.

Now, if the policy is to stick the player's sum of the card (*21* or *20)*, if not then hits. We have to find the value state function for this policy by the Monte Carlo approach. One way is to simulate a lot of *Blackjack* game simulations using this policy and return the average for each state.

Blackjack game implementation

In this section, we will implement a complete *Blackjack* game in Python. I have put all the required comments so that you can understand the game implementation; it is important to understand the code as we need to learn how to play the game with machine learning.

The implementation of this game is by using the functional approach; we are not concerned with following an object-oriented approach. It is just the functions; transform the data and return some data.

Now let's dive into the code to implement the *Blackjack* game:

```python
import math
import random

#Following are the values of the var_Card_s: Jack (10), King (10), Queen
(10), Ace (1), 2, 3, 4, 5, 6, 7, 8, 9, 10,


def meth_var_Card__Random_():
  var_Card_ = random.randint(1,13)
  if var_Card_ > 10:
    var_Card_ = 10
  return var_Card_


def meth_Ace_Useable(_var_Hand_):
  _var_value_, ace = _var_Hand_
  return ((ace) and ((_var_value_ + 10) <= 21))


def _meth_Value_Total(_var_Hand_):
  _var_value_, ace = _var_Hand_
  if (meth_Ace_Useable(_var_Hand_)):
    return (_var_value_ + 10)
  else:
    return _var_value_
def _meth_Add_Card_Value_(_var_Hand_, var_Card_):
  _var_value_, ace = _var_Hand_
  if (var_Card_ == 1):
    ace = True
  return (_var_value_ + var_Card_, ace)



def _meth_Dealer_Eval(var_Hand_Dealer):
```

```
        while (_meth_Value_Total(var_Hand_Dealer) < 17):

            var_Hand_Dealer = _meth_Add_Card_Value_(var_Hand_Dealer,
    meth_var_Card__Random_())
        return var_Hand_Dealer



    def meth_Play_(state, dec):
        #evaluate
        var_Hand_Player = state[0] #val, useable ace
        var_Hand_Dealer = state[1]
        if dec == 0: #action = stay
            #evaluate game; dealer plays
            var_Hand_Dealer = _meth_Dealer_Eval(var_Hand_Dealer)

            player_tot = _meth_Value_Total(var_Hand_Player)

            dealer_tot = _meth_Value_Total(var_Hand_Dealer)

            status = 1

            if (dealer_tot > 21):
                status = 2 #player wins
            elif (dealer_tot == player_tot):
                status = 3 #draw
            elif (dealer_tot < player_tot):
                status = 2 #player wins
            elif (dealer_tot > player_tot):
                status = 4 #player loses


    #Now we are cheking that if hit then we add on player hand a new var_Card_

        elif dec == 1: #action = hit
            var_Hand_Player = _meth_Add_Card_Value_(var_Hand_Player,
    meth_var_Card__Random_())
            d_hand = _meth_Dealer_Eval(var_Hand_Dealer)
            player_tot = _meth_Value_Total(var_Hand_Player)
            status = 1
            if (player_tot == 21):
                if (_meth_Value_Total(d_hand) == 21):
                    status = 3 #It means draw game
                else:
                    status = 2 #It means that player win the game
            elif (player_tot > 21):
                status = 4
            #It means player lose the game
```

```
        elif (player_tot < 21):
    #It means player lose the game
            status = 1
    state = (var_Hand_Player, var_Hand_Dealer, status)

    return state

#Now we are ready to start the blackjack

def initGame():

#4 = Player lose the game and dealer won
#3 = Game draw
#2 = Player won the game
#1 = The game is in process


    status = 1

    var_Hand_Player = _meth_Add_Card_Value_((0, False),
meth_var_Card__Random_())

    var_Hand_Player = _meth_Add_Card_Value_(var_Hand_Player,
meth_var_Card__Random_())

    var_Hand_Dealer = _meth_Add_Card_Value_((0, False),
meth_var_Card__Random_())

    #We will check here that the player win the game

    if _meth_Value_Total(var_Hand_Player) == 21:
        if _meth_Value_Total(var_Hand_Dealer) != 21:
            status = 2 #After first deal player win the game
        else:
            status = 3 #means its draw game

    state = (var_Hand_Player, var_Hand_Dealer, status)
    return state
```

We have just implemented a very simplified version of *Blackjack*. We wrote very few methods that consist of if/else logic. Now we are going to play a sample game; then you will be able to understand it better:

```
state = initGame()
print(state)
```

The output of the previous line of code:

((7, False), (5, False), 1)

```
#Here the Player has 7 as total, now let's hit
state = meth_Play_(state, 1)
print(state)
```

The output is as follows:

((9, False), (5, False), 1)

```
#Here the player has 9 as total, now let's hit

state = meth_Play_(state, 1)
print(state)
```

The output of the previous code:

((15, False), (5, False), 1)

```
##Here the player has 15 as total, now let's hit

state = meth_Play_(state, 0)
print(state)
```

The output is:

((15, False), (20, False), 4)

Now we are ready to start building an Monte Carlo-based RL algorithm:

```python
import numpy as np

#First we create list of all the states

def meth_State_Space_Init():
    states = []
    for var_Card_ in range(1,11):
        for _var_value_ in range(11,22):
            states.append((_var_value_, False, var_Card_))
            states.append((_var_value_, True, var_Card_))
    return states


#Now we are going to create a key value pair dictionary
#for all the possible action-state and the values

#Below method will create a Q look up table

def initStateActions(states):
    av = {}
    for state in states:
        av[(state, 0)] = 0.0
        av[(state, 1)] = 0.0
    return av

#Now we will set-up a dictionary that contains
#all the actions-state to capture the record


def math_S_Account_Init(stateActions):
    counts = {}
    for sa in stateActions:
        counts[sa] = 0
    return counts


#Now we will write a code that calculate our reward,
#it is +1 for winning a game
#-1 for losing a game
#0 for tie a game


#We will substract it with 3 to get the value

def math_Reward_Calc(outcome):
    return 3-outcome
```

```
#Now this function will recalculate the reward average in the Q lookup
table


def meth_QTable_Update(av_table, av_count, returns):
    for key in returns:
        av_table[key] = av_table[key] + (1.0 / av_count[key]) *
(returns[key]- av_table[key])
    return av_table

#This value returning a Q value or average rewards for all the states

def meth_QValue_Reward_Average(state, av_table):
    stay = av_table[(state,0)]
    hit = av_table[(state,1)]
    return np.array([stay, hit])



#Now we convert the state of the game to ((ace total , player)
#and (ace total, dealer), status)

def getRLstate(state):
    var_Hand_Player, var_Hand_Dealer, status = state
    player_val, player_ace = var_Hand_Player
    return (player_val, player_ace, var_Hand_Dealer[0])
```

We've defined in the previous code all the basic methods to run a Monte Carlo algorithm. We have initialized the state and action-state space and we've also defined the function to reward calculation and update our Q-lookup take.

Now we will do it for 5000000 Monte Carlo simulations of our game:

```
#Now we set the value for number of run
#It just take 1-2 minutes to run
var_epochs_ = 5000000
var_Eepsilon_ = 0.1


state_space = meth_State_Space_Init()

av_table = initStateActions(state_space)

av_count = math_S_Account_Init(av_table)


for i in range(var_epochs_ ):
```

```
    #Now we will initialize a new game

    state = initGame()

    var_Hand_Player, var_Hand_Dealer, status = state


    while var_Hand_Player[0] < 11:
        var_Hand_Player = _meth_Add_Card_Value_(var_Hand_Player,
meth_var_Card__Random_())
        state = (var_Hand_Player, var_Hand_Dealer, status)
    rl_state = getRLstate(state) #convert to compressed version of state
    #Now set-up to temp hold action-state for current episode
    #return, action, state
    returns = {}

    while(state[2] == 1): #while in current episode
        #var_Eepsilon_ greedy action selection
        act_probs = meth_QValue_Reward_Average(rl_state, av_table)

        if (random.random() < var_Eepsilon_ ):
            action = random.randint(0,1)

        else:
            action = np.argmax(act_probs)#select an action

        sa = ((rl_state, action))

        returns[sa] = 0
      #For average calculation we increment the counter


        av_count[sa] += 1

      #Start the game now

        state = meth_Play_(state, action)

        rl_state = getRLstate(state)

    #Now once an episode complete then reward will be assign to all the
actions-state

    for key in returns:
        returns[key] = math_Reward_Calc(state[2])
    av_table = meth_QTable_Update(av_table, av_count, returns)

print("Done")
```

We can run the Monte Carlo simulation for a *Blackjack* game 5000000 times and build a value-action Q-table. We used it to determine the optimal action in a specific state.

Monte Carlo for control

Monte Carlo methods for prediction (also called **passive**) are a little bit different from Monte Carlo methods for control (also called **active**). We can say that the Monte Carlo control problem is more accurate because we need to estimate the policy that is not provided. Monte Carlo for control works similar to the techniques we used in dynamic programming. We explained it in the policy iteration algorithm in Chapter 3, *Dynamic Programming*. Policy iteration allows us to find the utility value for each state, and at the same time, it finds the optimal policy $\pi*$. The policy iteration approach includes two steps:

1. **Policy evaluation**: $U \rightarrow U^\pi$.
2. **Policy improvement**: $\pi \rightarrow greedy(U)$.

The first step is called policy evaluation; it makes the function of utility consistent as per the current policy. The second step is called policy improvement; it makes the current function of utility as policy π greedy. Both the changes work against each other and creates a target moving to the other:

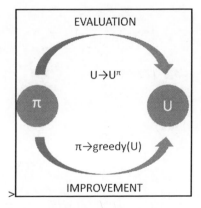

Figure 5.5: Monte Carlo for control

Look at the second step and you'll notice that we've used a new term called **greedy**. What is the meaning of greedy? A greedy algorithm is used for each step to make a local optimal choice. As per our scenario, greedy means the action taken at each step with the highest utility and updating the policy for that action. This is only for the local optimal choice, so it generally does not get to the optimal solution.

Now we will discuss how the greedy strategy works. It works because the local choice evaluates using the function utility, which changes with time. At the start, the agent will follow the lot of suboptimal paths, but after some time, the greedy strategy will lead to a positive reward and the utilities will start converging to the true values. All reinforcement learning algorithms can be seen in terms of policy iteration. Now, keeping this policy iteration idea in mind will allow you to easily understand the control methods.

In Monte Carlo for control, it is important to guarantee uniform exploration of all action-state pairs. By following a policy, it is possible that specific action-state pairs will never be visited.

Now we will implement the algorithm and see how it works in code.

Monte Carlo Exploring Starts

Here's the algorithm for Monte Carlo **Exploring Starts (ES)**:

```
Initialize, for all s ∈ S, a ∈ A(s):
   Q(s, a) ← arbitrary
   π(s) ← arbitrary
   Returns(s, a) ← empty list

Repeat forever:
   Choose S₀ ∈ S and A₀ ∈ A(S₀) s.t. all pairs have probability > 0
   Generate an episode starting from S₀, A₀, following π
   For each pair s, a is appearing in episode:
      G ← it return following the first occurrence of a, s
      Append G to Returns(a, s)
      Q(a, s) ← average(Returns(a, s))
   For each s in the episode:
      π(s) ← argmaxₐ Q(a, s)
```

We are again going to the function `fuc_return_get()`, but this time the input would be a list containing the tuple (action, observation, reward):

```python
def fuc_return_get(par_list_state_, par_gamma_df):
    var_count_ = 0
    var_value_return = 0
    for var_visit in state_list:
        var_rewards_ = var_visit[2]
        var_value_return += var_rewards_ * numP.power(par_gamma_df,
var_count_)
        var_count_ += 1
    return var_value_return
```

Now I am going to use another function, `fun_Policy_Update_()`, which makes the greedy policy with respect to the action-state function:

```python
def fun_Policy_Update_(var_list_episode, var_matrix_policy,
parm_Matrix_Action_State_):
    """ Now we will update the policy in the function

    With respoect to action-state
    this fuction make the policy greedy.
    and it return the updated policy
    """
    for var_visit in var_list_episode:
        var_obser_ = var_visit[0]
        var_col_ = var_obser_[1] + (var_obser_[0]*4)
        if(var_matrix_policy[var_obser_[0], var_obser_[1]] != -1):
            var_matrix_policy[var_obser_[0], var_obser_[1]] = \
                numP.argmax(parm_Matrix_Action_State_[:,var_col_])

    return var_matrix_policy
```

The `fun_Policy_Update_()` function is for improvement of the policy and it is required to get the convergence of an optimal policy. We will also implement `fun_print_policy()`; we will use it to print the policy into a terminal with the symbols #, &, <, >, v, and ^. We will initialize the action-state matrix and the random matrix policy in the main function. The matrix can be initialized with random values or zero:

```python
# Random policy matrix
var_matrix_policy = numP.random.randint(low=0, high=4,
                                        size=(3, 4)).astype(numP.float32)
#for obstacle for Nan at (1,1)

var_matrix_policy[1,1] = numP.NaN
var_matrix_policy[0,3] = var_matrix_policy[1,3] = -1
```

```
# Matrix action-state (intilize with random values)

parm_Matrix_Action_State_ = numP.random.random_sample((4,12))
```

Finally, we have the main loop of the algorithm, which is not so different from the loop used for the Monte Carlo prediction:

```
for var_epochs_ in range(var_Eepsilon_):

# New episode starting
var_list_episode = list()

# First observation would reset and return
_var_obser_ = environment.reset(var_Exploring_Starts=True)
_var_IsStarting_ = True

for _ in range(1000):
    # Now we will take the action from the matrix action
    var_action_ = var_matrix_policy[_var_obser_[0], _var_obser_[1]]
    # It is nessary to chose the random action
    # As the state just started
  if(_var_IsStarting_):
        var_action_ = numP.random.randint(0, 4)
        _var_IsStarting_ = False
    # Get a new observation and reward from the next move
    new_observation, var_reward_, done = environment.step(var_action_)
    #In the episode list we will append the visit
    var_list_episode.append((_var_obser_, var_action_, var_reward_))
    _var_obser_ = new_observation

  if done: break

    # For estimating the utility at the end of the episode
_var_count_ = 0

# Have to check that is this the first visit to action-state

var_matrix_checkup = numP.zeros((4,12))

# Here we will implement the Fist visit MC.
# We will store the list of episode for each action-state

for var_visit in var_list_episode:
    _var_obser_ = var_visit[0]
    var_action_ = var_visit[1]
    _var_col_ = _var_obser_[1] + (_var_obser_[0]*4)
    _var_row_ = var_action_
    if(var_matrix_checkup[_var_row_, _var_col_] == 0):
```

```
              _var_value_return_ = get_return(var_list_episode[_var_count_:],
gamma)
              _var_Matrix_RunningMean_[_var_row_, _var_col_] += 1
              state_action_matrix[_var_row_, _var_col_] += _var_value_return_
              var_matrix_checkup[_var_row_, _var_col_] = 1
          _var_count_ += 1

  # Update Policy for improvement

var_matrix_policy = fun_Policy_Update_(var_list_episode,
                            var_matrix_policy,
                            state_action_matrix/_var_Matrix_RunningMean_)
# Now we will do the printing to terminal here

if(var_epochs_ % print_epoch == 0):

    print("")

    print("matrix Action-State later " + str(var_epochs_+1) + " times")

    print(state_action_matrix / _var_Matrix_RunningMean_)

    print("Matrix Policy later " + str(var_epochs_+1) + " times")

    print(var_matrix_policy)

    print_policy(var_matrix_policy)

# Here we will check the matrix of utility

print("Matrix utility later " + str(var_Eepsilon_) + " times")

print(state_action_matrix / _var_Matrix_RunningMean_)
```

Now if we check out the code as follows, we can notice some differences from the Monte Carlo prediction as we implemented it earlier:

```
if(_var_IsStarting_):
    _var_action_ = numP.random.randint(0, 4)
    _var_IsStarting_= False
```

The previous condition simply states that the exploring start is true, meaning it satisfies the start condition. Only when the exploring start will assure, the Monte Carlo algorithm converges to an optimal policy. In the control problem, we cannot start from random starting states. The algorithm will improve the policy during the iteration if the action has chosen a non-zero probability. This means only for the start when the states episode start, the random action has to be taken.

There is another important difference that needs to be analyzed. In the following code, you can notice the two variables `_var_obser_` and `new_observation` at time t and time t+1 respectively. We store in the list of episodes at time t the reward received at t+1 for the action taken at t.

The optimal policy is defined as follows:

```
Policy (Optimal):

    > > > *
    ^ # ^ *
    ^ < < <
```

As seen in the previous code, the agent's optimal policy is to move at state *(4, 2)* and this will take us to the longest path. Now we will run the policy evaluation for Monte Carlo control and get the following results:

```
Policy later 1 times
    ^ > v *
    < # v *
    v > < >


. . .


Policy later 3001 times
    > > > *
    > # ^ *
    > > ^ <


. . .


Policy later 78001 times
    > > > *
    ^ # ^ *
    ^ < ^ <


. . .


Policy later 405001 times
```

```
> > > *
^ # ^ *
^ < < <


. . .


Policy later 500000 times
> | > | > | *
^ | # | ^ | *
^ | < | < | <
```

As we saw earlier that the first policy is completely useless and nonsense, we start with a random policy. However, after *3,000* iterations, we can see that the algorithm finds a suboptimal policy. After *78,000* iterations, it finds another policy that is better than the earlier policy but still a suboptimal policy. At the end of about *405,000* iterations, our algorithm finds the optimal policy and uses the same policy until the end.

Monte Carlo methods never converge to the optimal policy. Now you need to understand that if the algorithm converges to a suboptimal policy, then the function utility also converges for that specific policy.

Example - Blackjack

It is very easy to apply the Monte Carlo exploring start to a *Blackjack* game. It is easy to arrange the Monte Carlo exploring start algorithm by including all the possibilities because it is an episodic and simulated game. It simply picks the cards and checks the player's sum of card values and whether the player has any usable aces. All these checks are done with equal probability. We used the initial policy from the previous example of *Blackjack*, that stick on *21* or *20*. The initial function value-action can be zero for all action-state pairs. We are not completely certain about the reason for this discrepancy, but having said that, we are confident that it is indeed the optimal policy for the *Blackjack* game.

Summary

In this chapter, we started by defining Monte Carlo methods. We discussed that Monte Carlo is a model-free algorithm and it learns with episodes of direct experience. We discussed two approaches in Monte Carlo: every visit Monte Carlo and first visit Monte Carlo.

The major disadvantage of the Monte Carlo method is that we only learn with episodes, so we have to wait until we complete an episode to update the policy. A policy cannot be updated in between.

Then we also learned how to play *Blackjack;* we discussed its basic rules and techniques. We implemented the game using Python and then applied Monte Carlo methods to the game. Our agent tried to learn the policy.

Furthermore, we discussed Monte Carlo for control and defined the algorithm and the complete implementation of that algorithm in Python.

In the next chapter, we will discuss planning and learning algorithms in reinforcement learning. We will discuss in detail what Q-learning is, how it works, and why it is important? Later in the chapter, we'll see practical code examples using the Q-learning algorithm.

6

Learning and Planning

In the earlier chapters, we saw how to use planning and learning algorithms. In reinforcement learning, there are three ways to think about it: model-based learning, value-based learning, and policy-based learning. We discussed earlier that learning comes from experience and reaches a policy; on the other hand, planning comes from a model and then reaches a policy.

In this chapter, we will discuss **Q-learning** in detail. We will see in this chapter what Q-learning is and why it is important in reinforcement learning. Here, we will learn from scratch how to create or extend our own algorithm for learning and planning. We will start with a Q-learning example and then solve the Q-learning example by writing it down to better understand the algorithm. Later in the chapter, we will use the full functionality of BURLAP libraries to ease our development efforts. In this chapter, we will implement both learning algorithms and planning algorithms. Specifically, we will go through the implementation of Q-learning and value iteration.

Q-learning

Q-learning is a way to optimize solutions in an MDP problem. The distinguishing feature of Q-learning is its ability to choose between delayed rewards and instant rewards. At each time step, an agent notices the vector of state, Z_t. Then the agent chooses an action, a_t. When the process moves to the next state, Z_{t+1}, an agent receives a reward, $r(z_t, u_t)$. The overall goal of this training is to find the sequence of actions that maximizes the sum of future rewards, thus leading to the shortest path from the start state to the finish state:

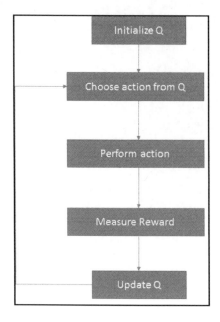

Figure 6.1: Structure of a Q-learning algorithm

Now we are going to discuss a very important topic in reinforcement learning called Q-learning. First I will directly jump into an example; then I will explain the concepts in detail.

Let's say we have **5** rooms in a building that are connected by doors as shown in *Figure 6.2*. I will number the rooms from **0** to **4**. The outside environment of the building is marked as **5**. Note that it is possible to go in and out of the building from room **1** and room **4** only:

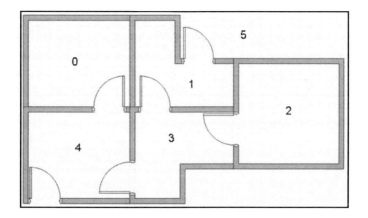

Figure 6.2: Q-learning example - building map

We can convert this building diagram into a graph. Each node represents a room and each link represents a door:

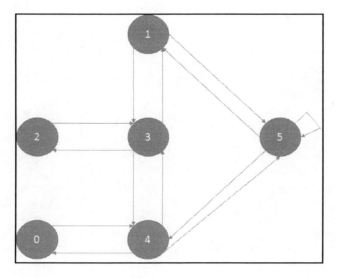

Figure 6.3: Converting our building map into a graph

To start this example, suppose the agent is in any one of the rooms and he needs to leave the building. In other words, he needs to go to room **5**, which represents the outside of the building. So, room **5** is our goal room or goal state. Now we will define the rewards for each door (link). For the door that reaches room **5**, we set the reward as 100, and the rest of them that do not take us to goal state are set to **0**. As the doors are two-way, such as the door between room **2** and **3**, each room has two arrows representing one door. Each arrow has a reward value as shown in *Figure 6.4*:

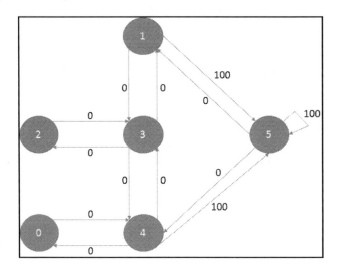

Figure 6.4: Adding rewards into the graph

One more thing to note is that from room **5**, the loop-back reward (going to the same state) is **100**. In Q-learning, the goal is to get maximum rewards. For the agent to get maximum rewards, it's looping back again and again, and it will be in that state forever. We called this type of goal an absorbing goal.

Now let's assume that our agent is a dumb robot that only learns through experience. The agent can roam around the building from one room to another and it has no prior knowledge of the environment. It also has no information about which sequence of doors it will use to go outside:

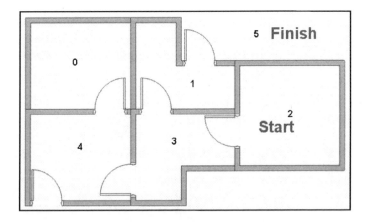

Figure 6.5: Building a map with agent start state 2

The terminology in Q-learning includes the terms action and state. We call each room (including the outside environment) a state and the movement of the agent from one room to another is through a door called **link**. In the below figure 6.6, nodes represent states and arrows represent doors as actions

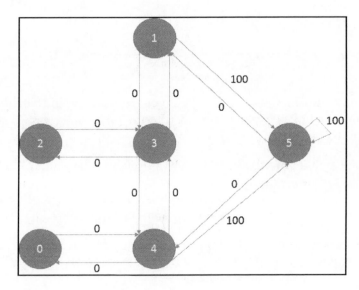

Figure 6.6: Graph with agent start state 2

Now we want to create a model that depicts the agent exit plan for an agent from any room to room **5** (the outside environment). To implement it, let's suppose the agent is in room **2** and our aim is to take it outside the building; so the agent needs to go to room **5**.

Now from state **2**, the agent can only reach state **3** because that's the only connection possible. From state **3**, it has multiple options to choose from. It can go to room **1**, room **4**, or back to room **2** as shown in the *Figure 6.6*. Now if the agent is in room **4** then also it has three choices: room **0**, room **3**, or room **5**. If the agent is in room **1**, then it has two choices: room **3** or the goal in room **5**. If the agent is in room **0**, then it has only one option: room **4**.

As our agent is already in room **3**, it needs to select one of the three possible rooms: **1, 2** or **4**.

We will create the state diagram and put all the instant rewards into the reward table; we call it the *R* matrix:

$$R = \begin{array}{c} \\ \text{State} \\ 0 \\ 1 \\ 2 \\ 3 \\ 4 \\ 5 \end{array} \begin{array}{c} \text{Action} \\ \begin{array}{cccccc} 0 & 1 & 2 & 3 & 4 & 5 \end{array} \\ \begin{bmatrix} -1 & -1 & -1 & -1 & 0 & -1 \\ -1 & -1 & -1 & 0 & -1 & 100 \\ -1 & -1 & -1 & 0 & -1 & -1 \\ -1 & 0 & 0 & -1 & 0 & -1 \\ 0 & -1 & -1 & 0 & -1 & 100 \\ -1 & 0 & -1 & -1 & 0 & 100 \end{bmatrix} \end{array}$$

Figure 6.7: Reward matrix

In *Figure 6.7*, we have three types of values. *-1* means there are no links between the rooms; for example, there is no link between room *1* and room *0*. The other values are the *0* and *100* rewards as shown in *Figure 6.6*.

Now we will create another matrix called *Q* that is similar to the R matrix. The Q-matrix will act like a brain for the agent, representing the memory of whatever the agent learns while roaming around the building. Each row of the matrix will represent the agent's current state and the columns will represent the actions that lead to the next state.

In the beginning, the agent knows nothing and we represent it as zero. For simplicity, in this example, we will assume that the total number of states is known to be six. Note that if the total number of states is not known, then we set it only to one element. Later on, when we discover more states, we add more columns and rows into the matrix.

The learning formula is very simple, as follows:

*Q(state, action) = R(state, action) + Gamma * Max[Q(next state, all actions)]*

Now as per the previous formula, the Q value is equal to the sum of R values and the discounted factor *Gamma* multiplied by the maximum Q value for all the states and actions.

The agent will roam or explore the environment until it reaches the goal state. Each exploration is called an **episode**. Each exploration starts from the initial state. Once the agent reaches the goal state, it means it finishes one episode and the program moves to the next episode.

The algorithm for Q-learning is defined as follows:

1. Set the discounted factor (gamma) parameter and the reward in R matrix.
2. Initialize the Q-matrix to *0*.
3. For each episode:
    1. We select the random initial state.
    2. We run a Do-While loop until the goal (target) state cannot be reached.
    3. Select any one action from all the possible actions from the current state.
    4. From that selected action, move to the next state.
    5. For the next state, get the maximum Q-value.
    6. Now compute *Q(state, action) = R(state, action) + Gamma (discounted factor) * Max[Q(next state, all actions)]*.
    7. Set the next state as the current state. Which can be:
        1. End Do.
        2. End For.

The agent will use this algorithm to learn from experience. Each episode is actually one session of training. And in each training session, the agent will explore the environment (denoted by R matrix) and keep receiving the reward it until reaches the goal state. The major purpose of this training is to explore the environment, meaning our agent will store the values in its brain called Q-matrix.

The Q-matrix or Q-table will update throughout the lifetime of the agent. Now, an important thing to consider is that some actions look like the best possible actions for the time being, but once the agent has spent some time in the environment, the same action will not be the best. This is because the agent has already learned from the environment and experience.

The gamma or discounted factor parameter always has a range from *0* to *1*.

The learning rate, sometimes called **step size**, is actually used to determine when the newly obtained information will override the previous information. If it is *0* or close to *0*, it means the agent did not learn anything. On the other hand, if it is *1* or close to *1*, it means that the agent is very close to being well trained for its environment.

This is the algorithm for utilizing the Q-value:

1. Set *current state = initial state*.
2. From the current state, find the highest Q-value action (learning and planning).
3. Then we will set *current state = next state*.
4. Repeat steps 2 and 3 until *current state = goal (target) state*.

The preceding algorithm will return the states' sequence from the initial state to the goal (target) state.

> This is the key feature of Q-learning: when feedback is provided, it might be long after an important decision has been made. The reality is that a large number of important decisions change after the agent gains experience in the environment. All wrong actions decrease the chances of selecting the same actions again in the future.

Q-learning example by hand

Now, to understand the Q-learning algorithm completely, we will go through it step by step and write it down. Later we will do the implementation of Q-learning in code.

We will start our example by setting up the initial state as room *1* and discount factor learning parameter as *0.8*.

Now let's initialize our Q-matrix as a zero matrix:

$$Q = \begin{array}{c c} & \begin{array}{c c c c c c} 0 & 1 & 2 & 3 & 4 & 5 \end{array} \\ \begin{array}{c} 0 \\ 1 \\ 2 \\ 3 \\ 4 \\ 5 \end{array} & \begin{bmatrix} 0 & 0 & 0 & 0 & 0 & 0 \\ 0 & 0 & 0 & 0 & 0 & 0 \\ 0 & 0 & 0 & 0 & 0 & 0 \\ 0 & 0 & 0 & 0 & 0 & 0 \\ 0 & 0 & 0 & 0 & 0 & 0 \\ 0 & 0 & 0 & 0 & 0 & 0 \end{bmatrix} \end{array}$$

Figure 6.8: Initializing Q as zero

Let's take the matrix *R* defined earlier for our example and look at its second row (state *1*). There are two actions possible: either to go to room *3* with reward *0* or go to room *5* with reward *100*.

$$R = \begin{array}{c c} & \begin{array}{c} \textbf{Action} \end{array} \\ \begin{array}{c} \textbf{State} \end{array} & \begin{array}{c c c c c c} 0 & 1 & 2 & 3 & 4 & 5 \end{array} \\ \begin{array}{c} 0 \\ 1 \\ 2 \\ 3 \\ 4 \\ 5 \end{array} & \begin{bmatrix} -1 & -1 & -1 & -1 & 0 & -1 \\ -1 & -1 & -1 & 0 & -1 & 100 \\ -1 & -1 & -1 & 0 & -1 & -1 \\ -1 & 0 & 0 & -1 & 0 & -1 \\ 0 & -1 & -1 & 0 & -1 & 100 \\ -1 & 0 & -1 & -1 & 0 & 100 \end{bmatrix} \end{array}$$

Figure 6.9: Initialize the matrix with rewards

Now we computer the Q-value as follows:

$$Q(state, action) = R(state, action) + Gamma * Max[Q(next\ state, all\ actions)]$$

$$Q(1, 5) = R(1, 5) + 0.8 * Max[Q(5, 1), Q(5, 4), Q(5, 5)] = 100 + 0.8 * 0 = 100$$

As the Q-matrix is initialized to zero, Q(5, 5), Q(5, 4), and Q(5, 1) all become zero. This computation gives Q(1, 5) as 100.

Now the agent moves to the next state and it is state 5, so it has become the current state. As 5 is the goal (target) state, it means we've finished one episode. Now the agent will store this information in the Q-matrix as follows:

$$Q = \begin{array}{c} \\ 0 \\ 1 \\ 2 \\ 3 \\ 4 \\ 5 \end{array} \begin{array}{cccccc} 0 & 1 & 2 & 3 & 4 & 5 \\ \begin{bmatrix} 0 & 0 & 0 & 0 & 0 & 0 \\ 0 & 0 & 0 & 0 & 0 & 0 \\ 0 & 0 & 0 & 0 & 0 & 100 \\ 0 & 0 & 0 & 0 & 0 & 0 \\ 0 & 0 & 0 & 0 & 0 & 0 \\ 0 & 0 & 0 & 0 & 0 & 0 \end{bmatrix} \end{array}$$

Figure 6.10: Updated Q-matrix

To start the next episode, the agent will randomly choose the initial state. Suppose this time our initial state is 3.

As per the R matrix, the agent has three possible actions to choose from. It can go from state 3 to state 1, 2, or 4. We apply random selection and go to state 1:

$Q(state, action) = R(state, action) + Gamma * Max[Q(next state, all actions)]$

$Q(1, 3) = R(1, 3) + 0.8 * Max[Q(3, 1), Q(3, 2), Q(3, 1)]$
$0 + 0.8 * Max(0, 100) = 80$

We use the previously updated Q-matrix and update the current transition for $Q(1, 3) = 0$ and $Q(1, 5) = 100$.

We are now using the Q-matrix as updated in the last episode. $Q(1, 3) = 0$ and $Q(1, 5) = 100$. The computation result is $Q(3, 1) = 80$ as the reward is zero. The Q-matrix now becomes:

$$Q = \begin{array}{c} \\ 0 \\ 1 \\ 2 \\ 3 \\ 4 \\ 5 \end{array} \begin{array}{cccccc} 0 & 1 & 2 & 3 & 4 & 5 \\ \begin{bmatrix} 0 & 0 & 0 & 0 & 0 & 0 \\ 0 & 0 & 0 & 0 & 0 & 100 \\ 0 & 0 & 0 & 0 & 0 & 0 \\ 0 & 80 & 0 & 0 & 0 & 0 \\ 0 & 0 & 0 & 0 & 0 & 0 \\ 0 & 0 & 0 & 0 & 0 & 0 \end{bmatrix} \end{array}$$

Figure 6.11: Updated Q-matrix

The next initial state is state **1**. We do the same procedure and run through the inner loop of Q-learning as state **1** is not our goal (target) state.

From state **1**, we can see in R matrix that there are two possibilities: either state **5** or state **3**. Luckily, our agent chooses the action to move to state **5**:

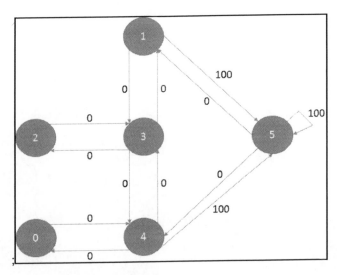

Figure 6.12: The current state is 1

We've reached state **5** and there are three possibilities to go to: **1, 4,** or **5**. In this case, we compute the Q-value and then take the maximum value of possible actions:

$$Q(state, action) = R(state, action) + Gamma * Max[Q(next\ state, all\ actions)]$$

$$Q(1, 5) = R(1, 5) + 0.8 * Max[Q(1, 2), Q(1, 5)]$$

$$= 100 + 0.8 * 0 = 100$$

Now we need to update the Q-matrix as $Q(5, 5)$, $Q(5, 4)$, and $Q(5, 1)$ are all zero. The result computes $Q(1, 5)$ as *100*.

As 5 is our goal (target) state, we've finished the episode. Now we update the Q-matrix as follows:

$$Q= \begin{matrix} & 0 & 1 & 2 & 3 & 4 & 5 \\ 0 & 0 & 0 & 0 & 0 & 0 & 0 \\ 1 & 0 & 0 & 0 & 0 & 0 & 100 \\ 2 & 0 & 0 & 0 & 0 & 0 & 0 \\ 3 & 0 & 80 & 0 & 0 & 0 & 0 \\ 4 & 0 & 0 & 0 & 0 & 0 & 0 \\ 5 & 0 & 0 & 0 & 0 & 0 & 0 \end{matrix}$$

Figure 6.13: Updated Q-matrix

If the agent learns more from future episodes, it will reach a convergence value in the Q-matrix like this:

$$Q= \begin{matrix} & 0 & 1 & 2 & 3 & 4 & 5 \\ 0 & 0 & 0 & 0 & 0 & 400 & 0 \\ 1 & 0 & 0 & 0 & 320 & 0 & 500 \\ 2 & 0 & 0 & 0 & 320 & 0 & 0 \\ 3 & 0 & 400 & 256 & 0 & 400 & 0 \\ 4 & 320 & 0 & 0 & 320 & 0 & 500 \\ 5 & 0 & 400 & 0 & 0 & 400 & 500 \end{matrix}$$

Figure 6.14: Convergence value in the Q-matrix

Now we will apply normalization to the Q-matrix (convert it to percentages). To do this, we need to divide all the non-zero entries by the highest number (which in this case is *500*):

$$Q= \begin{matrix} & 0 & 1 & 2 & 3 & 4 & 5 \\ 0 & 0 & 0 & 0 & 0 & 80 & 0 \\ 1 & 0 & 0 & 0 & 64 & 0 & 100 \\ 2 & 0 & 0 & 0 & 64 & 0 & 0 \\ 3 & 0 & 80 & 51 & 0 & 80 & 0 \\ 4 & 64 & 0 & 0 & 64 & 0 & 100 \\ 5 & 0 & 80 & 0 & 0 & 80 & 100 \end{matrix}$$

Figure 6.15: Normalized Q-matrix

When the Q-matrix is close to the state of convergence, we know that our agent has learned the optimal path to reach the goal (target) state. Now, for the sake of understanding, we will trace the best sequence by following the links to each state with the highest value.

In our example, the agent is currently in state 2. It can use the Q-matrix as a guide or brain as we explained earlier.

From state 2, it checks the maximum Q-value, and from there it gets a suggestion on what is the best action to reach state 3.

Now from state 3, it again checks the maximum Q-values, and from there it has two possibilities to select: go to state 4 or go to state 1. Suppose we choose state 1.

This time from state 1, it again checks the maximum Q-value and the suggestion is to go to state 5.

Thus, the overall sequence is *2 -3 - 1 - 5*.

Value iteration

We discussed the value iteration algorithm in Chapter 3, *Dynamic Programming*. We will implement it here in this section through a practical example. It's a really simple algorithm. We start with some arbitrary utilities, but then we update them based on their neighbors, and then we will simply repeat:

1. Start with arbitrary utilities.
2. Update the utilities based on the neighbors.
3. Repeat until convergence.

What does based on neighbors mean? It actually means we are going to update the utility for a state based on all the states that it can reach.

To start the implementation, we first create a class for value iteration, and we will call it `ValueIterationTutorial`. It will extend the `MDPSolver` class to gain many of the useful data structures used in solving an MDP, and it will implement the `QProvider` and `Planner` interfaces. We implement the `Planner` interface because we want to implement the `planFromState` method and the `QProvider` interface because we want to compute the value iteration function. The `QProvider` interface extends the `ValueFunction` interface:

```
package project;


//We will import all the required libraries
```

```
import java.util.*;

//Now we will import all the BURLAP libraries,
//there are lot of them to implement and it ease all our development
//We already introduce the implementation of BURLAP in earlier chapters
import burlap.behavior.policy.GreedyQPolicy;

//This library is related to implement policies
import burlap.behavior.policy.Policy;

//This library is related to implement Utitlities policies
import burlap.behavior.policy.PolicyUtils;

//This library is related to implement Single agent and episodic
import burlap.behavior.singleagent.Episode;

//This library is related to implement MDP
import burlap.behavior.singleagent.MDPSolver;

//This library is related to implement Episode Visualizer
import burlap.behavior.singleagent.auxiliary.EpisodeSequenceVisualizer;

//This library is related to implement States in MDP
import burlap.behavior.singleagent.auxiliary.StateReachability;

//This library is related to implement Single agent planner
import burlap.behavior.singleagent.planning.Planner;

//This library is related to implement Value functions constants
import burlap.behavior.valuefunction.ConstantValueFunction;

//This library is related to implement Q Provider
import burlap.behavior.valuefunction.QProvider;

//This library is related to implement Q Value
import burlap.behavior.valuefunction.QValue;

//This library is related to implement Value function
import burlap.behavior.valuefunction.ValueFunction;

//This library is related to implement Grid world
import burlap.domain.singleagent.gridworld.GridWorldDomain;

//This library is related to implement Grid world terminal function
import burlap.domain.singleagent.gridworld.GridWorldTerminalFunction;

//This library is related to implement Grid World visualization
import burlap.domain.singleagent.gridworld.GridWorldVisualizer;
```

```
//This library is related to implement Grid Agent
import burlap.domain.singleagent.gridworld.state.GridAgent;

//This library is related to implement states in Grid World
import burlap.domain.singleagent.gridworld.state.GridWorldState;

//This library is related to implement actions
import burlap.mdp.core.action.Action;

//This library is related to implement states
import burlap.mdp.core.state.State;

//This library is related to implement SA Domain
import burlap.mdp.singleagent.SADomain;

//This library is related to implement full model
import burlap.mdp.singleagent.model.FullModel;

//This library is related to implement transition probabilities
import burlap.mdp.singleagent.model.TransitionProb;

//This library is related to implement hashable states
import burlap.statehashing.HashableState;

//This library is related to implement hashable state factory
import burlap.statehashing.HashableStateFactory;

//This library is related to implement simple hashable state factory
import burlap.statehashing.simple.SimpleHashableStateFactory;

//This library is related to implement visualization
import burlap.visualizer.Visualizer;


public class ValueIterationTutorial extends MDPSolver implements QProvider,
Planner{

  @Override
   public double value(State st)
     {
         return 0.0;
     }

  @Override
  public List<QValue> qValues(State st) {
    {
         // We will implement it later
    }
```

```
@Override
  public double qValue(State st, Action act) {
  {
  // We will implement it later
  }

@Override
public GreedyQPolicy planFromState(State _initial_State_) {
  {
   // We will implement it later
  }

@Override
public void resetSolver() {
  {
   // We will implement it later
  }
}
```

As we extend MDPSolver, this will auto-build the data members that define the task and our domain (the HashableStateFactory, discount factor, domain, and state). Now the critical data that value iteration requires is to store its estimates for the value function. It is actually a mapping from states to real values. Moreover, for faster access, we can use HashableStateFactory and HashMap to provide the HashableState object from the states. One of the ways to make value iteration run faster is to initialize it to the optimal value function. This is why we use the value function as the initial value state.

We should also have a parameter that tells us how long the value iteration algorithm will run and when it's going to terminate.

Now we will define the constructor and create data members with the following code:

```
protected Map<HashableState, Double> functionValue;
protected ValueFunction vfinit;
protected int _iterations_Num;

public ValueIterationTutorial(SADomain domain_SA, double
  gamma_discount_factor, HashableStateFactory _hashFactory_,
  ValueFunction vfinit, int _iterations_Num)
  {
  this.solverInit(domain_SA, gamma_discount_factor, _hashFactory_);
  this.vfinit = vfinit; this._iterations_Num = _iterations_Num;
  this.functionValue = new HashMap<HashableState, Double>();
  }
```

There is a major component that value iteration requires and which is not defined as part of the data we provided to the constructor. Because it is an MDP, it is not demanding it upfront, and it is actually possible that the entire state space is infinite. When the input states are given there is a possibility that the finite set of states are in range.

Now we write a method to get all the reachable states from the input state:

```
public void ReachableFrom(State stateSeed)
    {
    Set<HashableState> Hashedstates =
StateReachability.getReachableHashedStates(stateSeed, this.domain,
this.hashingFactory);

    //initialize the value function for all states

    for(HashableState stateHash : Hashedstates)
    {
        if(!this.functionValue.containsKey(stateHash))
        {
            this.functionValue.put(stateHash,
this.vfinit.value(stateHash.s()));
        }
    }
}
```

Let me explain the previous code. First we use the `StateReachability` tool to find all the reachable states. Then we just iterate the complete list and for all the `HashableState` for which we do not have an entry. You can also note that the function is passed `stateHash.s()` by its `s()` method. As our states are sets of `HashableState` objects, we can get the `State` instance that is stored in the `HashableState` and it can be accessed from its `s()` method.

The other important method that we need to do is the implementation of the Bellman equation. We are already aware from the earlier chapters that the Bellman equation is simply a max over the Q-values. As we've already defined the methods that get the Q-values of the states, we can easily implement these methods and then the Bellman method:

```
@Override
public List<QValue> qValues(State st) {
    List<Action> actionsApplicable = this.applicableActions(st);
    List<QValue> qvalueSt = new ArrayList<QValue>
    (actionsApplicable.size());
    for(Action act : actionsApplicable){
        qvalueSt.add(new QValue(st, act,
            this.qValue(st, act)));
    }
```

```
        return qvalueSt;
   }



   @Override
   public double qValue(State st, Action act) {

     if(this.model.terminal(st)){
     return 0.;
     }

     //We will check the all the possible outcomes
     List<TransitionProb> tansProb =
       ((FullModel)this.model).transitions(st, act);

     //aggregating all possible outcomes
     double q_Value = 0.;
     for(TransitionProb transp : tansProb){
     //we will check the reward for this transition
     double _rr = transp.eo.r;

     //We will find the value for the next state
     double valuep = this.functionValue.get
       (this.hashingFactory.hashState(transp.eo.op));

     //Now we will add the contribution weighted by the transition
probability and
     //it discounting the next state
     q_Value += transp.p * (_rr + this.gamma * valuep);
   }

     return q_Value;
   }
```

You will note that the qValues function returns a lot of QValue objects, that consist of an Action object, a State object, and a Q-value that is a double data type.

In this method, we've found all possible actions (we are using this method that is extended from the MDPSolver class).

In the qValues function, the first thing we check is whether the input state is a terminal state. If it is a terminal state, then the Q-value will be zero. For all other transitions, the value for each outcome is the discounted factor value and the reward received; based on that, we estimate the outcome state.

You might wonder where the model data member comes from. Because we are extending the MDPSolver class, when we call the solverInit method, it automatically unpacks the model included with the domain into a model data member that we can use. This is convenient because we also allow a client to change the model that the solver uses to something other than what comes out of the domain object with the setModel method. Note that the model is cast to the super interface SampleModel. To perform dynamic programming, we require a FullModel, and we assume the model is of that type, so we typecast to that and call the FullModel transitions method:

```
@Override
public GreedyQPolicy planFromState(State _initial_State_) {
        HashableState InitialStatehashed =
           this.hashingFactory.hashState(_initial_State_);
        if(this.functionValue.containsKey(InitialStatehashed))
        {
           //planning perform here!
                return new GreedyQPolicy(this);
        }

        //We find all the possible reachable states
        this.ReachableFrom(_initial_State_);

        //Over the complete state space we perform multiple iterations
        for(int i = 0; i < this._iterations_Num; i++){
                //iterate over each state
                for(HashableState shKey : this.functionValue.keySet())
                {
                   //Now update the value from the bellman equation
                   this.functionValue.put(shKey,
                     QProvider.Helper.maxQ(this, shKey.s()));
                }
        }

        return new GreedyQPolicy(this);


}
```

We are almost done. Now the only thing pending is to implement each `MDPSolver` object and the function `resetSolve`. When we call `resetSolve`, it has the effect of resetting all of the data if no planning calls have been made. For our value iteration implementation, we need to clear all the value functions:

```
@Override
public void resetSolver() {
  this.functionValue.clear();
}
```

Testing the value iteration code

Now we need to test our code. We can try to use the planning algorithm with our GridWorld. Alternatively, we implement the following main method, which we can add in the value iteration implementation that creates a GridWorld. We can plan it, evaluate a single policy, and visualize the results:

```
public static void main(String [] args){
    GridWorldDomain gridDomain = new GridWorldDomain(11, 11);
    gridDomain.setTf(new GridWorldTerminalFunction(10, 10));
    gridDomain.setMapToFourRooms();

    //we implement it as 0.8 means 80% will go to intended direction
    gridDomain.setProbSucceedTransitionDynamics(0.8);

    SADomain domain_sa = gridDomain.generateDomain();

    //Initialize the agent to initial state 0, 0
    State st = new GridWorldState(new GridAgent(0, 0));

    //setup value iteration with discount factor as 0.99,
    //a value function initialization that initializes all states to
value 0, and which will
    //run for 30 iterations over the state space
    ValueIterationTutorial valueIteration = new
        ValueIterationTutorial(domain_sa, 0.99, new
SimpleHashableStateFactory(), new ConstantValueFunction(0.0), 30);

    //we will now run the planning from our initial state
    Policy pol = valueIteration.planFromState(st);

    //we will evaluate the policy
    Episode episode = PolicyUtils.rollout(pol, st,
    domain_sa.getModel());

    Visualizer visualize =
```

```
        GridWorldVisualizer.getVisualizer(gridDomain.getMap());
        new EpisodeSequenceVisualizer(visualize, domain_sa,
          Arrays.asList(episode));
}
```

Now it's time to implement an example of Q-learning.

Q-learning code

Now it's time to implement the Q-learning algorithm. Our class called
QLearningTutorial will again extend the MDPSolver and implement the QProvider and
LearningAgent interfaces. The interface LearningAgent specifies for the function a
learning algorithm to be implemented, so it enables us to use it with other BURLAP tools.

This is the class we created as a skeleton code:

```
package project;

//Required java libraries
import java.util.Map;
import java.util.HashMap;
import java.util.ArrayList;
import java.util.List;

//Now we will import all the BURLAP libraries,
//there are lot of them to implement and it ease all our development
import burlap.behavior.policy.EpsilonGreedy;

//This library is related to implement policies
import burlap.behavior.policy.Policy;

//This library is related to implement Utitlities policies
import burlap.behavior.policy.PolicyUtils;

//This library is related to implement Single agent and episodic
import burlap.behavior.singleagent.Episode;

//This library is related to implement MDP
import burlap.behavior.singleagent.MDPSolver;

//This library is related to implement Episode Visualizer
import burlap.behavior.singleagent.auxiliary.EpisodeSequenceVisualizer;

//This library is related to Learning Agent
import burlap.behavior.singleagent.learning.LearningAgent;
```

```
//This library is related to implement States in MDP
import burlap.behavior.singleagent.auxiliary.StateReachability;

//This library is related to implement Single agent planner
import burlap.behavior.singleagent.planning.Planner;

//This library is related to implement Value fuctions constants
import burlap.behavior.valuefunction.ConstantValueFunction;

//This library is related to implement Q Provider
import burlap.behavior.valuefunction.QProvider;

//This library is related to implement Q Value
import burlap.behavior.valuefunction.QValue;

//This library is related to implement Value function
import burlap.behavior.valuefunction.ValueFunction;

//This library is related to implement Grid world
import burlap.domain.singleagent.gridworld.GridWorldDomain;

//This library is related to implement Grid world terminal function
import burlap.domain.singleagent.gridworld.GridWorldTerminalFunction;

//This library is related to implement Grid World visualization
import burlap.domain.singleagent.gridworld.GridWorldVisualizer;

//This library is related to implement Grid Agent
import burlap.domain.singleagent.gridworld.state.GridAgent;

//This library is related to implement states in Grid World
import burlap.domain.singleagent.gridworld.state.GridWorldState;

//This library is related to implement actions
import burlap.mdp.core.action.Action;

//This library is related to implement states
import burlap.mdp.core.state.State;

//This library is related to implement SA Domain
import burlap.mdp.singleagent.SADomain;

//This library is related to implement full model
import burlap.mdp.singleagent.model.FullModel;

//This library is related to implement transition probabilities
import burlap.mdp.singleagent.model.TransitionProb;
```

```java
//This library is related to implement hashable states
import burlap.statehashing.HashableState;

//This library is related to implement hashable state factory
import burlap.statehashing.HashableStateFactory;

//This library is related to implement simple hashable state factory
import burlap.statehashing.simple.SimpleHashableStateFactory;

//This library is related to implement visualization
import burlap.visualizer.Visualizer;

//These libraries are related to Environment
import burlap.mdp.singleagent.environment.Environment;
import burlap.mdp.singleagent.environment.EnvironmentOutcome;
import burlap.mdp.singleagent.environment.SimulatedEnvironment;


//This library is related to QFunction
import burlap.behavior.valuefunction.QFunction;




public class QLearningTutorial extends MDPSolver implements QProvider,
LearningAgent {

        @Override
        public Episode runLearningEpisode(Environment environment)
    {
                return null;
        }

        @Override
        public Episode runLearningEpisode(Environment environment, int
          maximumSteps)
    {
                return null;
        }

        @Override
        public void resetSolver()
        {
          // We will implement it later

        }

        @Override
```

```
    public List<QValue> qValues(State st)
    {
        // We will implement it later

                return null;
    }

    @Override
    public double qValue(State st, Action act)
    {
        // We will implement it later

                return 0.0;
    }


    @Override
    public double value(State st)
    {
                return 0.0;
    }

}
```

As per the value iteration we implemented earlier, we extend MDPSolver; this will auto-build the data members and estimate the Q-value that defines the task and our domain (the HashableStateFactory, discount factor, domain, and state). Now consider the critical data that value iteration requires to store its estimates for the value function. It is actually a mapping from states to real values. Moreover, for faster access, we can use HashableStateFactory and HashMap to provide the HashableState object from states. One way to make value iteration run faster is by initializing it to the optimal value function. That is why we use the value function as the initial value state:

```
    Map<HashableState, List<QValue>> _q_Values_;

    QFunction _initQ_;

    double _learn_Rate_;

    Policy _learn_Policy_;
```

Now we will add a constructor that will initialize some of the data members inherited from `MDPSolver`:

```
public QLearningTutorial(SADomain domain_sa, double
  _gamma_discount_factor, HashableStateFactory factoryHash, QFunction
  _initQ_, double _learn_Rate_, double _eps_)
   {

    this.solverInit(domain_sa, _gamma_discount_factor,
      factoryHash);

    this._initQ_ = _initQ_;

    this._learn_Rate_ = _learn_Rate_;

    this._q_Values_ = new HashMap<HashableState, List<QValue>>();

    this._learn_Policy_ = new EpsilonGreedy(this, _eps_);

   }
```

Now you can see that the `EpsilonGreedy` instance we created takes an input `QProvider`.

Consider the following code for storing and getting `Qvalue`. We will implement it as follows:

```
@Override
  public List<QValue> qValues(State st)
   {
       //get the hashed state first
       HashableState hashSt = this.hashingFactory.hashState(st);

       //We will check if it is stored the values already
       List<QValue> qValueSt = this._q_Values_.get(hashSt);

       //If we dont have Q-values stored then add and create Q-values
       if(qValueSt == null){
           List<Action> act = this.applicableActions(st);
           qValueSt = new ArrayList<QValue>(act.size());
           //Now we will create the Q-value for all the actions
           for(Action a : act){
               //Now we will add the q value
               qValueSt.add(new QValue(st, a, this._initQ_.qValue(st,
                 a)));
           }
           //we will store this for later use
           this._q_Values_.put(hashSt, qValueSt);
       }
```

```
            return qValueSt;
    }

    @Override
    public double qValue(State st, Action act)
    {
        return Qstored(st, act).q;
    }
    protected QValue Qstored(State st, Action act)
    {
        //we will get all Q-values first
        List<QValue> qValueSt = this.qValues(st);

        //then we iterate through all the stored Q-values
        for(QValue qVal : qValueSt){
            if(qVal.a.equals(act)){
                return qVal;
            }
        }

        throw new RuntimeException("Matching Q-value not found");
    }

    @Override
    public double value(State st) {
        return QProvider.Helper.maxQ(this, st);
    }
```

Now you can see the preceding code for the qValue function; it checks whether we have already stored the QValue for the state. If it is not stored, then we add and create it with initial value as defined by our QFunction.

Now that we have all the methods defined, it's time to implement the learning algorithm. The interface LearningAgent is required to implement two methods; we will define it in the following code:

```
@Override
public Episode runLearningEpisode(Environment environment)
{

        return this.runLearningEpisode(environment, -1);

}

@Override
public Episode runLearningEpisode(Environment environment, int
  maximumsteping)
```

```
{
        //We will initialize the episode object with the environment
initial state
        Episode episode = new
          Episode(environment.currentObservation());

        //behave until a terminal state or max steping is reached
        State state_Current = environment.currentObservation();
        int steping = 0;
        while(!environment.isInTerminalState() && (steping <
          maximumsteping || maximumsteping == -1)){

                //now we will select the action
                Action act = this._learn_Policy_.action(state_Current);

                //take the action and observe outcome
                EnvironmentOutcome envn_Out_Come =
                  environment.executeAction(act);

                //Now we will record the results
                episode.transition(envn_Out_Come);

                //get the max Q value of the resulting state if it's
                not terminal, 0 otherwise
                double maximumQ = envn_Out_Come.terminated ? 0. :
                  this.value(envn_Out_Come.op);

                //Now we will update the old Q value
                QValue oldQValue = this.Qstored(state_Current, act);

                oldQValue.q = oldQValue.q + this._learn_Rate_ *
                  (envn_Out_Come.r + this.gamma * maximumQ -
                    oldQValue.q);


                //Now point to the next enviornment and update the
                state
                state_Current = envn_Out_Come.op;
                steping++;


        }

        return episode;


}
```

Let me explain this code. First we construct an object for a new episode that points to the current state in the environment. From that, it returns an environment function, `getCurrentObservation()`. After that, we start executing a loop that ends either when the number of steps we have taken is more than the number required or when the environment has reached the terminal state.

Now in the execution loop, using the learning policy, we select an action. Then we execute an action in the environment using the method `executeIn(Environment)`, which returns an `EnvironmentOutcome` instance.

 Notice that the environment uses the term observation instead of state.

Now, as we are using a new observation for our environment, we store the transition to our episode and the previous Q-value. To update the Q-value, we need the maximum Q-value for the encountered next state. But if it is the terminal state, then the value store should be zero because there is no further state possible.

Finally, we will implement the `resetSolve` method, which just clears the Q-values:

```
@Override
public void resetSolver()
{
    this._q_Values_.clear();
}
```

Testing Q-learning code

As we did it earlier in value iteration, we are again doing a test for our learning algorithm. We will use the main method to implement a GridWorld and do an implementation of the Q-learning algorithm.

The implementation of the `main` method is defined in the following code:

```
public static void main(String[] args) {

    GridWorldDomain gridDomain = new GridWorldDomain(11, 11);
    gridDomain.setMapToFourRooms();
    gridDomain.setProbSucceedTransitionDynamics(0.8);
    gridDomain.setTf(new GridWorldTerminalFunction(10, 10));

    SADomain _domain_sa = gridDomain.generateDomain();
```

```
//now we get the agent as 0,0 state
State st = new GridWorldState(new GridAgent(0, 0));

//now we will create an environment for our agent
SimulatedEnvironment environment = new
    SimulatedEnvironment(_domain_sa, st);

//now we will create Q-learning element
QLearningTutorial _QL_agent_ = new
    QLearningTutorial(_domain_sa, 0.99, new
    SimpleHashableStateFactory(),
    new ConstantValueFunction(), 0.1, 0.1);

//Now we will run the Q learning algorithm and results will be
store in a list
List<Episode> _episodes_ = new ArrayList<Episode>(1000);
for(int i = 0; i < 1000; i++)
{
    _episodes_.add(_QL_agent_.runLearningEpisode(environment));
        environment.resetEnvironment();
}

Visualizer visualizer =
    GridWorldVisualizer.getVisualizer(gridDomain.getMap());
    new EpisodeSequenceVisualizer(visualizer, _domain_sa,
    _episodes_);

}
```

Now we are ready to compile and run the program.

```
mvn compile
mvn exec:java -Dexec.mainClass="project.QLearningTutorial"
```

Output of the Q-learning program

Here is the output of our Q-learning program as shown in *Figure 6.6*:

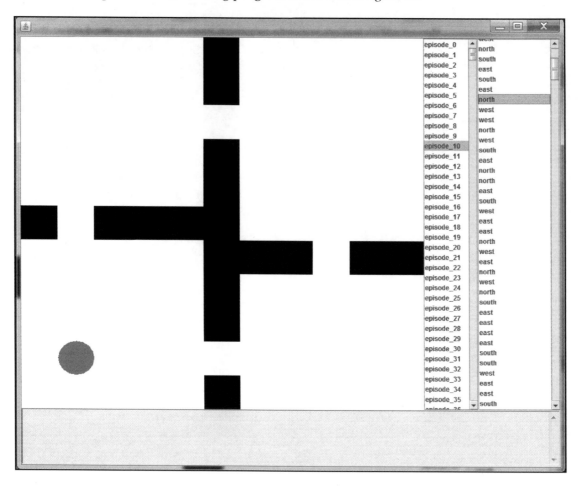

Figure 6.16: Q-learning program output

Summary

In this chapter, we saw how to implement our own learning and planning algorithms. We started this chapter with a Q-learning example and then we went through the example to solve it by hand. Later in the chapter, we did a complete implementation of value iteration and proceeded to implement the value iteration algorithm in code. After that, we jumped into the implementation of a Q-learning example in code. We utilized the BURLAP libraries to ease our development efforts. This is the reason I strongly advise you to use BURLAP for new and existing implementations of Q-learning or value iteration--because there are lots of features supported by BURLAP, such as learning rate, options, and so on.

The next chapter is very important as we will discuss neural networks in detail; then we'll go through deep learning and the connection between deep learning and neural networks. Later in the chapter, we'll explain in detail what deep reinforcement learning is. Then we will go through deep Q-learning and see how Q-learning is applied to a deep neural network (thus it becomes a deep Q-network). We will also see practical implementations of deep Q-networks.

7
Deep Reinforcement Learning

Humans are always trying to solve different types of problems, from low-level controls of a motor to very-high-level computer cognitive tasks. The goal of researchers in the domain of **Artificial Intelligence (AI)** is to achieve the same level of performance from an agent. Agents should learn from any kind of environment and perform successful strategies themselves without any supervision.

Like a human, an agent should learn successful strategies that will allow it to get the greatest long-term reward. We've already learned that this paradigm of trial and error exactly follows rewards or punishments and is called **reinforcement learning**. Humans learn from their senses, such as vision, touching some objects, and so on. Similarly agents learn or construct their knowledge from raw inputs; these inputs can come from sensors, cameras, or other hand-engineered features. These can be achieved from deep learning and neural networks; we will look into these approaches in detail in this chapter.

In this chapter, we'll start by discussing neural networks. Then we will see what deep learning is. Later in the chapter, we will combine these approaches as deep reinforcement learning. We will also discuss **Deep Q Networks (DQN)** in detail and learn the complete implementation of DQN. We will do an implementation of the *Flappy Bird* game and see how to write an agent that will learn to play the game itself.

What is a neural network?

We'll discuss neural networks in this section because deep learning always works together with neural networks. To understand or work on deep learning, we have to be very clear about neural networks.

A neural network's structure is similar to any other network. There is a web of nodes that are interconnected; they are called neurons and the edges join them together. The neural network receives a set of inputs and then it performs some complex operations and provides the output.

A neural network is considered to be very highly structured and is always in layers. The first layer is called the **input layer**, the in-between layers are called **hidden layers**, and the final layer is called the **output layer**, as defined in *Figure 7.1*:

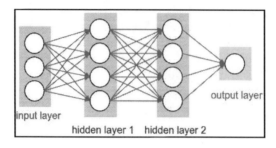

Figure 7.1: Neural network

A single neuron

In a neural network, a neuron (sometimes also called a node) is the basic unit of computation. Neurons receive inputs from other nodes, do the processing, and determine the output. Now each of the inputs has an associated weight, that depends on the relative importance. In each node, the function **(w1.x1+w2.x2+b)** is applied to the weighted sum of its inputs as shown in *Figure 7.2*:

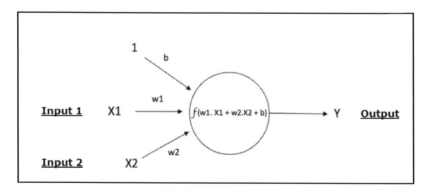

Figure 7.2: A single neuron

In the previous diagram, we can see that for each input (**X1** and **X2**), there is a weight associated. Furthermore, there is an additional **Input 1** with a corresponding weight **b**; this is called **bias**. We will look into the functionality of the bias function later.

As per *Figure 7.2*, the output **Y** is computed. Here the function **f** is called **activation function** and it is non-linear. The purpose of the activation function is to provide non-linearity in the output because most real-world data is non-linear.

Feed-forward neural network

Feed-forward neural networks receive a lot of attention and are being used in many types of applications. This is the most simplified type of **Artificial Neural Network (ANN)**. It consists of neurons that are arranged in layers. Nodes have edges or connections from adjacent layers. Weights are associated with all the connections. You can refer to *Figure 7.3* to see a feed-forward neural network:

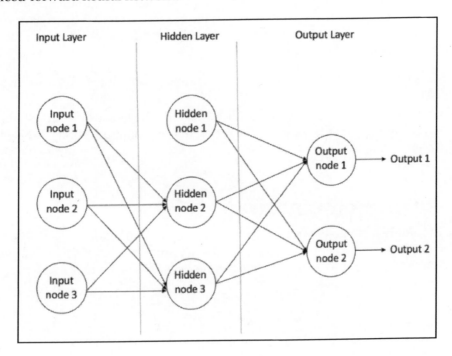

Figure 7.3: Feed-forward neural network

There are three types of nodes in a feed-forward neural network:

- **Input nodes:** The outside world provides data to the network and it goes through the input nodes. All the input nodes are referred to as the input layer. At the level of the input layer, computations are not performed; they just pass data to the hidden nodes.
- **Hidden nodes:** These don't have a direct connection with the outside world. All information or data will only be transferred from the input layer to the hidden nodes. Hidden nodes will do the computations and pass the relevant information to the output nodes. A collection of all hidden nodes is referred to as the hidden layer. There can be zero or multiple hidden layers in each network.
- **Output nodes:** These receive the data from the hidden nodes. They can perform some computations and provide information to the outside world. Their main responsibility is to provide data or information to the outside world.

As we just discussed each type of node, you might notice that information is flowing only in the forward direction. It starts from input nodes; then it passes on to hidden nodes and finally to output nodes. There is no way it can go back in the network; that's why this is called a feed-forward network.

1. **Single-layer perceptron**: These are the simplest form of feed-forward networks. They don't have any hidden layer.
2. **Multi-Layer Perceptron (MLP)**: These networks have one or multiple hidden layers and they are mostly used in different types of applications. We will discuss these in detail.

Multi-Layer Perceptron

Compared to single-layer perceptrons, MLPs have one or more hidden layers. They also have one input layer and one output layer. Single-layer perceptrons can learn only linear functions while MLP can also learn non-linear functions. This is the reason they are more useful in our real-life problems.

Figure 7.4. shows an MLP with only one hidden layer. Just note that all the connections have weights, but for simplicity, they are not depicted in the picture and we've just put weights **w0**, **w1**, and **w2**.

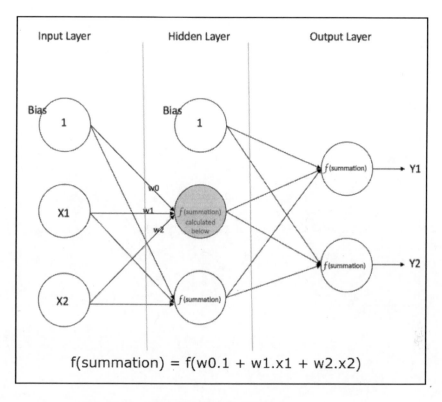

$$f(summation) = f(w0.1 + w1.x1 + w2.x2)$$

Figure 7.4: An MLP with one hidden layer

From the previous figure, you can see that the function applied to the hidden layer is **f(summation) = f(w0.1 + w1.X1 + w2.X2)**; they learn this relationship in an MLP.

Deep learning

What are the problems we can solve with the help of deep learning? Or, can our problem be solved from deep learning? The answer is not straightforward; it all depends on what our problem is. We need to check the exact problem and see how deep learning can apply to our solution.

We also need to see the outcomes we are looking for. The outcomes are labeled and they are applied to the data. Let me give you an example, in customer relationship management or call center solutions, we need to identify happy customers or an angry customer. Or for an email archiving system, we need to predict that the employees are satisfied with the company or identify some employees who are going to leave the company soon. Then we need to determine whether we have the data available to predict the outcomes. We need to see the data that is labeled as happy customers or angry customers, and we need to teach an algorithm that correlates between inputs and labels.

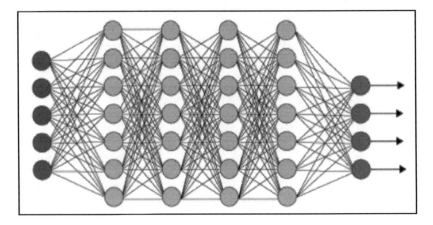

Figure 7.5: Deep neural network

Deep Q Network

I explained in `Chapter 1`, *Reinforcement Learning*, that two years ago, a London-based company named *DeepMind* published a paper called *Playing Atari with Deep Reinforcement Learning*. This paper explained how a computer can learn and play 2,600 games just by observing the pixels and receiving the reward signals. The same architecture can be used to learn and play seven other Atari games without any change. The performance of the computer player is much better than a human player.

Now let's think about the *Breakout* game as shown in *Figure 7.6*. In this game, you have to bounce a ball by controlling the paddle and clear the bricks in the upper half of the screen. Whenever you hit the brick, the score (reward) will increase.

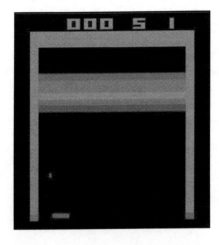

Figure 7.6: Breakout game

The environment of a state covers the paddle location, each individual brick's absence or presence, and the direction and location of the ball.

Neural networks are excellent when it comes to features for highly structured data. Q-functions can represent neural networks; they take the actions as inputs and outputs with the corresponding Q-values and also take the states (game screens).

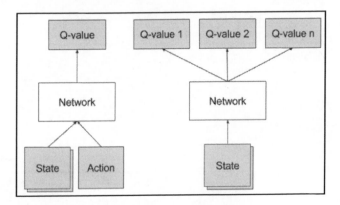

Figure 7.7: A DQN used in the DeepMind paper

The preceding network is a **Convolutional Neural Network (CNN)** and has three convolutional layers and two fully connected layers.

Experience replay

Now we will discuss the experience replay memory. We've already seen how the future reward is estimated in each state by using Q-learning and how to approximate the Q-function using CNN. By now, we know that the approximation of Q-values is non-linear and not very stable. There are lots of tricks that we can apply to make it converge but they take a long time; in some instances, it can even take a week on a single GPU.

The major trick to solve it is by using experience replay. At the time of playing the game, the experience $<a, s, r, s'$ is stored in a replay memory. At the time of training the neural network, random small batches are used from the replay memory. Note that random batches are used, not the most recent transitions.

The DQN algorithm

In this section, we will discuss the DQN algorithm:

```
Initialize replay memory D
Initialize action-value function Q with random weights
Observe initial state s
repeat
    select an action a
        with probability ε select a random action
        otherwise select a = argmax_a' Q(s,a')
    carry out action a
    observe reward r and new state s'
    store experience <s, a, r, s'> in replay memory D

    sample random transitions <ss, aa, rr, ss'> from replay memory D
    calculate target for each minibatch transition
        if ss' is terminal state then tt = rr
        otherwise tt = rr + γ max_a' Q(ss', aa')
    train the Q network using (tt - Q(ss, aa))^2 as loss

    s = s'
until terminated
```

In the next section, we will look into an implementation of DQN.

DQN example – PyTorch and Gym

In this example, we will understand the usage of `PyTorch`; we will see how to train a deep Q-learning agent. We will use the environment CartPole that is available in the `Gym` libraries.

Task

The agent can take two actions--either go right or go left--and the pole attached should stay upright:

Figure 7.8: CartPole-v0

The agent from the current environment will choose the action and environment transitioned to a new state and return a reward that is a feedback signal of how good the result of the action was. The environment will terminate when the pole falls over too far.

We are considering the difference between the current screen and the previous screen, taking the velocity of the pole into account.

Packages

We first need to import all the required libraries. We will use two types of libraries in this program. The first is the `gym` library because we need to use the environment (we discussed it in `Chapter 1`, *Reinforcement Learning*). Second, we need to use the following libraries for `PyTorch`:

- `torch.nn`: A neural network library
- `torch.autograd`: An automatic differentiation library
- `torch.optim`: An optimization library
- `torchvision`: A separate package that determines utilities for vision tasks

```
# provides access to reinforcement algorithms and other environments
import gym

# provides mathematical fucntions
```

```
import math

# provides access to random module and its fucntions
import random

# provides support for multidimension arrays, metrices, high level
mathematical fucntions
import numpy as numP

# provides matlab style functions
import matplotlib

# provides matlab style functions
import matplotlib.pyplot as imp_Plt_

# provides access to dictionaries
from collections import namedtuple

# provide access to efficient looping
from itertools import count

# provides access to copying list
from copy import deepcopy

#defined the image module
from PIL import Image


# provides access to Tensor computation and Deep Neural Networks
import torch

#provides easier way to build and train models for Neural Networks
import torch.nn as imp_nn_

#Numerical Package for torch Deep Neural Networks
import torch.optim as imp_Optim_

#Functional interface for Neural Networks
import torch.nn.functional as imp_F_

#provide automatic differentiation
from torch.autograd import Variable

#provides access to models,image,video datasets for torch Deep Neural
Networks
import torchvision.transforms as T
```

```
var_Environment_ = gym.make('CartPole-v0').unwrapped

# set up matplotlib

var_is_ipython_ = 'inline' in matplotlib.get_backend()


if var_is_ipython_:
    from IPython import var_Display_

imp_Plt_.ion()


# if we are using gpu

var_Cuda_Use_ = torch.cuda.is_available()

FloatTensor = torch.cuda.FloatTensor if var_Cuda_Use_ else
torch.FloatTensor

LongTensor = torch.cuda.LongTensor if var_Cuda_Use_ else torch.LongTensor

ByteTensor = torch.cuda.ByteTensor if var_Cuda_Use_ else torch.ByteTensor

var_Tensor_ = FloatTensor
```

Replay memory

To train the DQN, we have to use the experience replay memory. The replay memory stores the complete transition that is coming from the agent observation and it allows us to reuse this information later. From the sampling that we did randomly, it can be noted that the transitions combined as a batch are de-correlated. This is what improves the DQN's performance.

To implement this functionality, we need to create two classes:

- `ReplayMemory`: This class will hold the recently observed transitions. It has a function, `sample()`, that selects a random transition batch for training.
- `Transition`: This represents a single-transition tuple in our environment.

```
var_Transition_ = namedtuple('Transition',
                    ('state', 'action', 'next_state', 'reward'))


class cls_Memory_Replay(object):

    def __init__(self, parm_Capacity):
        self.var_Capacity_ = parm_Capacity
        self.var_Memory_ = []
        self.var_Position_ = 0

    def func_Push(self, *args):
      if len(self.var_Memory_) < self.var_Capacity_:
            self.var_Memory_.append(None)
            self.var_Memory_[self.var_Position_] = var_Transition_(*args)
            self.var_Position_ = (self.var_Position_ + 1) %
self.var_Capacity_

    def func_Sample(self, var_Size_Batch_):
        return random.func_Sample(self.var_Memory_, var_Size_Batch_)

    def __len__(self):
        return len(self.var_Memory_)
```

Now we are ready to define our model.

Q-network

The model we designed is a CNN that takes the variance from the previous screen and the current screen patches:

```
class cls_DQN_(imp_nn_.Module):


    def __init__(self):
        super(cls_DQN_, self).__init__()
        self.var_conv1_ = imp_nn_.Conv2d(3, 16, kernel_size=5, stride=2)
        self.var_bn1_ = imp_nn_.BatchNorm2d(16)
        self.var_Conv2_ = imp_nn_.Conv2d(16, 32, kernel_size=5, stride=2)
        self.var_Bn2_ = imp_nn_.BatchNorm2d(32)
```

```
        self.var_Conv3_ = imp_nn_.Conv2d(32, 32, kernel_size=5, stride=2)
        self.var_Bn3_ = imp_nn_.BatchNorm2d(32)
        self.var_Head_ = imp_nn_.Linear(448, 2)

    def forward(self, parm_x_):
        var_x_ = imp_F_.relu(self.var_bn1_(self.var_conv1_(parm_x_)))
        var_x_ = imp_F_.relu(self.var_Bn2_(self.var_Conv2_(parm_x_)))
        var_x_ = imp_F_.relu(self.var_Bn3_(self.var_Conv3_(parm_x_)))
        return self.var_Head_(var_x_.view(var_x_.size(0), -1))
```

Input extraction

Now we will do the coding for the utilities that will do the extraction and process the rendered images. The package we will use here is torchvision; it will help us transform the compose image:

```
var_Resize_ = T.Compose([T.ToPILImage(),
T.Scale(40, interpolation=Image.CUBIC),
T.ToTensor()])


var_Width_Screen = 600


def func_Get_Location_Cart_():
    var_Width_World_ = var_Environment_.x_threshold * 2
    var_Scale_ = var_Width_Screen / var_Width_World_
    return int(var_Environment_.state[0] * var_Scale_ + var_Width_Screen /
2.0)


def func_Get_Screen_():

    var_Screen_ = var_Environment_.render(mode='rgb_array').transpose(
        (2, 0, 1))


    var_Screen_ = var_Screen_[:, 160:320]
    var_Width_View_ = 320
    var_Location_Cart = func_Get_Location_Cart_()

    if var_Location_Cart < var_Width_View_ // 2:
        var_Range_Slice_ = slice(var_Width_View_)

    elif var_Location_Cart > (var_Width_Screen - var_Width_View_ // 2):
        var_Range_Slice_ = slice(-var_Width_View_, None)
```

```
    else:
        var_Range_Slice_ = slice(var_Location_Cart - var_Width_View_ // 2,
                        var_Location_Cart + var_Width_View_ // 2)


    var_Screen_ = var_Screen_[:, :, var_Range_Slice_]
    var_Screen_ = numP.ascontiguousarray(var_Screen_, dtype=numP.float32) /
255

    var_Screen_ = torch.from_numpy(var_Screen_)
    return var_Resize_(var_Screen_).unsqueeze(0).type(var_Tensor_)

var_Environment_.reset()

imp_Plt_.figure()

imp_Plt_.imshow(func_Get_Screen_().cpu().squeeze(0).permute(1, 2,
0).numpy(),
            interpolation='none')

imp_Plt_.title('Example extracted screen')

imp_Plt_.show()
```

Training

Now we initiate the training as per the following code:

```
var_Size_Batch_ = 128
var_Gamma_ = 0.999
var_Start_EPS_ = 0.9
var_End_EPS_ = 0.05
var_Decay_EPS_ = 200

var_Model_ = cls_DQN_()

if var_Cuda_Use_:
    var_Model_.cuda()

var_Optimizer_ = imp_Optim_.RMSprop(var_Model_.parameters())
var_Memory_ = cls_Memory_Replay(10000)


var_Done_Steps = 0
```

```
def func_Action_Select_(var_State_):
    global var_Done_Steps
    var_Sample_ = random.random()
    var_Threshold_EPS_ = var_End_EPS_ + (var_Start_EPS_ - var_End_EPS_) * \
        math.exp(-1. * var_Done_Steps / var_Decay_EPS_)
    var_Done_Steps += 1
    if var_Sample_ > var_Threshold_EPS_:
        return var_Model_(
            Variable(var_State_,
volatile=True).type(FloatTensor)).data.max(1)[1].view(1, 1)
    else:
        return LongTensor([[random.randrange(2)]])


_var_Durations_Episode_ = []


def func_Durations_Plot_():

    imp_Plt_.figure(2)
    imp_Plt_.clf()
    vat_T_Durations = torch.FloatTensor(_var_Durations_Episode_)
    imp_Plt_.title('Training...')
    imp_Plt_.xlabel('Episode')
    imp_Plt_.ylabel('Duration')
    imp_Plt_.plot(vat_T_Durations.numpy())
    if len(vat_T_Durations) >= 100:
        var_Means_ = vat_T_Durations.unfold(0, 100, 1).mean(1).view(-1)
        var_Means_ = torch.cat((torch.zeros(99), var_Means_))
        imp_Plt_.plot(var_Means_.numpy())

    imp_Plt_.pause(0.001)
    if var_is_ipython_:
        var_Display_.clear_output(wait=True)
        var_Display_.display(imp_Plt_.gcf())
```

Training loop

Now we are ready to provide the training to our agent. We need to implement the training functionality in the following code. To perform a single step of the optimization, we need to define a function called `func_Model_Optimize_`.

We set V(s) = 0; here is a terminal state:

```
var_Sync_Last = 0

def func_Model_Optimize_():

    global var_Sync_Last
    if len(var_Memory_) < var_Size_Batch_:
        return
    _var_Transitions_ = var_Memory_.func_Sample(var_Size_Batch_)
    _var_Batch_ = Transition(*zip(*_var_Transitions_))

    _var_Mask_Non_Final_ = ByteTensor(tuple(map(lambda s: s is not None,
                                        _var_Batch_.var_State_Next_)))

    var_Next_States_Final_ = Variable(torch.cat([s for s in
_var_Batch_.var_State_Next_
                                                if s is not None]),
                                volatile=True)
    var_Batch_State_ = Variable(torch.cat(_var_Batch_.state))
    var_Batch_State_ = Variable(torch.cat(_var_Batch_.action))
    var_Batch_Reward_ = Variable(torch.cat(_var_Batch_.reward))
    var_Values_Action_ = model(var_Batch_State_).gather(1,
var_Batch_State_)

    _var_Values_Next_State_ =
Variable(torch.zeros(var_Size_Batch_).type(var_Tensor_))
    _var_Values_Next_State_[_var_Mask_Non_Final_] =
model(var_Next_States_Final_).max(1)[0]
    _var_Values_Next_State_.volatile = False
    var_State_Expected_Values_Actions_ = (_var_Values_Next_State_ *
var_Gamma_) + var_Batch_Reward_

    _var_loss_ = imp_F_.smooth_l1_loss(var_Values_Action_,
var_State_Expected_Values_Actions_)

    var_Optimizer_.zero_grad()
    _var_loss_.backward()
    for var_Param_ in model.parameters():
        var_Param_.grad.data.clamp_(-1, 1)
        var_Optimizer_.step()
```

In the code, you would be able to identify the main training loop. At the beginning, we reset the environment and initialize the state variable. Then, we sample an action, execute it, observe the next screen and the reward (always 1), and optimize our model once. When the episode ends (our model fails), we restart the loop.

`num_episodes` is set small. You should download the notebook and run a lot more episodes:

```
var_Episode_Num_ = 10
for var_Episode_i_ in range(var_Episode_Num_):
    var_Environment_.reset()
    var_Screen_Last_ = func_Get_Screen_()
    var_Screen_Current_ = func_Get_Screen_()
    var_State_ = var_Screen_Current_ - var_Screen_Last_
    for var_T_ in count():
        var_Action_ = func_Action_Select_(var_State_)
        _, var_Reward_, var_Done_, _ = var_Environment_.step(var_Action_[0,
0])

        var_Reward_ = var_Tensor_([var_Reward_])

        var_Screen_Last_ = var_Screen_Current_
        var_Screen_Current_ = func_Get_Screen_()
        if not var_Done_:
            var_State_Next_ = var_Screen_Current_ - var_Screen_Last_
        else:
            var_State_Next_ = None

        var_Memory_.func_Push(var_State_, var_Action_, var_State_Next_,
var_Reward_)

        var_State_ = var_State_Next_

        func_Model_Optimize_()
        if var_Done_:
            _var_Durations_Episode_.append(var_T_ + 1)
            func_Durations_Plot_()
            break

print('Complete')
var_Environment_.render(close=True)
var_Environment_.close()
imp_Plt_.ioff()
imp_Plt_.show()
```

Example – Flappy Bird using Keras

Now we are going to implement another example of DQN. This example will play a *Flappy Bird* game by itself. It will use the DQN algorithm with the power of Keras.

Dependencies

We need the following dependencies to implement this example:

- Python 2.7
- Keras 1.0
- Pygame
- scikit-image

qlearn.py

Let's go though the example in `qlearn.py` line by line. If you are familiar with Keras and DQN, you can skip this session.

The `qlearn.py` code simply does the following:

1. The code receives the game screen input in the form of a pixel array.
2. It does some image preprocessing.
3. The processed image will be fed into a neural network (CNN), and the network will then decide the best action to execute (flap or no flap).
4. The network will be trained millions of times via an algorithm called Q-learning to maximize the future expected reward.

Game screen input

Just take note that *Flappy Bird* is already written in Python via Pygame, so here is the code snippet to access the *Flappy Bird* API:

```
import wrapped_flappy_bird as game
```

The idea is quite simple. The input is a_t (0 means don't flap and 1 means flap). The API will give you the next frame, `_var_X_T1_Color` and the reward (*0.1* if alive, *+1* if the bird passed the pipe, and *-1* if dead). `var_Terminal_` is a Boolean flag that indicates whether the game is finished or not:

```
_var_X_T1_Color, _var_R_T_, var_Terminal_ =
var_State_Game_.frame_step(_var_A_T_)
```

Image preprocessing

In order to make the code train faster, it is vital to do some image processing. Here are the key steps:

1. I first convert the color image into grayscale.
2. I crop the image size to 80x80 pixels.
3. I stack four frames together before I feed them into the neural network.

Why do I need to stack four frames together? Because this is one way for the model to be able to infer the velocity information of the bird:

```
_var_X_T1_ = imp_skimage_.color.rgb2gray(_var_X_T1_Color)
_var_X_T1_ = imp_skimage_.transform.resize(_var_X_T1_,(80,80))
_var_X_T1_ = imp_skimage_.exposure.rescale_intensity(_var_X_T1_,
out_range=(0, 255))


_var_X_T1_ = _var_X_T1_.reshape(1, _var_X_T1_.shape[0],
_var_X_T1_.shape[1], 1)
_var_S_T1_ = numP.append(_var_X_T1_, var_S_T_[:, :, :, :3], axis=3)
```

x_t1 is a single frame with shape *1x1x80x80* and s_t1 is the stacked frame with shape *1x4x80x80*. You might ask, "Why is the input dimension *1x4x80x80* instead of *4x80x80*?" Well, it is a requirement in Keras, so let's stick to it.

Convolution Neural Network

Now we will build the model. We provide the preprocessed input screen to the CNN:

```
def func_Build_Model_():

 print("Now we build the model")
 var_Build_Models_ = Sequential()
 var_Build_Models_.add(Convolution2D(32, 8, 8, subsample=(4, 4),
border_mode='same',input_shape=(_var_Image_Rows_,_var_Image_Columns_,_var_I
mage_Channels_))) #80*80*4

 var_Build_Models_.add(Activation('relu'))
 var_Build_Models_.add(Convolution2D(64, 4, 4, subsample=(2, 2),
border_mode='same'))
 var_Build_Models_.add(Activation('relu'))
 var_Build_Models_.add(Convolution2D(64, 3, 3, subsample=(1, 1),
border_mode='same'))
```

```
var_Build_Models_.add(Activation('relu'))
var_Build_Models_.add(Flatten())
var_Build_Models_.add(Dense(512))
var_Build_Models_.add(Activation('relu'))
var_Build_Models_.add(Dense(2))

var_Adam_ = imp_Adam_(lr=_var_Learning_Rate_)
var_Build_Models_.compile(_var_Loss_='mse',optimizer=var_Adam_)

print("We completed building the model")
return var_Build_Models_
```

The exact architecture is as follows: the input to the neural network consists of *4x80x80* images. The first hidden layer convolves 32 filters of *8x8* with stride 4 and applies the ReLU activation function. The second layer convolves 64 filters of *4x4* with stride 2 and applies the ReLU activation function. Then the third layer convolves 64 filters of *3x3* with stride 1 and applies the ReLU activation function. The final hidden layer is fully connected and consists of 512 rectifier units. The output layer is a fully connected linear layer with a single output for each valid action.

DQN implementation

Finally, we can use the Q-learning algorithm to train the neural network:

```
#If done ovserving then only do a training
 if _vat_T_ > _var_Observe_:
  _var_Mini_Batch_ = random.sample(var_D_, _var_Batch_)

 #32, 80, 80, 4
 _var_Inputs_ = numP.zeros((_var_Batch_, var_S_T_.shape[1],
 var_S_T_.shape[2], var_S_T_.shape[3]))

 print (_var_Inputs_.shape)

 _var_Targets_ = numP.zeros((_var_Inputs_.shape[0], _var_Actions_))

 #Now we will do the experience replay

 for i in range(0, len(_var_Mini_Batch_)):

  _var_State_T_ = _var_Mini_Batch_[i][0]


  #index action
  _var_Action_T_ = _var_Mini_Batch_[i][1]
```

```
_var_Reward_T_ = _var_Mini_Batch_[i][2]
_var_State_T1_ = _var_Mini_Batch_[i][3]
var_Terminal_ = _var_Mini_Batch_[i][4]


#saved down var_S_T_
_var_Inputs_[i:i + 1] = _var_State_T_

# Now we will hit the probability of each
_var_Targets_[i] = var_Build_Models_.predict(_var_State_T_)
_var_Q_sa__ = var_Build_Models_.predict(_var_State_T1_)

if var_Terminal_:
 _var_Targets_[i, _var_Action_T_] = _var_Reward_T_
else:
 _var_Targets_[i, _var_Action_T_] = _var_Reward_T_ + _var_Gama_ *
numP.max(_var_Q_sa__)


 _var_Loss_ += var_Build_Models_.train_on_batch(_var_Inputs_,
_var_Targets_)

var_S_T_ = _var_S_T1_
_vat_T_ = _vat_T_ + 1
```

Complete code

Here's the complete code:

```
#First import all the required libraries

from __future__ import print_function
import argparse as imp_parse_
import skimage as imp_skimage_
from skimage import transform, color, exposure
from skimage.transform import rotate
from skimage.viewer import ImageViewer

# We include the sys libraries here
import sys
sys.path.append("game/")

# The game flappy bird libraries included here
import wrapped_flappy_bird as game
```

```python
# We include the random function libraries here
import random

# All the scientific libraries include here
import numpy as numP

# Now include the collection libraries
from collections import deque as imp_DQ

#Also include the JSON libraries here
import json

#Here we will use the keras libraries
from keras import initializers
from keras.initializers import normal, identity
from keras.models import model_from_json
from keras.models import Sequential

from keras.layers.core import Dense, Dropout, Activation, Flatten
from keras.layers.convolutional import Convolution2D, MaxPooling2D
from keras.optimizers import SGD as imp_SGD_ , Adam as imp_Adam_


#Now we will use the import the tensor flow libraries
import tensorflow as imp_ten_Flow

var_Game_ = 'bird' # It is the game name that we store it in log file

_var_Config_ = 'nothreshold'
_var_Actions_ = 2 # no. of valid actions
_var_Gama_ = 0.99
_var_Observation_ = 3200.

_var_Explore_ = 3000000.
_var_Epsilon_Final_ = 0.0001
_var_Epsilon_initital_ = 0.1
_var_Replay_Memory_ = 50000
_var_Batch_ = 32
_var_Action_Per_Frame_ = 1
_var_Learning_Rate_ = 1e-4

_var_Image_Rows_ , _var_Image_Columns_ = 80, 80

#Black and white image convertion

_var_Image_Channels_ = 4 #We stack 4 frames

def func_Build_Model_():
```

```
print("Now we build the model")
var_Build_Models_ = Sequential()
var_Build_Models_.add(Convolution2D(32, 8, 8, subsample=(4, 4),
border_mode='same',input_shape=(_var_Image_Rows_,_var_Image_Columns_,_var_I
mage_Channels_))) #80*80*4

var_Build_Models_.add(Activation('relu'))
var_Build_Models_.add(Convolution2D(64, 4, 4, subsample=(2, 2),
border_mode='same'))
var_Build_Models_.add(Activation('relu'))
var_Build_Models_.add(Convolution2D(64, 3, 3, subsample=(1, 1),
border_mode='same'))

var_Build_Models_.add(Activation('relu'))
var_Build_Models_.add(Flatten())
var_Build_Models_.add(Dense(512))
var_Build_Models_.add(Activation('relu'))
var_Build_Models_.add(Dense(2))

var_Adam_ = imp_Adam_(lr=_var_Learning_Rate_)
var_Build_Models_.compile(_var_Loss_='mse',optimizer=var_Adam_)

print("We completed building the model")
return var_Build_Models_



def func_Train_Network(var_Build_Models_,parm_Args_):

# We will open the game now on the emulator
var_State_Game_ = game.GameState()

# We will store the old observations into the replay memory
var_D_ = imp_DQ()


# Now we will get the first image and then pre-process the image to 80 x
80 x 4
var_Do_Nothing_ = numP.zeros(_var_Actions_)
var_Do_Nothing_[0] = 1
var_X_T_, var_R_0_, var_Terminal_ =
var_State_Game_.frame_step(var_Do_Nothing_)

var_X_T_ = imp_skimage_.color.rgb2gray(var_X_T_)
var_X_T_ = imp_skimage_.transform.resize(var_X_T_,(80,80))
var_X_T_ =
imp_skimage_.exposure.rescale_intensity(var_X_T_,out_range=(0,255))
```

```
   var_S_T_ = numP.stack((var_X_T_, var_X_T_, var_X_T_, var_X_T_), axis=2)

#Now we will use Keras library to reshape it.
   var_S_T_ = var_S_T_.reshape(1, var_S_T_.shape[0], var_S_T_.shape[1],
var_S_T_.shape[2]) #1*80*80*4

   if parm_Args_['mode'] == 'Run':

     _var_Observe_ = 999999999 #We keep _var_Observe_, never train
   _var_Epsilon_ = _var_Epsilon_Final_
   print ("Now we are going to load the weight")
   var_Build_Models_.load_weights("model.h5")
   var_Adam_ = imp_Adam_(lr=_var_Learning_Rate_)
   var_Build_Models_.compile(_var_Loss_='mse',optimizer=var_Adam_)
   print ("Here the load weight successful.")



while (True):
 _var_Loss_ = 0
 _var_Q_sa__ = 0
 _var_Index_Action_ = 0
 _var_R_T_ = 0
 _var_A_T_ = numP.zeros([_var_Actions_])

 #Now we will choose an action
if _vat_T_ % _var_Action_Per_Frame_ == 0:

 if random.random() <= _var_Epsilon_:

   print("----------Take Random Action----------")

   _var_Index_Action_ = random.randrange(_var_Actions_)

   _var_A_T_[_var_Index_Action_] = 1

 else:

 #Now from the input stack of 4 images, we will do the prediction here
  q = var_Build_Models_.predict(var_S_T_)
  _var_Max_Q_ = numP.argmax(q)
  _var_Index_Action_ = _var_Max_Q_
  _var_A_T_[_var_Max_Q_] = 1

#Now we will be reducing the epsilon gradually
 if _var_Epsilon_ > _var_Epsilon_Final_ and _vat_T_ > _var_Observe_:
  _var_Epsilon_ -= (_var_Epsilon_initital_ - _var_Epsilon_Final_) /
_var_Explore_
```

```
#Now we will run the chosen action and observed next reward and state
_var_X_T1_Color, _var_R_T_, var_Terminal_ =
var_State_Game_.frame_step(_var_A_T_)

_var_X_T1_ = imp_skimage_.color.rgb2gray(_var_X_T1_Color)
_var_X_T1_ = imp_skimage_.transform.resize(_var_X_T1_,(80,80))
_var_X_T1_ = imp_skimage_.exposure.rescale_intensity(_var_X_T1_,
out_range=(0, 255))

#1x80x80x1
_var_X_T1_ = _var_X_T1_.reshape(1, _var_X_T1_.shape[0],
_var_X_T1_.shape[1], 1)
_var_S_T1_ = numP.append(_var_X_T1_, var_S_T_[:, :, :, :3], axis=3)

# store the transition in var_D_
var_D_.append((var_S_T_, _var_Index_Action_, _var_R_T_, _var_S_T1_,
var_Terminal_))

if len(var_D_) > _var_Replay_Memory_:
 var_D_.popleft()

#If done ovserving then only do a training
 if _vat_T_ > _var_Observe_:
  _var_Mini_Batch_ = random.sample(var_D_, _var_Batch_)

#32, 80, 80, 4
_var_Inputs_ = numP.zeros((_var_Batch_, var_S_T_.shape[1],
var_S_T_.shape[2], var_S_T_.shape[3]))

print (_var_Inputs_.shape)

_var_Targets_ = numP.zeros((_var_Inputs_.shape[0], _var_Actions_))

#Now we will do the experience replay

for i in range(0, len(_var_Mini_Batch_)):

 _var_State_T_ = _var_Mini_Batch_[i][0]


 #index action
 _var_Action_T_ = _var_Mini_Batch_[i][1]
 _var_Reward_T_ = _var_Mini_Batch_[i][2]
 _var_State_T1_ = _var_Mini_Batch_[i][3]
 var_Terminal_ = _var_Mini_Batch_[i][4]


#saved down var_S_T_
```

```
_var_Inputs_[i:i + 1] = _var_State_T_

# Now we will hit the probability of each
_var_Targets_[i] = var_Build_Models_.predict(_var_State_T_)
_var_Q_sa__ = var_Build_Models_.predict(_var_State_T1_)

if var_Terminal_:
 _var_Targets_[i, _var_Action_T_] = _var_Reward_T_
else:
 _var_Targets_[i, _var_Action_T_] = _var_Reward_T_ + _var_Gama_ *
numP.max(_var_Q_sa__)


 _var_Loss_ += var_Build_Models_.train_on_batch(_var_Inputs_,
_var_Targets_)

var_S_T_ = _var_S_T1_
_vat_T_ = _vat_T_ + 1

# save the progress for every 10000 iterations
if _vat_T_ % 1000 == 0:

 print("Now we will save the model")
 var_Build_Models_.save_weights("var_Build_Models_.h5", overwrite=True)
 with open("var_Build_Models_.json", "w") as outfile:
  json.dump(var_Build_Models_.to_json(), outfile)

# Here we will print all the information
 _var_State_ = ""
 if _vat_T_ <= _var_Observe_:
  _var_State_ = "observe"
 elif _vat_T_ > _var_Observe_ and _vat_T_ <= _var_Observe_ + _var_Explore_:
  _var_State_ = "explore"
 else:
  _var_State_ = "train"

print("TIMESTEP", _vat_T_, "/ STATE", _var_State_, \
 "/ EPSILON", _var_Epsilon_, "/ ACTION", _var_Index_Action_, "/ REWARD",
_var_R_T_, \
 "/ Q_MAX " , numP.max(_var_Q_sa__), "/ Loss ", _var_Loss_)

print("Finally here our episode finished")
print("-----------------------------")


 def func_Game_Play_(parm_Args_):
  var_Build_Models_ = func_Build_Model_()
  func_Train_Network(var_Build_Models_,parm_Args_)
```

```
def func_Main_():
 parser = imp_parse_.ArgumentParser(description='Description of your
program')
 parser.add_argument('-m','--mode', help='Train / Run', required=True)
 parm_Args_ = vars(parser.parse_args())
 func_Game_Play_(parm_Args_)

if __name__ == "__main__":
 _var_Config_ = imp_ten_Flow.ConfigProto()
 _var_Config_.gpu_options.allow_growth = True
 _var_Sess_ = imp_ten_Flow.Session(config=_var_Config_)
 from keras import backend as imp_Ks_
 imp_Ks_.set_session(_var_Sess_)
 func_Main_()
```

Now we will run the program with the following command:

```
python PRL_Learn_Flappy_Bird.py -m "Run"
```

Output

Here is the output of the program:

Figure 7.9: Output of the Flappy Bird program

Photo credit: UhThiLaHuVo via Visual Hunt /CC BY</a>

Summary

In this chapter, we discussed in detail the combination of reinforcement learning and deep learning. We started with an explanation of neural networks and saw that neural networks are highly structured and in layers. The first layer is called the input layer and the last layer is called the output layer; the layers in between are called hidden layers. Then we discussed that there are several types of neural networks: single neuron, feed-forward neural network, and MLP.

We also learned in detail about deep learning and how we can combine it with a neural network. Then we discussed a very famous and important algorithm, DQN, introduced by *DeepMind* in a paper called *Playing Atari with Deep Reinforcement Learning*. We went through the DQN algorithm and then finished up with the implementation of a DQN example-- PyTorch--to train a deep Q-learning agent on the `CartPole-v0` task from `OpenAIGym`.

At the end of the chapter, we implemented a deep Q-learning algorithm with Keras to play *Flappy Bird*.

In the next chapter, we will discuss some advanced topics in reinforcement learning such as **Inverse Reinforcement Learning (IRL)** and **Hierarchical Reinforcement Learning (HRL)**.

8

Game Theory

In this chapter, we are going to look into game theory. What does game theory have to do with machine learning? That's an interesting question, because game theory comes from a traditional way which is outside of machine learning in AI, but you will see in a moment why I care about game theory. Really, this is a very natural extension to all the stuff I have been writing about reinforcement learning.

Reinforcement learning was originally developed for MDPs. For a single agent, it allows learning a policy in a stochastic stationary environment to maximize a possibly delayed reward. On the optimal policy, it guarantees convergence on a condition; that is, the agent can experiment the environment that is Markovian. However, the important thing to note here is what happens when multiple agents are involved and we apply reinforcement learning to a shared environment. Then it might not be an MDP model. In that case, the optimal policy depends on the policies of other agents and not just on the environment. These situations can be seen in different domains such as telecom, traffic light control, banking, economics, air ticketing, economics, and so on. In these kinds of domains, multi-agent learning is involved because the environment is complex and control is decentralized.

In this chapter, we will cover strategies and see what pure and mixed strategies are. Then we will try to solve different games and also cover the **von Neumann theorem**. Later, we will proceed to solve a *Mini Poker* game.

Introduction to game theory

What is game theory? We can just try to define game theory and maybe it will be clear why we are worried about this at all. There are lots of definitions of game theory that we can use. One that I like in particular is that game theory is the mathematics of conflict. I think it's kind of interesting. Generally, it's the mathematics of conflicts of interest when trying to make optimal choices.

How can worrying about the mathematical conflict be a sort of natural next thing to think about after you've learned a lot about reinforcement learning? We have been talking about decision making and it's almost always in the context of a single agent that lives in a world trying to maximize its reward but that's a kind of lonely way to think about things. What if there are other agents in the world with you? Evidence suggests that there are in fact other agents in the world with you and what we have been doing with reinforcement learning (which, as you know, has worked out very well for us) is mostly pretending that those other agents are just a part of the environment. Somehow, all the stuff that the other agents do is hidden inside of the transition model. But it probably makes sense if you want to make optimal decisions to try to take into account explicitly the desires and goals of all other agents in the world with you.

So, that's what game theory helps us to do. In the end, I think we will be able to tie what we are going to learn directly back into the reinforcement learning stuff that we have covered and even into the **Bellman equation**.

This is going to work out pretty well, but we have to get there first and there's a lot of stuff that we have to do to get there. Right now, what I want you to think about is that we are going to move from the reinforcement learning world of single agents to a game theory world of multiple agents and then tie it back together. It's a sort of general note that, I think, game theory comes from economics. Then, in fact, if you think about millions and millions of multiple agents, that's economics in some sense. Economics is a kind of math, science, and the art of thinking about what happens when there are lots and lots of people with their own goals conflicting, trying to work together to accomplish something. So, game theory gives us mathematical tools to think around. I think other fields would care about some of these things too.

Let's try to make this concrete with a very simple example.

Example of game theory

Let's pretend that we are no longer in the world of a single agent as we have been learning so far with reinforcement learning, but we have gone with full-blown generality to two agents. Let's call them *A* and *B*. They are going to be in a very simple game where *A* gets to make a choice. Then, *B* gets to make a choice and then *A* might be able to make a choice. So, this tree that I have drawn is going to capture the dynamics of this specific game. The little nodes in it (circles) represent states. We can think about those states in the same way as we saw in reinforcement learning in the past. The edges between the nodes represent the actions that one can take. So, this should look familiar; this is basically a game tree like what anyone who has taken an AI course might have seen:

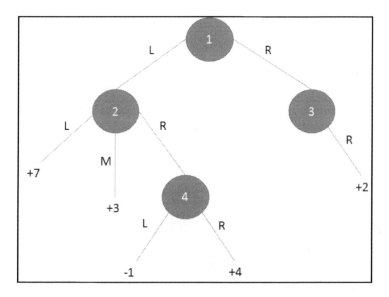

Figure 8.1: A simple game example

It's a very simple game, so that we can get a hand on some basic concepts. In particular, if you look at the details of this game, you start out in state one. *A* gets to make a choice between two actions, going left or going right. If *A* goes right, it ends up in state three. If it goes left, it ends up in state two. Regardless of this, *B* gets to make a choice. From state three, it can choose to go right, and really that's all that can happen. What happens if *B* goes right from state three? A value of +2 is assigned to *A*.

All of these numbers at the bottom are going to be values or rewards if you want to think about the way they are assigned to player *A*. And, in fact, for the purposes of this game, it's going to be the case that *B* always gets the opposite of what *A* gets. So if *A* gets +2, then *B* gets -2; if *A* gets +4, then *B* gets -4; and if *A* gets -1, *B* gets +1.

By the way, this is a very specific type of game and it has a name, which I want to get right. This is a two-player, zero-sum, finite, deterministic game of perfect information. It is two-player because we have *A* and *B*. It is zero-sum because the leaves are *A* rewards and *B* rewards are the negations, so if you add the two rewards, you're always going to get zero. It's not exactly right. Actually, zero sum just means that the sum of the rewards is always a constant and that the constant needs to be zero. So, if it added up to eleven, that would still be zero sum.

Everything seems to be finite here. There are no infinite number of choices, states, or depth. Deterministic means thinking about it in an MDP kind of way; there's no casting transitions in this particular picture.

So, this is about the simplest or the least complicated game that you can think about: a two-player, zero sum, finite, and deterministic game of perfect information. You know, basically, I can look at this tree, I know everything I need to know, and I can make decisions about what action I might want to take in order to maximize my reward. Now, in the MDP, we had this notion of policies. You remember what a policy was? It is the mapping of states to actions. So, in the game theory world, we have something very similar to policies. We call them strategies. A strategy is a mapping of all possible states to actions. So, for example, here's a strategy that *A* might have: when in state one, go left, and when in state four, also go left. But it's a strategy for one of the players and each player has their own strategy.

There was only one player before--only one agent--and so we did not have to worry about other strategies. Here, when we discuss a strategy, it's always with respect to one of the players of the game. So, I have just given you one strategy, which is what A does in all the states. Now, how many other strategies are there for *A*? How many different strategies are there for *A* and how many different strategies are there for *B*?

Let's think about *A*. In state *1*, it can go either left or right and the same is true in state 4. So, it sounds a lot like two times two equals four.

Now, how did we get two times two? We had a little choice. One is that in some sense, if you go right from one, then you don't really have to make another choice. But if you go left, then you have this other choice to make of either left or right. So if you are just writing it down as a mapping from state to action, you have got two choices at state one, and two choices at state four. and so that is two times two. So, in fact it's important there that, even though if we can gone right on one, we would never have to make another choice because we can't reach state 4. In order to be a strategy, you have to basically say what you would do in all states where you might end up.

Now *B* seems a little trickier because here it can only ever matter whether you're in like if player *A* sends us down to the left then we have a choice of three. If player one sends us down the right, we have a choice of one, which is really no choice at all.

So, by the definition of how many reachable strategies it would be, one answer is that it's three times one or, three.

Let's actually write down all the possible strategies of *A*:

```
State 1        State 4
   L              L
   L              R
   R              L
   R              R
```

Now, let's write all the possible strategies of *B:*

```
State 2:    L    M    R
State 3:    R    R    R
```

Why did I write it this way? Well, because if I write it this way with all the strategies that *B* has up here and all the strategies that *A* has here, I actually form a matrix. I can put in each of cells of the matrix the value of taking a particular strategy from *A* and a particular strategy from *B*:

```
[ 7     3    -1
  7     3     4
  2     2     2
  2     2     2 ]
```

Now, let me explain the preceding matrix. See how I derived the first index; since A goes first and *A* chooses to go left in State 1, it ends up in State 2. Then *B* goes left in the first strategy, which means we will end up going down this path and the value there is +7. The value of the first index in this game with respect to *A* is +7.

Now take the first column and second row, start with the agent *A* from State 1 goes left and end up in State 2. Then agent *B* from State 2 goes to M, so it gets a reward of 3.

Then take the first column and third row, start with the agent *A* from State 1 goes left and ends up in State 2. Then agent *B* from State 2 goes to R and ends up in State 4. Then, agent *A* takes L and ends up with reward –1. It will go further and we'll derive the matrix:

```
[ 7     3    -1
  7     3     4
  2     2     2
  2     2     2 ]
```

Now we have this nice matrix. What's really interesting about it? As we've written out this matrix, nothing else matters. The complete tree as per *Figure 8.1* and all the rules defined in the diagram are not needed anymore, because everything about the game is captured in the previous matrix.

So, what was the whole point in doing reinforcement learning? It was to optimize your long-term expected reward. So, you picked the policy that would get you to the best place possible.

This matrix is all we need to know; then we also have all the policies *A* can choose from and we are calling them strategies here. There are four for *A* three for *B*. What will you think *A* and *B* will actually do?

A wants the reward to be high, so 7 is the highest and *A* chooses the upper-left corner of the matrix. However, take note that this is a two-player game and *A* cannot choose the upper-left corner directly. Because *A* can only choose a strategy and *B* gets to choose some strategy based on the selection of *A*. So, *A* is choosing the row and then *B* gets to choose the column. Then *B* should choose that also because what *A* wants. However, it's actually opposite. The reason is that *B* wants to maximize what *B* gets, and remember *B* always gets the opposite of *A*, as it is a zero-sum game.

If *A* chooses the first row, which is the left, left strategy, *B* now has a choice between three values (7 3 −1). B will choose the one that is worst for *A*, which would be −1.

Now, *A* chooses the second row; again *B* has a choice between three values (7 3 4) and *B* will choose 3. So, it's 3 for *A* and −3 for *B*.

Thus, the best strategy for *A* is to select the second row, where *A* get a plus 3 reward.

These are the selections we did by assuming that *A* makes the first choice. Now, we will do the other way; so if *B* chooses first, then *B* should choose the far-right column because that's where the −1 is. Let say *B* chooses that column (−1 4 2 2), then *A* want to choose the second row and gets 4.

Now *B* can choose the middle column (3 3 2 2); then *A* would choose the 3 from one of the first two rows.

Let's say *B* chooses the 1st column (7 7 2 2); then *A* should choose one of the 7s from the top two rows.

We wind up with *B* choosing the middle column, where *A* gets the lowest reward, 3. *A* chooses the top or the second row. That's exactly the same answer we got where player *A* had to move first.

Minimax

In particular, *A* must consider the sort of worst-case counter-strategy by B. When *A* chooses the row, *B* will make things bad for *A* along that row, so that's the counter-strategy.

In fact, when we try to do it the other way with *B*, *it* has to do the same thing. *B* has to consider the worst-case counter-strategy as well. *B* is always trying to minimize *A*, which works out to be the same thing as maximizing itself.

A is trying to maximize, *B* is trying to minimize; they both have to consider the worst case that the other will do. So, that's going to force them through exactly the same process we went through. I am going to make the choice so that if my opponent makes the counter-choice, or the worst case choice, I will end up as best as I can. So, *A* is going to try to find the maximum minimum, and *B* is trying to find the minimum maximum.

In fact that strategy has a name: minimum maximum or minimax.

Minimax is the algorithm that we use for game search and many of you must have already heard about it in the university subject of AI.

So in the end, this matrix induces a game tree if you want to think about it that way. Or, the game tree induces a matrix if you want to think about it other way. The strategy in basic AI search, and the strategy in game theory is minimax when you are in a two-player game.

The minimax strategy would actually give you a sort of answer. In this case, we say the best value of this game for *A* is 3. If A acts rationally and so does B (trying to maximize their own value), you end up in this situation.

There is in fact a theorem, as we will see in the next section.

Fundamental results

Here's the theorem. In a two-player zero-sum deterministic game of perfect information, *Minimax* equals *Maximin*.

> *In a 2 player, zero - sum deterministic game of perfect information*
>
> *Minimax = Maximin*
>
> *AND</em>*
>
> *There always exists an optimal pure strategy for each player*

We discussed earlier what minimax is. Now, what is maximin? Well, maximin is like minimax but the other way around. One side is trying to minimize the maximum, the other side is trying to maximize the minimum. It's exactly what we described before; it just depends upon whether you are looking at it from $A's$ or $B's$ point of view.

For example, do you choose a column first or a row first? So, whether it A followed by B or B followed by A, you are going to end up with the same result. More importantly, or at least equally importantly, there always exists an optimal pure strategy for each player. In other words, you can solve those games and know for sure what the answer is once you write down the matrix. You just do minimax or maximin and you end up with the proper answer; thus you know what the optimal players would do.

There is a subtlety here, however. When we discussed rational agents, what we were assuming is that people are always trying to maximize their rewards. So we defined the reinforcement learning problem that way. My goal is to find a policy that maximizes my long-term expected reward. So I am trying to find the best reward that I can. What we are assuming here is that everyone else is doing the same thing and they too are assuming that everyone else is doing the same thing!

Now what is optimal in the above theorem? Optimal here really means that I am maximizing the reward I can get, and I am assuming everyone else is doing the same thing. Furthermore, I am assuming that they are assuming that everyone else is doing the same thing!

So we have got this fundamental result and now we are going to try to be a bit more interesting. But it is important to go through this because now we have got some basic vocabulary and some basic building blocks.

Game tree

Here's another game tree. There are again two players, A and B. A gets to make a choice first to go left or right, and then B will have to choose to go left or right.

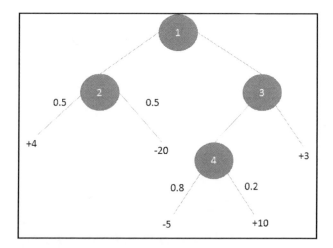

Figure 8.2: Game tree

As shown in the previous figure that if *A* goes left, you end up in a chance box where you flip a coin; 50 percent of the time you end up with right and 50 percent of the time you end up with left. Along a similar vein, if *A* goes right and then *B* goes left, you end up in another chance node; 80 percent of the time you end up left and 20 percent of the time you end up right. Alternatively, if *B* goes right, you always end up with **+3** rewards.

What we have done is we have gone from a two-player zero-sum, deterministic game of perfect information to a two-player, zero-sum non-deterministic game of perfect information. So, we've gone at least one level up in complexity!

The stochasticness is happening essentially at the leaves. There's no choice to make for either player after this randomness happens. It could be that later you end up in a different state where you can then make more choices, but I don't have enough room, or maybe I want to make it simple. So, it just ends.

However, this tree can keep going on and there can be choice and chance nodes everywhere. There can be a chance node at the very beginning.

How do we go about working out the value of the game? The first thing that we would do, at least if we were patterning after what we just did, is try to write down a matrix.

We have to figure out what the strategies are. What are strategies of *A*? We would have called them left and right but they are not labeled. *A* can go left or *A* can go right. What about the strategies of *B*? *B* can go left or right.

In a world where *A* can go left or right and *B* can go left or right, what are the values that we would put in the cells of this matrix? These values are from *A's* point of view, and implicitly we know the values for *B*. So, we are just looking for the values from *A's viewpoint*.

Thus, if *A* goes left, it doesn't matter what *B* does. At that point, there's a chance node, and it's *50/50* for *-20*, which ought to be *-8*:

$$-20/2 = -10$$
$$4/2 = 2$$
$$-10+2 = -8$$

So then *-8* is in the upper row of the matrix.

The next one is easy if both go right. *A* goes right and *B* goes right; then we get 3.

The last thing requires some multiplication. If *A* goes right and *B* goes left, then *-5* times *0.8* is *-4* and *10* times *0.2* is *2*. So, *-4+2* is **-2**:

	B:	
	Left	**Right**
Left:	-8	-8
Right:	-2	3

A:

Now we have the matrix. What do we notice here? Remember what I mentioned about matrices before? It has all the information that you need.

So what is the solution for the game? **A** is trying to maximize, right? So **A** would never ever want to go left. **A** goes right and then **B** tries to minimize. So **B** will go left and we'll get **-2**.

von Neumann theorem

In fact here's another theorem. It turns out that the theorem that we wrote down before is still true in the case of non-deterministic games of perfect information. It is von Neumann theorem. We discussed von Neumann architectures in computer science; the basic design of a microprocessor is still following the ideas that he worked out.

What we've learned so far is that the only thing that matters is the matrix. Once you have the matrix, you use minimax, at least if you are in a two-player, zero-sum game of perfect information, or at least if you are in a world of two-player, zero-sum games of perfect information. We can simply write down this matrix, throw everything else away, and use minimax or maximin to figure out what the value of the game is, which is the same thing as the policy.

Mini Poker game

So, here is another little game to play, and what I want you to notice about this game before I describe it to you in detail is that we have relaxed yet another of the constraints. We started out playing a two-player, zero-sum, finite deterministic games of perfect information. What we did last time was relaxing the deterministic part; so we got to a two-player, zero-sum, non-deterministic game of perfect information. Now, we are going to relax the requirement for perfect information as well.

So, we're going to look at two-player, zero-sum, and possibly non-deterministic games of hidden information. This is really important because this last little bit of relaxation--going from perfect information to hidden information--is a sort of quantum leap into the difficult problems of game theory. So, this is where it actually starts to get interesting; we have been building a foundation so far and now we are going to get into the interesting and complicated stuff.

Here we go! Let me describe the game. This is a version of Mini Poker where there is a set of cards, but they have no numbers or faces on them; they are just red or black. Red is bad for our hero, Player A, and black is good for him.

So, here are the rules. A is the delta card. It will be red or black and the probability of it being red or black is 50 percent each. So, we have a uniform priority over the color. Remember, red is bad for A and black is good for A. So, it's going to turn out without loss of generality that if A gets a black card, A is definitely going to hold on to the card. When A gets this card, Player B does not get to see the card. A can choose to either resign or hold. If A resigns when given a red card, then he loses 20 cents. So A is dealt red. A may resign only if it is red and then A loses 20 cents.

So, this is a betting game. It's not strange that it makes perfect sense; it's a sort of metaphor for life. Now, A can choose to hold instead, thus requiring B to do something. If A holds the card, B can either resign or demand to see the card. If B resigns, then A gets 10 cents regardless of the color of the card.

If *B* chooses, or in fact demands, to see the card, then two things are possible:

- If the card is red, then *A* loses *40* cents
- If the card is black, then *A* gets *30* cents

Since we are betting, it means that whatever *A* wins, *B* loses, and vice versa. That makes it zero-sum.

The basic pattern here is that red is bad and black is good. If *A* gets a bad card, he can essentially fold or resign or kind of bluff like, *Hey I have got this great card!* If *B* believes that the card is bad then he calls *A* and just folds then *A* wins that. But if *B* says, *No I think you are bluffing* and calls him, then everybody's rewards are more extreme.

This is a simple version of poker; nonetheless there's a tiny little detail here that is not so important. Notice it's written that *A* may resign if it's red. Basically, *A* will never resign on a black card because it just doesn't make any sense. So, there's really no point in writing it out. Because black is always good--sort of--nothing bad can ever happen to *A* if he gets a black card. So, there's really no point in writing this. However, that's just a minor detail. Regardless these are the rules.

Now, I am going to redraw this as a game tree, which might make it a little easier to keep all the rules in your head:

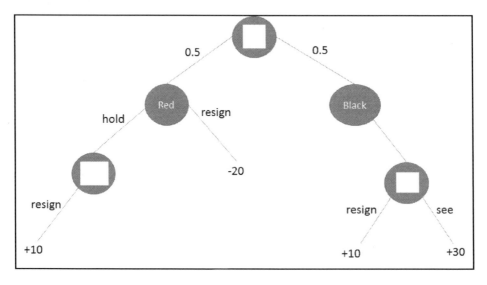

Figure 8.3: Mini Poker game

Here's the tree version. Remember, I draw squares as chance nodes. So, chance takes *A*. Half the time we end up in a state where *A* has a red card and half the time in a state where he has a black card. If *A* has a black card, then *B* gets to choose whether to hold or not.

This is the place where *A* gets to make a decision and then this is the place where *B* gets to make a decision. So, *A* is going to be either in a red state or in a black state. Only *A* knows this. *B* does not know what state he is in. So, let's say *A* is in a black state. Well, *A* can only hold in that case, in part because it makes no sense to resign. Then *B* gets to decide whether to resign (which gives *A* 10 cents) or to see (in which case *A* gets 30 cents). By contrast, when we're in the red state, *A* can either hold or resign. If he resigns, he loses 20 cents. If he holds then *B* gets to decide whether to resign (in which case *A* gets 10 cents) or to see the card (in which case *A* loses 40 cents and *B* of course gains 40 cents). So, this is just a tree version of what I wrote.

Let me point out something: *B* has no idea which of these two states he is in. It is hidden information and, because *B* doesn't know what state he's in, he doesn't know whether to resign or to see. In particular, *B* knows that if he is in this leftmost state, then he would always see. If *B* knows that he is always in the rightmost state, then he would always resign. However, he doesn't know, so it's not entirely clear what to do.

I wrote down a bunch of words that describe the game and then I made it a tree because I could do that. This makes it nice and easy to see what's going on. We want to make a little matrix. So, we want to figure out the values for different strategies for *A* and *B*. I'm going to assert (and I think it's pretty easy I hope) that *A* basically has only two strategies. *A* is either the type of person who resigns when a card is red or the type of person who holds when a card is red.

It is really a conditional policy. Consider if red and black hold to resign. The point is that black isn't really a choice; red is a choice and we have only two choices. So, I can see these as the two strategies. This does kind of say that when in the case of black, you know you're going to hold. So you know what's going to happen. Ultimately, *B* can be either the kind of person who resigns whenever *A* holds or the kind of person who chooses to see whenever *A* holds.

As in the previous trees, *B* would have four different strategies in the left and the right state. Here there's an extra connection. This sort of quantum entanglement between these two states concludes that they have to be the same. So, there are really just two choices. Although I probably wouldn't have used the phrase *quantum entanglement*, there's certainly an entanglement because we can't tell which state we're in. We'll either resign or see, and we just do not know what else to do. So, **A** is a **Resigner** or **Holder**. **B** is a **Resigner** or **Seer**. The question is: what numbers go into this matrix?

Let's start with **Resigner-Resigner**. If **A** is a **Resigner**, it means whenever he gets a red card he resigns. That would be a -20, but that's not going to be the answer. This is because **A** doesn't always get a red card. He sometimes gets a black card, and if he does, then **Resigner** means **B** is going to resign and a +10 will happen. These are the two possibilities and they're equally likely, so it's a -10 divided by 2, which is **-5**.

Now, we will do **Resigner-Seer**. Again, this is a good choice because now it's the same argument as before, except when we end up in that far-right node; that means -20 in half the cases and +30 in half the cases. This means +10 divided by 2, or **+5**.

The next one is **Holder-Resigner**. This means when **A** gets a card, he is going to hold the card and it's red or black. Then, it's **B's** turn, and **B** resigns. That takes us to those two leaves, both of which are +10. So, it's the average of +10 and +10, *which is* **+10**.

That's a case where **A** holds; so we go down those branches and always end up in one of the blue circled states. **B** reaches half-time that leads to -40, half the time that leads to +30. So, that's -10 divided by 2, which is **-5** again:

		B	
		Resigner	Seer
	Resigner	−5	+5
A			
	Holder	+10	−5

What is the value of this game? **A** chooses the first row or the second row. If he chooses the first row and then **B** has to choose the column, then **B** is going to choose the first column. So, **A** is going to get **-5**.

The same applies to the bottom row. If **A** chooses the bottom row, then **B** is going to choose the **Seer** position, which gets the **-5**.

So from this, it seems that the value of the game is **-5**.

Now let's do the same thing on the **B** column. If **B** resigns, **A** can choose to resign or hold and he gets a **+10**. If **B** is a **Seer**, then **A** chooses between **Resigner** and **Holder** and gets **+5**.

Then, from this perspective, the value of the game is **+5**. So, here's a case where it better not be that we take a perfect information game, put it into a matrix, and get this out, because this is something unfavorable; it doesn't fit our theorem. We can't get its value by doing minimax or maximin.

The problem here is that, once we move the hidden information, *Minimax* is not necessarily--and in this case, definitely not--equal to *Maximin*. So, von Neumann theorem fails:

Minimax NOT EQUAL Maximin

Anyway, we seem to have a problem here. The problem is that once we get this hidden information, as I promised, complexity increases. We cannot do anything very simple with the matrix to find a pure strategy that's going to work. *A's* strategy depends upon what *B* will do and *B's* strategy depends upon what *A* will do. If you don't know what that's going to be, you don't actually have a value for the game.

Everything we have discussed so far--pure strategies--is exactly the same thing as was discussed about consistency. So, the way we are going to get around this is by ceasing to be consistent, or at least, consistent in the same way. To cheat here, we are going to introduce mixed strategies instead of pure strategies.

Mixed strategies

What's the difference between a pure strategy and a mixed strategy? A mixed strategy simply implies, or means, some distribution over strategies. So, take the case of two strategies where **A** can be either a **Resigner** or a **Holder**. We are going to simply say that the mixed strategy for **A** is some value for *P*, which is the probability of choosing to be a **Holder**. The only difference between a mixed strategy and a pure strategy is that for a mixed strategy, we choose some probability over all the different strategies that we might choose. So, we decide that before selecting the **Resigner** or **Holder**, we flip the coin; half the time we are going to be a **Resigner** and half the time we are going to be a holder. Or say, *30* percent of the time we will be a **Resigner** and *70* percent of the time we will be a **Holder**.

As with pure strategies, we always choose one or the other. So technically, it's the case that a pure strategy is also a mixed strategy where all of the probability mass is on a single strategy. In this case, we use *P* to represent the probability of **A** choosing to be a holder rather than a **Resigner**. So, *P* can be *0* or *1* or any value in between.

I've copied the previous matrix for quick reference:

		B	
		Resigner	Seer
A	Resigner	−5	+5
	Holder	+10	−5

Let's say B is always a **Resigner**; then what is the expected profit of **A**? If **B** is the **Resigner**, we don't really care about the other column anymore. Then **A** mixes between resigning and holding and P is the probability of being a holder; whenever that happens, it gets +10, and whenever the opposite of it happens, it gets -5. So, the profit of A will be $10P - (1-P)5$. Let me simplify it:

$$10P - (1-P)5$$
$$10P - 5 + 5P$$
$$15P - 5$$

A chooses to be a **Resigner**, and so it's just the weighted average between those two values. Just double-check it. If P is 0, that means it never holds; it always resigns and it gets -5. If P is 1, that means it always holds, so it should get a +10. And $15 - 5$ is 10.

If B is always a seer, then what is the expected profit of A? It's the same story, except we are using another column that is a seer. It is $-5P + (1-P)5$:

$$-5P + (1-P)5$$
$$-5P + 5 - 5P$$
$$-10P + 5$$

Let's check the results. So, again, if P is 1, then that means we will get the value of -5, and if we put in a 1 there, we get $5 - 10 = -5$. If P is 0, it means we are always a **Resigner**, and we should get a 5 for that.

So, this is how well a mixed strategy does, but not against another mixed strategy. This is against two deterministic strategies.

Now, note that these two equations we derived are actually line equations. Draw these equations in a graph:

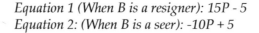

Equation 1 (When B is a resigner): 15P - 5
Equation 2: (When B is a seer): -10P + 5

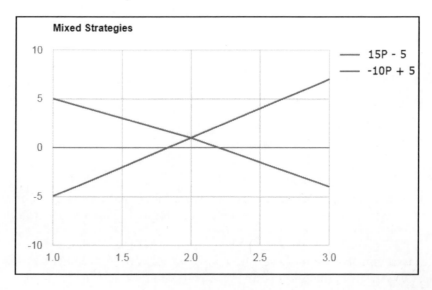

Figure 8.4: Mixed strategies line graph

What do you notice about these two lines? They make an X, so they intersect. Where do they intersect? I will make both the line equations equal and do a little bit of algebra, as follows:

$$15P - 5 = -10P + 5$$
$$15P + 10P = 5 + 5$$
$$25P = 10$$
$$P = 10/25$$
$$P = 2/5$$
$$P = 0.4$$

Both the lines are intersects at *p=0.4*. What is the value of the game at *p=0.4*?

$$= -10P + 5$$
$$= -10 (0.4) + 5$$
$$= -4 + 5$$
$$= 1$$

The value of the game at *P=0.4* is +1.

OpenAI Gym examples

In Chapter 1, *Reinforcement Learning*, we installed and configured the OpenAI Gym. Now it's time to start using it.

Agents

We discussed the agents in the earlier chapter in much detail. An agent in reinforcement learning is the one who performs an action. It actually runs the algorithms of reinforcement learning. So, the agent just contains the algorithms to itself or provides an integration between Gym and algorithm.

Environments

Gym comes out with lots and lots of environments. It inherits a common API around lots of environments and that's the reason it is fantastic. The following are the environments included in gym:

- **Classic control and toy text**: These are a variety of classic control tasks--small-scale tasks from the reinforcement learning literature. You can get started with the classic environment as follows:

```
import gym
environment = gym.make('CartPole-v0')
environment.reset()
environment.render()
```

- **Algorithmic**: This performs computations such as adding multi-digit numbers and reversing sequences. Most of these tasks require memory, and their difficulty can be chosen by changing the sequence length.

- **Atari**: Classic Atari games, with screen images or RAM as input, using the **Arcade Learning Environment** (**ALE**). This has a variety of Atari video games. You can get started with the Atari environment as follows:

```
import gym
environment = gym.make('SpaceInvaders-v0')
environment.reset()
environment.render()
```

- **Board games**: The board game environment has a variety of board games. You can get started with board games as follows:

```
import gym
environment = gym.make('Go9x9-v0')
environment.reset()
environment.render()
```

- **2D and 3D robots**: **Box2D** is a 2D physics engine control for a robot in simulation. These tasks use the **MuJoCo** physics engine, which was designed for fast and accurate robot simulation. You can get started with Box2D as follows:

```
import gym
environment = gym.make('LunarLander-v2')
environment.reset()
environment.render()
```

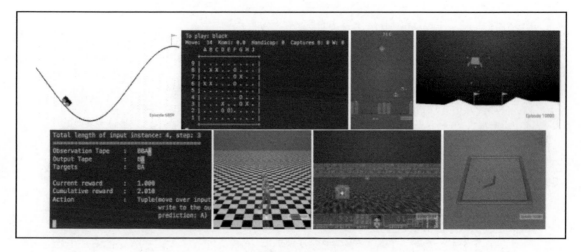

Figure 8.5: Sample environments

This is the code to display a list of all environments in gym:

```
from gym import envs

environment_ID = [spec.id for spec in envs.registry.all()]

for env_ID in sorted(environment_ID):

    print(env_ID)
```

Example 1 – simple random agent

This example implements a random agent and it will upload the results to the scoreboard:

```
import argparse
import logging
import sys

import gym
from gym import wrappers


class RandomAgent(object) :

#It is the world simplest agent

    def __init__(self_Agent, action_state_space) :
        self_Agent.action_space = action_state_space

    def act(self_Agent, observations, rewards, complete) :
        return self_Agent.action_space.sample()


if __name__ == '__main__':
    parser = argparse.ArgumentParser(description = None)
    parser.add_argument('env_id', nargs = '?', default = 'CartPole-v0',
help = 'Select which environment you want to run')

    argument = parser.parse_args()

  # We need to call the method undo_logger_setup , it will undo the
  # Gym's logger setup and we need to configure it manually
  # If we dont call it then most of of the time default should be fine

    gym.undo_logger_setup()

    logger_Details = logging.getLogger()
    formating = logging.Formatter('[%(asctime)s] %(message)s')

    handling = logging.StreamHandler(sys.stderr)

    handling.setFormatter(formating)

    logger_Details.addHandler(handling)

  #We can setup the level to logging.WARN or logging.DEBUG
  #if we want it to change the amount of output.
```

```
      logger_Details.setLevel(logging.INFO)
      environment = gym.make(argument.env_id)
```

  #We need to provide the output directory to write(It can be an#existing directory, we are including one with existing data.#Kindly notr that all files must be with namespaced).We can also put it to temporary#directory

```
      outdir = '/tmp/results_agent'
      environment = wrappers.Monitor(environment, directory = outdir, force
= True)
      environment.seed(0)
      agent = RandomAgent(environment.action_space)
      episode_count = 100
      rewards = 0
      complete = False

for i in range(episode_count) :
      ob = environment.reset()
   #Note there 's no environment.render() here.
            # But the environment still can open window and
            # render if asked by environment.monitor: it calls
environment.render('rgb_array ')
            # to record video.
            # Video is not recorded every episode, see
capped_cubic_video_schedule for details.
            # Close the environment and write monitor result info to disk
      environment.close()

   # Upload to the scoreboard. We could also do this from another
   # process if we wanted.

      logger.info("Successfully ran RandomAgent. Now trying to upload
results to the scoreboard. If it breaks, you can always just try re-
uploading the same results.")
      gym.upload(outdir)
```

Example 2 – learning agent

Now, we are going to implement an example of a learning agent; in this example, we are using the cross-entropy method, which will upload the results to the scoreboard:

```
from __future__ import print_function

#import the required gym libraries
import gym
from gym import wrappers
```

```python
#import the logging functionality
import logging

#import scientific libraries
import numpy as np

#import the pickle libraries

try:
    import cPickle as pickle
except ImportError:
    import pickle
import json, sys, os
from os import path
#from _policies import BinaryActionLinearPolicy # Different file so it can
be unpickled
import argparse

class BinaryActionLinearPolicy(object):
    def __init__(self, theta):
        self.w = theta[:-1]
        self.b = theta[-1]
    def act(self, ob):
        y = ob.dot(self.w) + self.b
        a = int(y < 0)
        return a

class ContinuousActionLinearPolicy(object):
    def __init__(self, theta, n_in, n_out):
        assert len(theta) == (n_in + 1) * n_out
        self.W = theta[0 : n_in * n_out].reshape(n_in, n_out)
        self.b = theta[n_in * n_out : None].reshape(1, n_out)
    def act(self, ob):
        a = ob.dot(self.W) + self.b
        return a


def cem(f, th_mean, batch_size, n_iter, elite_frac, initial_std=1.0):
    n_elite = int(np.round(batch_size*elite_frac))
    th_std = np.ones_like(th_mean) * initial_std

    for _ in range(n_iter):
        ths = np.array([th_mean + dth for dth in
th_std[None,:]*np.random.randn(batch_size, th_mean.size)])
        ys = np.array([f(th) for th in ths])
        elite_inds = ys.argsort()[::-1][:n_elite]
        elite_ths = ths[elite_inds]
        th_mean = elite_ths.mean(axis=0)
```

```
            th_std = elite_ths.std(axis=0)
            yield {'ys' : ys, 'theta_mean' : th_mean, 'y_mean' : ys.mean()}

    def do_rollout(agent, env, num_steps, render=False):
        total_rew = 0
        ob = env.reset()
        for t in range(num_steps):
            a = agent.act(ob)
            (ob, reward, done, _info) = env.step(a)
            total_rew += reward
            if render and t%3==0: env.render()
            if done: break
        return total_rew, t+1

    if __name__ == '__main__':
        logger = logging.getLogger()
        logger.setLevel(logging.INFO)

        parser = argparse.ArgumentParser()
        parser.add_argument('--display', action='store_true')
        parser.add_argument('target', nargs="?", default="CartPole-v0")
        args = parser.parse_args()

        env = gym.make(args.target)
        env.seed(0)
        np.random.seed(0)
        params = dict(n_iter=10, batch_size=25, elite_frac = 0.2)
        num_steps = 20000

        outdir = '/tmp/cem-agent-results'
        env = wrappers.Monitor(env, outdir, force=True)

        def writefile(fname, s):
            with open(path.join(outdir, fname), 'w') as fh: fh.write(s)
        info = {}
        info['params'] = params
        info['argv'] = sys.argv
        info['env_id'] = env.spec.id
        # ------------------------------------------

        def noisy_evaluation(theta):
            agent = BinaryActionLinearPolicy(theta)
            rew, T = do_rollout(agent, env, num_steps)
            return rew

        # Train the agent, and snapshot each stage
        for (i, iterdata) in enumerate(
            cem(noisy_evaluation, np.zeros(env.observation_space.shape[0]+1),
```

```
    **params)):
        print('Iteration %2i. Episode mean reward: %7.3f'%(i,
iterdata['y_mean']))
        agent = BinaryActionLinearPolicy(iterdata['theta_mean'])
        if args.display: do_rollout(agent, env, 20000, render=True)
        writefile('agent-%.4i.pkl'%i, str(pickle.dumps(agent, -1)))
    writefile('info.json', json.dumps(info))

    env.close()

    logger.info("Successfully ran cross-entropy method. Now trying to
upload results to the scoreboard. If it breaks, you can always just try re-
uploading the same results.")
    gym.upload(outdir)
```

Example 3 - keyboard learning agent

This is an example of running a keyboard agent where the user will pass the environment name and it will run it in the specified environment:

```
import sys
import gym

#In this program we will do the test
for learning agent,
and environment name through command line

environment = gym.make('LunarLander-v2'
if len(sys.argv) < 2
else sys.argv[1])

if not hasattr(environment.action_space, 'n') : raise Exception('The agent
only supporting the discrete action space')

PERFORM_ACTION = environment.action_space.n

_ROLLINGOUT_TIME = 1000

CONTROL_SKIP = 0

#we can test is the skip is still usable ?

_action_agent_human_ = 0
_restart_want_human_ = False
_pause_set_human_ = False

def _key_pressed_(_key_pressed, mod) : global _action_agent_human_,
```

```
_restart_want_human_,
_pause_set_human_
if _key_pressed == 0xff0d: _restart_want_human_ = True
if _key_pressed == 32 : _pause_set_human_ = not _pause_set_human_ aaa =
int(_key_pressed - ord('0')) if aaa <= 0 or aaa >= PERFORM_ACTION: return
_action_agent_human_ = aaa

def _key_released_(_key_pressed, mod) : global _action_agent_human_
aaa = int(_key_pressed - ord('0'))
if aaa <= 0 or aaa >= PERFORM_ACTION: return if _action_agent_human_ ==
aaa: _action_agent_human_ = 0

environment.render()
environment.unwrapped.viewer.window.on__key_press_ = _key_pressed_
environment.unwrapped.viewer.window.on__key_release_ = _key_released_

def _rollingout_(environment) : global _action_agent_human_,
_restart_want_human_,
_pause_set_human_
_restart_want_human_ = False

observation = environment.reset()
skip = 0
for t in range(_ROLLINGOUT_TIME) : if not skip: aaa = _action_agent_human_
skip = CONTROL_SKIP
else: skip -= 1

observation,
r,
_done_,
info = environment.step(aaa)
environment.render()

if _done_: break
if _restart_want_human_: break
while _pause_set_human_: environment.render()

#Now importing the time libraries
import time

time.sleep(0.1)

print("PERFORM_ACTION={}".format(PERFORM_ACTION))
print("Please press one of the following keys 1, 2 or 3 and it take
PERFORM_ACTION 1 or 2 or 3 ...")
print("if you did not press any keys then it takes an action 0")

while 1 : _rollingout_(environment)
```

Summary

In this chapter, we learned how game theory is related to machine learning and how we apply reinforcement learning in gaming practices.

We learned that in reinforcement learning, it is common to imagine an underlying MDP. Then the goal of reinforcement learning is to learn a good policy for the MDP, which is normally only partially specified. MDPs can have different objectives such as discounted reward, average, and total; here, discounted reward is the most common assumption for reinforcement learning. There are other extensions that are well studied for MDPs' two-player (that is, game) settings as we saw in the examples.

We discussed pure and mixed strategies. Then, we discussed the von Neumann theorem. We learned the meaning of, and how to construct, the matrix normal form of a game. We also understood the principles of decision making in games with hidden information.

We also discussed that there is an underlying theory shared by MDPs and their extensions to two-player zero-sum games, including, value iteration, policy iteration / strategy improvement, Bellman optimality, and so on. However, there are close connections between these specific types of games and MDPs.

We implemented three different examples and used the OpenAI Gym API. All the results were simulated in an Atari environment. The first example was a simple random agent; then, we saw the implementation of learning agents.

In the upcoming chapter, we will look into lots of other frameworks for reinforcement learning and we will learn how to set up and work using those frameworks.

9
Reinforcement Learning Showdown

In this chapter, we will look at different reinforcement learning frameworks. We have already learnt about OpenAI Gym, and BURLAP. Now we will look at other very interesting reinforcement learning frameworks, such as PyBrain, RLPy, Maja, and so on. We will also discuss in detail about **Reinforcement Learning Glue (RL-Glue)** that enables us to write the reinforcement learning program in many languages.

Reinforcement learning frameworks

There are lot of useful reinforcement frameworks. We have already discussed OpenAI Gym, OpenAI Universe, and BURLAP. Now we will discuss the following reinforcement frameworks:

- PyBrain
- RLPy
- Maja
- RL-Glue
- Mindpark

PyBrain

PyBrain is a reinforcement learning framework. It has components such as task, agent, environment, and experiments that help us to program the reinforcement learning problem. In this section, we will learn how to setup the environment and create one simple task using Python code.

Setup

To setup the environment, the first step is to clone it from GitHub:

```
git clone https://github.com/pybrain/pybrain
```

Then the user needs to enter into the pybrain directory:

```
cd pybrain
```

Next step is to install all the files:

```
python setup.py install
```

Ready to code

First we need to import all the libraries that will help us to develop the reinforcement learning components from PyBrain:

```
//First thing to import all the required libraries here

import sys, time
from scipy import *

from pybrain.rl.environments import Task
from pybrain.rl.learners.valuebased import ActionValueTable
from pybrain.rl.environments.mazes import Maze, MDPMazeTask
from pybrain.rl.experiments import Experiment
from pybrain.rl.agents import LearningAgent
from pybrain.rl.learners import Q, SARSA
```

Environment

As we discussed earlier, an environment is a place where an agent can perform actions. For the agent, the environment is a complete world. In PyBrain, all environments are located at `pybrain/rl/environments`.

In a list of environments that are already present in PyBrain, one of them is called **maze environment** and we are going to use this environment in this section. When we create a maze environment, it creates a wall, a goal point, and free fields. The agent needs to find a goal point while he can freely move over the free fields.

Now let's define the maze structure in a simple 2D array, where 0 is the free field and 1 is the wall:

```
var_structure_arr_ = array([[1, 1, 1, 1, 1, 1, 1, 1, 1],
                    [1, 0, 0, 1, 0, 0, 0, 0, 1],
                    [1, 0, 0, 1, 0, 0, 1, 0, 1],
                    [1, 0, 0, 1, 0, 0, 1, 0, 1],
                    [1, 0, 0, 1, 0, 1, 1, 0, 1],
                    [1, 0, 0, 0, 0, 0, 1, 0, 1],
                    [1, 1, 1, 1, 1, 1, 1, 0, 1],
                    [1, 0, 0, 0, 0, 0, 0, 0, 1],
                    [1, 1, 1, 1, 1, 1, 1, 1, 1]])
```

Next, we will create the `var_environment_` with the `var_structure_arr_`:

```
var_environment_ = imp_Maze_(var_structure_arr_, (7, 7))
```

Agent

Now that the environment is created, we need an agent that can interact with the environment and take some actions.

In PyBrain, we represent the controller as a module; it takes an input and transforms the input into an action:

```
var_controller_ = imp_Table_Action_Value_(81, 4)
var_controller_.initialize(1.0)
```

In the previous code, the table requires the number of states and actions as inputs. The maze environment has four actions: west, east, north, and south. We will use the Q function in the following code:

```
var_learner_ = Q()
var_Agent_ = imp_L_var_Agent_(var_controller_, var_learner_)
```

Task

We have already created an environment and an agent, but till now there is no connection between them. PyBrain provides a special component that connects the agent and the environment. Task provides the details of the goal that the agent needs to achieve and the reward for all its actions. The task also decides when an episode is considered completed. Each environment has different sets of tasks. We are using the maze environment and the task here is `imp_MDP_Task_Maze_`. The maze task needs an environment into parameter and it stores the reference in `var_task_`:

```
var_task_ = imp_MDP_Task_Maze_(var_environment_)
```

Experiment

Let us create an experiment as `var_experiment_`. We create a task, an experiment, and an agent, in order to learn something:

```
var_experiment_ = imp_Experiment_(var_task_, var_Agent_)

while True:
    var_experiment_.doInteractions(100)
    var_Agent_.learn()
    var_Agent_.reset()

    pylab.pcolor(var_controller_.params.reshape(81,4).max(1).reshape(9,9))
    pylab.draw()
```

In the preceding code, the experiment performs 100 interactions between the environment and the agent, or we can say, between the task and the agent. The task performed is actually an agent action that is taken into the environment. In response, the environment returns the new state and the reward for taking that action.

Once the `100` iterations are complete, we call the agent `learn` method and then reset the environment. With the `reset` function, the agent forgets the previous step but it has already learnt from the environment which cannot be undone. The loop repeats until we reach the desired behavior.

For visualization, as we saw in the last two lines of the code, we can observe the learning progress.

RLPy

Now we are going to discuss another reinforcement learning framework, called RLPy. It is a framework that makes experiments on the function-value based approaches. Here the reinforcement learning components can be joined together to create different experiments.

As discussed earlier, setting up a reinforcement problem requires the following four components: agent, policy, representation, and domain.

 RLPy requires Python v2.6 or 2.7. It will not work on v3.5 or higher.

Setup

There are two ways to setup the environment of RLPy:

- Download the stable and the latest version directly from `pip`:

```
pip install -U rlpy
```

- Download it manually; we need to extract and execute the installer manually:

```
git clone https://github.com/rlpy/rlpy.git RLPy
cd RLPy
python setup.py install
```

Ready to code

The following program is a common program that we use throughout this book; the domain used is GridWorld. Here an agent needs to find the optimal policy while he can interact with the environment.

```
#Here we will import all the required libraries

import os

from rlpy.Domains import imp_Grid_World_
from rlpy.Agents import imp_Q_Learning_
from rlpy.Representations import imp_Tabular_
from rlpy.Policies import imp_eGreedy_
from rlpy.Experiments import imp_Experiment_




def meth_Experiment_Make_(parm_id_exp=1,
parm_log_path="./Log_Results/Practical_Reinforement_Learning/QLearning_Grid
World"):
    """
  This function would return an experiment class with everything setup
already
  It function will that takes 2 parameters
  @parm_id_exp: that i seed a random number generators
  @parm_log_path: that is the output directory to write the results and
logs
    """
  _var_opt_ = {}
    _var_opt_["parm_id_exp"] = parm_id_exp
    _var_opt_["parm_log_path"] = parm_log_path

    # We are define the maze domain here
  _var_maze_ = os.parm_log_path.join(imp_Grid_World_.default_map_dir,
'4x5.txt')
    _var_domain_ = imp_Grid_World_(_var_maze_, noise=0.3)
    _var_opt_["domain"] = _var_domain_

    # We are defining the representation here
  _var_Representation_ = imp_Tabular_(_var_domain_, discretization=20)

    # We are defining the policy here
  _var_Policy_ = imp_eGreedy_(_var_Representation_, epsilon=0.2)

    # We are defined the agent here
```

```
  _var_opt_["agent"] =
imp_Q_Learning_(_var_Representation_=_var_Representation_,
_var_Policy_=_var_Policy_,
                        discount_factor=_var_domain_.discount_factor,
                        initial_learn_rate=0.1,
                        learn_rate_decay_mode="boyan", boyan_N0=100,
                        lambda_=0.)
   _var_opt_["checks_per_policy"] = 100
     _var_opt_["max_steps"] = 2000
     _var_opt_["num_policy_checks"] = 10
     var_Experiments_ = imp_Experiment_(**_var_opt_)
   return var_Experiments_

if __name__ == '__main__':
   var_Experiments_ = meth_Experiment_Make_(1)
   var_Experiments_.run(visualize_steps=False, # should each learning step
be shown
                    visualize_learning=True, # policy / value function
should display
                    visualize_performance=1) # performance runs would
display
   var_Experiments_.plot()
   var_Experiments_.save()
```

The major components for an experiment are GridWorld and domain. In the preceding code, an agent uses Q_Learning which in turn uses an eGreddy policy. The experiment is handling the execution between the domain and the agent, also it stores the result on a disk.

Maja Machine Learning Framework

It is a general machine learning framework that also can be used for reinforcement learning problems. We can use it with Python libraries. It provides a set of benchmark domains and reinforcement learning algorithms. It is also easily extendable and allows the agents to automate the bench marking. Maja framework provides such reinforcement learning algorithms as Fitted R-MAX, TD(lambda), Monte Carlo methods, CMA-ES, actor critic architecture, and Dyna TD. It also provides different environments for us to choose in the reinforcement learning problems, such as maze, mountain car, pinball, pole balancing, and so on.

Setup

For installing the most recent version of the **Maja Machine Learning Framework (MMLF)**, download the file from `https://sourceforge.net/projects/mmlf/`. With this file, the MMLF can either be installed locally or globally (see the following image):

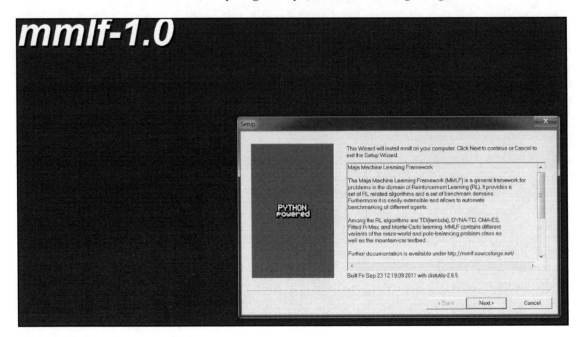

Figure 9.1: Maja installation

 The MMLF has been tested on Python v2.6 and v2.7, and requires that the Python packages `numpy` (tested on version 1.3.0), `scipy` (v0.7.0), `matplotlib` (v1.0), and `pyyaml` (v3.0.9) are installed.

RL-Glue

RL-Glue is a framework that allows the developer to write the code in many languages. It is a language independent framework. It provides the standard libraries that the developer can use and which can be extended easily. RL-Glue provides collaboration and code sharing facilities. Because of the code sharing feature, the developer can focus on his own reinforcement learning problem and not worry about re-engineering the task or algorithms. We can use RL-Glue in any language that supports network socket programming. All the communication between the libraries is through network sockets.

RL-Glue provides an interface that we can connect to the environment and the agent. We can experiment the programs together, even if they are written in any other language.

It also provides a standard interface that allows you to connect reinforcement learning agents, environments, and experiment programs together, even if they are written in different languages.

Setup

The first thing we need to do is to install the RL-Glue core and then install the codec in the language of our choice. Codec is actually a way that allows our preferred programming language to talk to RL-Glue libraries. Both codec and core projects are compatible on cross platforms; you can use macOS, Linux, Unix, or Windows.

You can download RL-Glue core from the following URL: `https://code.google.com/archive/p/rl-glue-ext/downloads`.

Select the package you want to download and then extract it. For Windows, just double click on the file `RL-Glue.exe`:

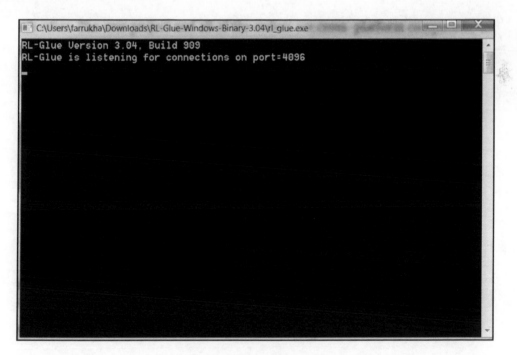

Figure 9.3: RL-Glue.exe

Now you need to download the codec. Again use the same link and select the language in which you want to download the codec: https://code.google.com/archive/p/rl-glue-ext/downloads.

After you download the codec, you need to extract it and run the setup:

Figure 9.4: RL-Glue codec

RL-Glue components

RL-Glue programs consist of the environment, experiment, and agent. We implement the environment program to define the task, and get the rewards and observations. The agent implements the learning algorithm and selection-action mechanism. The experiment program implements the sequence of environment-agent interactions and performance evaluation of the agent. RL-Glue uses the experiment program to manage the communication between the environment and the agent which is represented in *Figure 9.2* as follows:

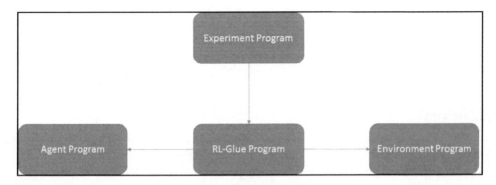

Figure 9.2: The four programs specified by the RL-Glue protocol

The experiment program contains the main function, that makes all the requests for information through RL-Glue. These requests are usually related to setting up, starting, and running the experiment and then gathering data about the agent's performance. The experiment program can never interact with the environment or the agent directly; all contact goes through the RL-Glue interface. There is also no direct contact between the agent and the environment. Any information that the agent or the environment returns is passed through RL-Glue to the module that needs it.

In RL-Glue, the agent is both the learning algorithm and the decision maker. The agent decides which action to take at every step.

The environment is responsible for storing all the relevant details of the world, or the problem of your experiment. The environment generates the observations, states, or perceptions that are provided to the agent, and also determines the transition dynamics and rewards.

The experiment is the intermediary that (through RL-Glue) controls all the communication between the agent and the environment. This structured separation is by design; the division of the agent and the environment helps create modularized code and captures our intuitions about how much the agent and the environment should know about each other.

RL-Glue can be used as external or internal mode. For external use, the environment, the agent, and the experiment are linked from different programs. Each of the programs has to connect with the RL-Glue server program, and all the communication happens through network sockets. We can use any programming language which uses sockets to write our code. Currently, the external mode supports Java, LISP, Python, C/C++, and MATLAB. Internal mode currently supports C/C++ and Java for experiment, agent, and environment setup.

Both external and internal mode have weaknesses and strengths. External mode is more portable and flexible, while the internal mode is faster in terms of execution speed, as the internal mode has less overheads. The environment and the agent are the same on the basis of their execution mode. The environment and agent are loaded and linked together.

Sample project

Two sample projects, skeleton and mines-sarsa are part of the codec installation, all the code files will be installed with this installation. They are located in the sample examples directory. Both the projects are written in C language and contain experiments, environments, and agents.

The skeleton project contains experiments, agents, and environments and it would be a good starting point for doing the further development. The mines-sarsa project has a fully functional sarsa learning algorithm. It combines the GridWorld problem and also has an experiment program.

Here we are going to define the skeleton project that uses the mines-sarsa program. We will provide an implementation of environment, agent and experiment, and compile them together and run it as an experiment. This example will help you to write future projects.

sample_sarsa_agent.py

First we will implement `sarsa_agent.py` as follows:

```
#Here we will import all the required libraries

import copy
import random
import pickle
import sys

from rlglue.agent.Agent import _imp_Agent_
from rlglue.agent import _imp_Agent_Loader_
from rlglue.types import _imp_Action_
from rlglue.types import _imp_observation
from rlglue.utils import imp_VRLGLUE3_TaskSpec_
from random import _imp_Random_



# We are creating a sarsa agent for action-discrete, state-discrete
environments.
```

```
class func_Agent_Sarsa(_imp_Agent_):
  var_Random_Generator=Random()
  var_Last_Action_=Action()
  var_Observation_Last=Observation()
  var_Stepsize_Sarsa = 0.1
  var_Epsilon_Sarsa = 0.1
  var_Gamma_Sarsa = 1.0
  var_States_Num = 0
  var_Actions_Num = 0
  var_Function_Value = None
  var_Frozen_Policy_=False
  var_Frozen_Exploring=False
  def func_Init_Agent_(self,var_String_Task_Specification_):
  var_Spec_Task =
imp_VRLGLUE3_TaskSpec_.TaskSpecParser(var_String_Task_Specification_)
  if var_Spec_Task.valid:
    assert len(var_Spec_Task.getIntObservations())==1,
      assert len(var_Spec_Task.getDoubleObservations())==0,
      assert not
var_Spec_Task.isSpecial(var_Spec_Task.getIntObservations()[0][0]),
      assert not
var_Spec_Task.isSpecial(var_Spec_Task.getIntObservations()[0][1]),
    self.var_States_Num=var_Spec_Task.getIntObservations()[0][1]+1;

      assert len(var_Spec_Task.getIntActions())==1,
      assert len(var_Spec_Task.getDoubleActions())==0,
      assert not
var_Spec_Task.isSpecial(var_Spec_Task.getIntActions()[0][0]),
      assert not
var_Spec_Task.isSpecial(var_Spec_Task.getIntActions()[0][1]),
    self.var_Actions_Num=var_Spec_Task.getIntActions()[0][1]+1;
      self.var_Function_Value=[self.var_Actions_Num*[0.0] for i in
range(self.var_States_Num)]

    else:
    print "The specification of task could not be parsed:
"+var_String_Task_Specification_;
    self.var_Last_Action_=Action()
  self.var_Observation_Last=Observation()
  def func_eGreedy_(self, var_State_):
  var_Index_Max=0
  a=1
  if not self.var_Frozen_Exploring and
self.var_Random_Generator.random()<self.var_Epsilon_Sarsa:
      return self.var_Random_Generator.randint(0,self.var_Actions_Num-1)

    return
self.var_Function_Value[var_State_].index(max(self.var_Function_Value[var_S
```

```
tate_]))
  def func_Start_Agent_(self,_var_Observation_):
    var_The_State_=_var_Observation_.intArray[0]
    var_This_Int_Action=self.func_eGreedy_(var_The_State_)

    var_Action_return=Action()
    var_Action_return.intArray=[var_This_Int_Action]
    self.var_Last_Action_=copy.deepcopy(var_Action_return)
    self.var_Observation_Last=copy.deepcopy(_var_Observation_)

    return var_Action_return
  def func_Step_Agent_(self,var_Reward_, _var_Observation_):
    var_State_New=_var_Observation_.intArray[0]
    var_State_Last=self.var_Observation_Last.intArray[0]
    var_Last_Action_=self.var_Last_Action_.intArray[0]

    var_New_Int_Action=self.func_eGreedy_(var_State_New)

    _var_Sa_Q_=self.var_Function_Value[var_State_Last][var_Last_Action_]
_var_aPrime_sPrime_Q_=self.var_Function_Value[var_State_New][var_New_Int_Ac
tion]

    _var_Sa_Q_New_=_var_Sa_Q_ + self.var_Stepsize_Sarsa * (var_Reward_ +
self.var_Gamma_Sarsa * _var_aPrime_sPrime_Q_ - _var_Sa_Q_)


    if not self.var_Frozen_Policy_:
self.var_Function_Value[var_State_Last][var_Last_Action_]=_var_Sa_Q_New_

    var_Action_return=Action()
    var_Action_return.intArray=[var_New_Int_Action]
    self.var_Last_Action_=copy.deepcopy(var_Action_return)
    self.var_Observation_Last=copy.deepcopy(_var_Observation_)

    return var_Action_return
  def func_End_Agent_(self,var_Reward_):

    var_State_Last=self.var_Observation_Last.intArray[0]
    var_Last_Action_=self.var_Last_Action_.intArray[0]

    _var_Sa_Q_=self.var_Function_Value[var_State_Last][var_Last_Action_]

    _var_Sa_Q_New_=_var_Sa_Q_ + self.var_Stepsize_Sarsa * (var_Reward_ -
Q_sa)

    if not self.var_Frozen_Policy_:
    self.var_Function_Value[var_State_Last][var_Last_Action_]=_var_Sa_Q_New_
```

```python
    def func_Cleanup_Agent(self):

      pass

    def func_Value_Function_Save_(self, var_File_Name_):
      var_The_File_ = open(var_File_Name_, "w")
      pickle.dump(self.var_Function_Value, var_The_File_)
      var_The_File_.close()

    def func_Value_Function_Load_(self, var_File_Name_):
      var_The_File_ = open(var_File_Name_, "r")
      self.var_Function_Value=pickle.load(var_The_File_)
      var_The_File_.close()
    def func_Message_Agent_(self,var_In_Message_):
      if var_In_Message_.startswith("freeze learning"):
        self.var_Frozen_Policy_=True
        return "message understand is, policy frozen"

     if var_In_Message_.startswith("unfreeze learning"):
        self.var_Frozen_Policy_=False
      return "message understand is, policy unfrozen"

    if var_In_Message_.startswith("freeze exploring"):
        self.var_Frozen_Exploring=True
      return "message understand is, exploring frozen"

    if var_In_Message_.startswith("unfreeze exploring"):
         self.var_Frozen_Exploring=False
        return "message understand is, exploring frozen"

    if var_In_Message_.startswith("save_policy"):
         var_String_Split=var_In_Message_.split(" ");
         self.func_Value_Function_Save_(var_String_Split[1]);
      print "Saved.";
      return "message understand is, saving policy"

    if var_In_Message_.startswith("load_policy"):
         var_String_Split=var_In_Message_.split(" ")
         self.func_Value_Function_Load_(var_String_Split[1])
      print "Loaded."
      return "message understand is, loading policy"

      return "Now able to understand your message."



    if __name__=="__main__":
    _imp_Agent_Loader_.loadAgent(func_Agent_Sarsa())
```

sample_mines_environment.py

Now we will implement `sample_mines_environment.py` as follows:

```
#First step is to include all the required libraries
import random
import sys
from rlglue.environment.Environment import imp_Environment_
from rlglue.environment import imp_Environment_Loader_
from rlglue.types import imp_Observation_
from rlglue.types import imp_Action_
from rlglue.types import imp_Terminal_Observation_Reward


class func_Environment_Mines_(imp_Environment_):
  _var_Free_World_ = 0
  _var_Obstacle_World = 1
  _var_Mine_World_ = 2
  _var_Goal_World_ = 3
  _var_Generator_Rand_=random.Random()
  _var_State_Fixed_Start_=False
  _var_Start_Row=1
  _var_Start_Col_=1
  _var_State_Current_=10
  def func_Init_Environment(self):
    self.var_Map_=[ [1, 1, 1, 1, 1, 1, 1, 1, 1, 1, 1, 1, 1, 1, 1, 1, 1, 1],
                    [1, 0, 0, 0, 0, 0, 0, 2, 2, 0, 0, 0, 0, 0, 0, 0, 0,
1],
                    [1, 0, 0, 0, 0, 2, 0, 0, 0, 0, 0, 0, 0, 0, 0, 0, 0,
1],
                    [1, 0, 0, 0, 0, 0, 0, 0, 0, 2, 2, 2, 0, 0, 0, 0, 1,
1],
                    [1, 0, 0, 0, 0, 0, 0, 0, 0, 0, 3, 0, 0, 0, 0, 0, 0,
1],
                    [1, 1, 1, 1, 1, 1, 1, 1, 1, 1, 1, 1, 1, 1, 1, 1, 1,
1]]

    return "VERSION RL-Glue-3.0."
  def func_Start_Environment(self):
    if self._var_State_Fixed_Start_:
var_Valid_Start_=self.func_Agent_State_Set_(self._var_Start_Row,self._var_S
tart_Col_)
      if not var_Valid_Start_:
        print "Not a valid fixed start state:
"+str(int(self._var_Start_Row))+","+str(int(self._var_Start_Row))
        self.func_State_Random_()
    else:
```

```
      self.func_State_Random_()

   var_Observation_Return_=imp_Observation_()
   var_Observation_Return_.intArray=[self.func_Flat_State_Calculate()]

   return var_Observation_Return_
 def func_Step_Environment(self,var_This_Action_):
 # We have to sure that the actions is valid
   assert len(var_This_Action_.intArray)==1,
   assert var_This_Action_.intArray[0]>=0,
   assert var_This_Action_.intArray[0]<4,
   self.func_Position_Update_(var_This_Action_.intArray[0])

   _var_The_Observation_(=imp_Observation_()
   _var_The_Observation_(.intArray=[self.func_Flat_State_Calculate()]

   _var_RO_Return_=imp_Terminal_Observation_Reward()
   _var_RO_Return_.r=self.func_Reward_Calculate()
   _var_RO_Return_.o=_var_The_Observation_(
   _var_RO_Return_.terminal=self.func_Current_Terminal_Check_()

   return _var_RO_Return_

 def _func_Cleanup_Environment_(self):
   pass

 def _func_Message_Environment(self,inMessage):
   if inMessage.startswith("set-random-start-state"):
    self._var_State_Fixed_Start_=False;
   return "Message is clearly understand. Now start state with random.";

   if inMessage.startswith("set-start-state"):
   splitString=inMessage.split(" ");
   self._var_Start_Row=int(splitString[1]);
     self._var_Start_Col_=int(splitString[2]);
     self._var_State_Fixed_Start_=True;
   return "Message is clearly understand. Now start state with fixed start
state.";

   if inMessage.startswith("print-state"):
     self.func_State_Print_();
   return "Message is clearly understand. Now print the state.";

   return "Python does not respond to that message.";

 def func_Agent_State_Set_(self,var_Row_, var_Col_):
   self._var_Row_Agent_=var_Row_
   self._var_Col_Agent_=var_Col_
```

```
      return self.func_Valid_Check(var_Row_,var_Col_) and not
self.func_Terminal_Check(var_Row_,var_Col_)

   def func_State_Random_(self):
     _var_Rows_Num_=len(self.var_Map_)
     _var_Cols_Num_=len(self.var_Map_[0])
     _var_Start_Row=self._var_Generator_Rand_.randint(0,_var_Rows_Num_-1)
    _var_Start_Col_=self._var_Generator_Rand_.randint(0,_var_Cols_Num_-1)

     while not self.func_Agent_State_Set_(_var_Start_Row,_var_Start_Col_):
        _var_Start_Row=self._var_Generator_Rand_.randint(0,_var_Rows_Num_-1)
        _var_Start_Col_=self._var_Generator_Rand_.randint(0,_var_Cols_Num_-1)

   def func_Valid_Check(self,var_Row_, var_Col_):
     valid=False
     _var_Rows_Num_=len(self.var_Map_)
     _var_Cols_Num_=len(self.var_Map_[0])

     if(var_Row_ < _var_Rows_Num_ and var_Row_ >= 0 and var_Col_ <
_var_Cols_Num_ and var_Col_ >= 0):
        if self.var_Map_[var_Row_][var_Col_] != self._var_Obstacle_World:
          valid=True
     return valid

   def func_Terminal_Check(self,var_Row_,var_Col_):
     if (self.var_Map_[var_Row_][var_Col_] == self._var_Goal_World_ or
self.var_Map_[var_Row_][var_Col_] == self._var_Mine_World_):
        return True
     return False

   def func_Current_Terminal_Check_(self):
     return
self.func_Terminal_Check(self._var_Row_Agent_,self._var_Col_Agent_)

   def func_Flat_State_Calculate(self):
     _var_Rows_Num_=len(self.var_Map_)
     return self._var_Col_Agent_ * _var_Rows_Num_ + self._var_Row_Agent_



   def func_Position_Update_(self, _var_The_Action_):

     _var_Row_New_ = self._var_Row_Agent_;
     _var_Col_New_ = self._var_Col_Agent_;

     if (_var_The_Action_ == 0):#move down
       _var_Col_New_ = self._var_Col_Agent_ - 1;
```

```
        if (_var_The_Action_ == 1): #move up
          _var_Col_New_ = self._var_Col_Agent_ + 1;

        if (_var_The_Action_ == 2):#move left
          _var_Row_New_ = self._var_Row_Agent_ - 1;

        if (_var_The_Action_ == 3):#move right
          _var_Row_New_ = self._var_Row_Agent_ + 1;

        if(self.func_Valid_Check(_var_Row_New_,_var_Col_New_)):
          self._var_Row_Agent_ = _var_Row_New_;
          self._var_Col_Agent_ = _var_Col_New_;

    def func_Reward_Calculate(self):
        if(self.var_Map_[self._var_Row_Agent_][self._var_Col_Agent_] ==
self._var_Goal_World_):
          return 10.0;
        if(self.var_Map_[self._var_Row_Agent_][self._var_Col_Agent_] ==
self._var_Mine_World_):
          return -100.0;
        return -1.0;
    def func_State_Print_(self):
      _var_Rows_Num_=len(self.var_Map_)
      _var_Cols_Num_=len(self.var_Map_[0])
      print "Agent is at:
"+str(self._var_Row_Agent_)+","+str(self._var_Col_Agent_)
     print "Columns:0-10 10-17"
     print "Col ",
     for var_Col_ in range(0,_var_Cols_Num_):
         print col%10,
       for var_Row_ in range(0,_var_Rows_Num_):
         print "Row: "+str(var_Row_)+" ",
       for var_Col_ in range(0,_var_Cols_Num_):
       if self._var_Row_Agent_==var_Row_ and self._var_Col_Agent_==var_Col_:
           print "A",
       else:
           if self.var_Map_[var_Row_][var_Col_] == self._var_Goal_World_:
               print "G",
         if self.var_Map_[var_Row_][var_Col_] == self._var_Mine_World_:
               print "M",
         if self.var_Map_[var_Row_][var_Col_] == self._var_Obstacle_World:
               print "*",
         if self.var_Map_[var_Row_][var_Col_] == self._var_Free_World_:
               print " ",

if __name__=="__main__":

    imp_Environment_Loader_.loadEnvironment(func_Environment_Mines_())
```

sample_experiment.py

Now we see the implementation of `sample_experiment.py` as follows:

```python
#We need to include all the required libraries
import sys
import math
import rlglue.RLGlue as imp_RL_Glue_



def func_Demo_Offline_():


  _var_Statistics_=[];
  _var_Score_This_=func_Agent_Evaluate_();

  func_Score_Print(0,_var_Score_This_);
  _var_Statistics_.append(_var_Score_This_);

  for i in range(0,20):
  for j in range(0,25):
     imp_RL_Glue_.RL_episode(0);
  _var_Score_This_=func_Agent_Evaluate_();
  func_Score_Print((i+1)*25,_var_Score_This_);
  _var_Statistics_.append(_var_Score_This_);
  func_Result_Save_To_CSV_(_var_Statistics_,"results.csv");

def func_Score_Print(afterEpisodes, score_tuple):
  print "%d\t\t%.2f\t\t%.2f" % (afterEpisodes, score_tuple[0],
score_tuple[1])



def func_Agent_Evaluate_():

  _var_Sum_=0;
  _var_Sum_Squares_=0;
  _var_This_Return_=0;
  _var_Mean_=0;
  _var_Variance_=0;
  n=10;
  imp_RL_Glue_.func_Message_RL_Agent_("freeze learning");
  for i in range(0,n):
  # In case a policy is bad then we will use a cutoff to end an episode
    imp_RL_Glue_.RL_episode(5000);
    _var_This_Return_=imp_RL_Glue_.RL_return();
    _var_Sum_+=_var_This_Return_;
    _var_Sum_Squares_+=_var_This_Return_**2;
```

```python
    _var_Mean_=_var_Sum_/n;
    _var_Variance_ = (_var_Sum_Squares_ - n*_var_Mean_*_var_Mean_)/(n - 1.0);
    _var_Standard_Dev_=math.sqrt(_var_Variance_);

    imp_RL_Glue_.func_Message_RL_Agent_("unfreeze learning");
    return _var_Mean_,_var_Standard_Dev_;


def func_Result_Save_To_CSV_(_var_Statistics_, _var_File_Name_):

    _var_The_File_ = open(_var_File_Name_, "w");
    _var_The_File_.write("#Results are displaying from sample_experiment.py.
First line is means, second line is standard deviations.\n");


    for _var_This_Entry_ in _var_Statistics_:
        _var_The_File_.write("%.2f, " % _var_This_Entry_[0])
    _var_The_File_.write("\n");


    for _var_This_Entry_ in _var_Statistics_:
        _var_The_File_.write("%.2f, " % _var_This_Entry_[1])
    _var_The_File_.write("\n");


    _var_The_File_.close();



def _funs_Evaluation_Single_():
    _var_Score_This_=func_Agent_Evaluate_();
    func_Score_Print(0,_var_Score_This_);



print "Starting offline demo \n"

print "After Episode \n"

imp_RL_Glue_.RL_init()

func_Demo_Offline_()


imp_RL_Glue_.func_Message_RL_Agent_("save_policy results.dat");
```

```
imp_RL_Glue_.RL_cleanup();
imp_RL_Glue_.RL_init();

print "Evaluating the agent's default policy \n"
_funs_Evaluation_Single_();

print "\nLoading up the value function we saved earlier."

imp_RL_Glue_.func_Message_RL_Agent_("load_policy results.dat");

print "Evaluating the agent after loading the value function:\n\t\tMean
Return\tStandardDeviation\n---------------------------------------------
------"

_funs_Evaluation_Single_();


imp_RL_Glue_.RL_env_message("set-start-state 2 3");

imp_RL_Glue_.RL_start();


imp_RL_Glue_.RL_env_message("print-state");

_funs_Evaluation_Single_();


imp_RL_Glue_.RL_env_message("set-random-start-state");

_funs_Evaluation_Single_();


imp_RL_Glue_.RL_cleanup();

print "\nProgram Complete."
```

Mindpark

In AI, reinforcement learning is a fundamental problem. In order to maximize a reward, the agent interacts with the environment. For example, we display the pixel bot screen of the game and we want it to choose the actions that give us high scores.

Mindpark provides us an environment where we can use it for testing, prototyping, and running different reinforcement learning algorithms to compare the results. The library provided in Mindpark makes it easier to program different algorithms and monitor the results. Mindpark can easily be integrated with Theano, TensorFlow, and other deep learning APIs. We can also integrate it with OpenAI's Gym environments as well.

Setup

The first step is to close the GitHub repository and install all the dependencies:

```
git clone github.com:danijar/mindpark.git
```

An experiment is actually a comparison between the environment, hyper parameters, and algorithms. We can start the experiment with –O, that turns an optimization in Python.

To start an experiment, run (–o turns on Python's optimizations):

```
python3 -O -m mindpark run definition/breakout.yaml
```

 Mindpark is a Python 3 package and it is not supported with Python 2.

Following are the algorithms that we already being implemented in Mindpark:

- **Deep Q-Network (DQN)**
- **Double Deep Q-Network (DDQN)**
- **Asynchronous Advantage Actor-Critic (A3C)**
- Reinforce

Summary

In this chapter, we went through the details of reinforcement learning frameworks. In the beginning of the chapter, we discussed the PyBrain framework, and then we went through the setup and also saw the implementation using this framework. After that, we went through RLPy, and we did the setup and then implemented the Grid World example.

We also discussed MMLF, which is also used for implementing a reinforcement learning problem using Python. We described how to setup the environment and also provided one simple example.

Later in the chapter, we discussed RL-Glue reinforcement learning framework. The advantage of the RL-Glue is that we can use any programming language that supports socket programming. We also saw how to setup the RL-Glue environment and provided an implementation of one example using Python code.

At the end of the chapter, we looked at the Mindpark framework, and we setup the environment and provided an implementation example.

In the next chapter, we will go through advance reinforcement learning topics, such as **Inverse Reinforcement Learning (IRL)** and **Partial Observable Markov Decision Process (POMDP)**.

10

Applications and Case Studies – Reinforcement Learning

In this chapter, we will cover advanced topics of reinforcement learning. To start with, we will discuss **Inverse Reinforcement Learning (IRL)**, and later in the chapter, we will discuss the **Partially Observable Markov Decision Process (POMDP)**.

Inverse Reinforcement Learning

Reinforcement learning is a type of machine learning that determines the action within a specific environment in order to maximize a reward. One of the characteristics of reinforcement learning is that the agent can only receive a reward after performing the action, and thus it must continue to interact with the environment in order to determine the optimal policy through trial and error.

On the other hand, assume that we only have the knowledge of the behavior (policy); then how we can estimate the reward structure from a specific behavior in the environment? This is the major problem of IRL, where, from the given optimal policy (we are assuming that it is optimal), we try to determine the underlying reward structure:

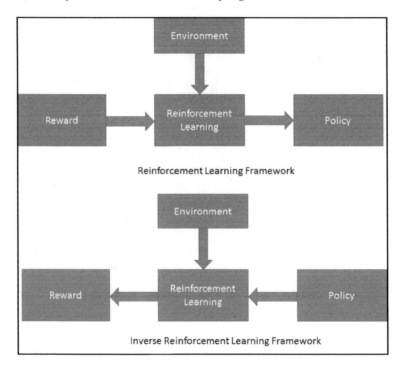

Figure 10.1: Framework of IRL

IRL is the problem of finding the environment's reward function given some observations of the behavior of an optimally behaving agent, that is, given either an optimal policy π^* or sample paths of an agent following π^*.

This is motivated by two main ideas. Firstly, we may want to replicate behavior of an entity using well-tested reinforcement learning methods, but a reward function suited to this task may be arbitrarily complex, abstract, or difficult to describe.

An example of this is the problem of driving a car. Despite being able to drive competently, we do not believe drivers can confidently specify a reward function for the task of *driving well*.

By finding a reward function, we can then train an agent to find a policy based on that reward function and hence replicate the original behavior. This kind of problem is called **apprenticeship learning**. By recovering a reward function and learning a policy from it, rather than directly learning a policy from behavior (for example, by function approximation of π'), we may be able to find more robust policies that can adapt to perturbations of the environment. We may also be able to solve the related problem of transfer learning, where the abstract goal the agent is trying to achieve is similar but the specifics of the environment differ; a policy learned directly from another environment's optimal policy will probably not be successful in the new environment.

Secondly, we may want to know the reward function itself to explain the behavior of an existing agent. In the example of modeling the behavior of bees, there is no real interest in recovering the behavior of the bees, but instead in modeling their motivations.

IRL, as stated, does have issues. The biggest issue is that of reward function multiplicity. For any given policy π, there are many reward functions for which π is optimal. As an example, for the reward function $R(s) = const$, every policy is optimal. In practice, degeneracy in reward functions is resolved with the use of heuristics to favor specific reward functions over trivial ones, but even this resolves the problem only partially as there can still be many non-trivial reward functions matching the observed policy.

IRL algorithm

The basic functions s' are basically observable in the state. We define $s'(st)$ to be the sum of all the feature expectations such that:

$$s'(st) = s1 + s2 + s3 + \ldots\ldots + sn$$

Implementing a car obstacle avoidance problem

In this example, we will implement the IRL algorithm in a 2D game to train a toy car. We will learn from given expert behaviors on a car obstacle avoidance problem.

First, we need to import the required dependencies and then define the parameters. Furthermore, we change the behavior as required. We also need to define the number of frames the reinforcement learning algorithm should run for. For this code, we will use 100000 frames and it will take approximately two hours:

```
#import all the required libraries
import scipy
```

```
import logging
import numpy as numP


#Reinforcement learning test agent dependency
from playing import _Library_play_

#now we will construct the neural network
from nn import _neural_network_

from cvxopt import _matrix_nn

#optimization convex library
from cvxopt import _solvers_CVX_

# environment dependencies will be added here
from flat_game import _munk_Car_

# Now we define the reinforcement learner
from learning import _helper_IRL_

_var_States_Num_ = 8

# brown/yellow/bumping/red
var_behavior_ = 'red'

# For each iterations we will define the number of training frames
var_Frame_ = 100000
```

After defining all the libraries and constants, we are going to implement the IRLAgent class, by which we implement random and expert behavior as per this code:

```
class IRLAgent:


  def __init__(_self, _parm_FE_random_, _expertFE, _parm_Epsilon_,
_parm_States_num_, _parm_Frames_, _parm_behavior_):
  _self.var_Policy_Random = _parm_FE_random_
  _self._var_Policy_Expert = _expertFE
  _self._var_States_Num_ = _parm_States_num_
  _self.var_Frame_ = _parm_Frames_
  _self.var_behavior_ = _parm_behavior_

 # when t<0.1 then terminate
  _self._var_Epsilon_ = _parm_Epsilon_


  _self._var_T_Random_ =
```

```
numP.linalg.norm(numP.asarray(_self._var_Policy_Expert)-
numP.asarray(_self.var_Policy_Random))

# Here we will store the t value and policy
 _self.policiesFE = {_self._var_T_Random_:_self.var_Policy_Random}
 print ("Expert Policy - Random Start (t) :: " , _self._var_T_Random_)
 _self._var_T_Current_ = _self._var_T_Random_
 _self.minimumT = _self._var_T_Random_
```

Now we will create a function named _func_Get_AgentFE_ that will use
_func_Helper_IRL_ from reinforcement learning to train a model and will get the feature
expectations. We will play this model up to 2000 iterations:

```
#Using Reinforcement learning agent we will get the expectations and new
policy
def _func_Get_AgentFE_(self, W, i):

# Now we will train the agent and save the model in a file
 _helper_IRL_(W, self.var_behavior_, self.var_Frame_, i)

# We will get the feature expectations (FE) from the saved model
 var_Model_Save = 'saved-
models_'+self.var_behavior_+'/evaluatedPolicies/'+str(i)+'_2000_iterations-
'+str(self.var_Frame_)+'.h5'

 var_Model_ = _neural_network_(self._var_States_Num_, [164, 150],
var_Model_Save)


 #It return the FE by executing the policy learned
 return _Library_play_(var_Model_, W)
```

Now we update the dictionary that is keeping the policies and the t values:

```
#now add the feature expectation policy list and its differences
 def _func_List_Updater_Policy_(self, W, i):

# Here get the FE of a new policy corresponding to the input weights
 _var_FE_Temp = self._func_Get_AgentFE_(W, i)

# t = _var_Hyper_Distance
 _var_Hyper_Distance = numP.abs(numP.dot(W,
numP.asarray(self._var_Policy_Expert)-numP.asarray(_var_FE_Temp)))

 self.policiesFE[_var_Hyper_Distance] = _var_FE_Temp
 return _var_Hyper_Distance
```

Here, we are implementing the main algorithm of IRL:

```python
def func_Weight_Finder_Optimal(self):

    f = open('weights-'+var_behavior_+'.txt', 'w')
    i = 1

    while True:

    # In the list of episode find a new weight for optimization
    W = self.func_Optimize()

    print ("weights ::", W )
    f.write( str(W) )
    f.write('\n')
    print ("Now the total distances :", self.policiesFE.keys())
    self._var_T_Current_ = self._func_List_Updater_Policy_(W, i)
    print ("The Current distance is: ", self._var_T_Current_ )

    # If the point reached to close enough then terminate
    if self._var_T_Current_ <= self.epsilon:
    break

    i += 1

    f.close()

    return W
```

Here, we will implement the functionality of convex optimization to get a new policy while updating the weight:

```python
# As an SVM problem implement the convex optimization

def func_Optimize(self):

var_m_ = len(self._var_Policy_Expert)
var_P_ = _matrix_nn(2.0*numP.eye(var_m_), var_tc_='d')
var_Q_ = _matrix_nn(numP.zeros(var_m_), var_tc_='d')
var_List_Policy = [self._var_Policy_Expert]
var_List_H = [1]

for i in self.policiesFE.keys():

var_List_Policy.append(self.policiesFE[i])

var_List_H.append(1)
```

```
var_Mat_Policy_ = numP._matrix_nn(var_List_Policy)

var_Mat_Policy_[0] = -1*var_Mat_Policy_[0]

var_G_ = _matrix_nn(var_Mat_Policy_, var_tc_='d')

var_H_ = _matrix_nn(-numP.array(var_List_H), var_tc_='d')

sol = _solvers_CVX_.qp(var_P_,var_Q_,var_G_,var_H_)

weights = numP.squeeze(numP.asarray(sol['x']))
norm = numP.linalg.norm(weights)
weights = weights/norm

# Now the normalized weights will return
return weights
```

Results and observations

After around 10-15 iterations, the algorithm converges in all the four chosen behaviors; I obtained the following results as shown in *Figure 10.2* and *Figure 10.3*:

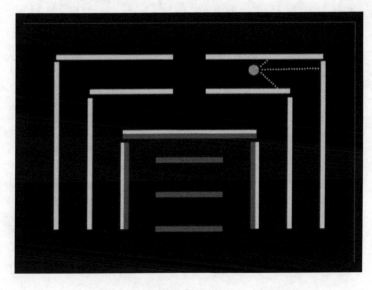

Figure 10.2: Agent yellow to move around yellow and avoid bumping

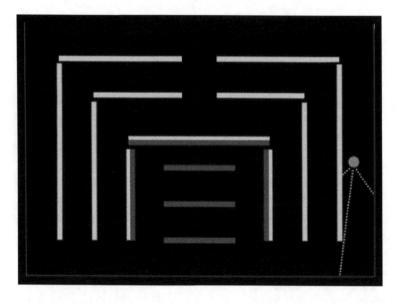

Figure 10.3: Agent red to move around red and avoid bumping

Partially Observable Markov Decision Process

In Chapter 2, *Markov Decision Process*, we discussed MDPs in detail. Now in this section, we will make the MDP partially observable.

A POMDP is simply an MDP, and similarly it has states, actions, transitions, and immediate rewards. Here, the action's effect on the state is similar to that in MDP. The only difference is that in MDP, we can observe the current state in the given process. In POMDP, we have to add a set of observations into the model. So, we will not directly observe the current state but the state which is given to us an observation (that has a hint about which state we are in). Sometimes, observations are probabilistic, so we need an observation function. The observation function tells us the probability of each observation for each state in the model.

There's a set of actions, states, transitions, and rewards. But the thing is that MDP inside POMDP cannot directly be observed by the agent. Instead, the agent has to make its decisions based on the observations it makes. So the z stands for *observable*:

$$A = action$$
$$s = state$$
$$t = transition$$
$$r = reward$$
$$z = observable$$
$$o = observation\ function$$

It's a set, like s and A. We need some kind of function that connects the states, actions, and observables, or actually, just the states and the observables. We're going to write it as o, which is the *observation function*:

$$O(s, z)$$

Actually, O consists of a mapping from the state and observation to the probability of actually seeing that observation, given that the agent is currently in that state s.

The key thing has always been what state are we in right now, and you never actually know what state you are in. So you get these observables or observations, and that's what gives you a hint about what state you are in.

Now, what's a concrete example of this in the real world? Let's say you either have chocolates or not. I can't directly observe that and I have to infer the presence of chocolates indirectly from whether or not you're teasing me. This is not a perfect indicator that you actually have chocolates; sometimes you may just tease me for fun. So what I need is some kind of observation function. I need to be able to predict, given whether or not you have chocolates? Let say you have chocolates, then what's the probability you tease me? It is very close to 1. And given that you don't have chocolates, what's the probability that you tease me? That's much lower, but not zero.

So, POMDP basically has an MDP inside of it and you can't see all of it. In particular, the part you cannot see is S and T. Now T *(transition)* relates to state and action? The T says, given that you are in a state and you take some action, what state you will go to next. You don't really know what state you were in and you may not know what state you end up in, because you as the agent have to make decisions based on what you can see.

POMDPs are generalizations of MDPs; in particular, anything that we can represent as an MDP, we can also represent the same as a POMDP. We can build an equivalent POMDP out of the same pieces. So, imagine that we've got an MDP consisting of **state, action, transition, reward** and we need to explain how we're going to create a POMDP out of it. For a POMDP, you need to specify the state, action, observables, transition, reward, and observation function. Let's say the states of the POMDP are going to be the same as the states the MDP. The actions of the POMDP are going to be the same as actions of the MDP. The transitions also are going to be the same and the rewards are going to be the same. Now have to define the set of observables and the observation function that makes the POMDP act just like the corresponding MDP.

As POMDP is a generalized MDP, if I have a true MDP, then a POMDP can represent it without any painful extra effort. That means there has to be a case where there's really a direct and simple connection between the parameters of the POMDP and parameters of the MDP. So what would the observables be? Well, if there is no uncertainty, there is no confusion about what the underlying state is, and one way to capture that would be simply to point out that z is s.

$$z = s$$

There's a one-to-one correspondence from every state to every observable. I would say it in a slightly different way which is the notion that the vocabulary of things you can see, we might as well reuse the vocabulary of the states because we are going to get to see them directly. So they are states *1, 2, 3, 4, 5,* and *6* and there are observables *1, 2, 3, 4, 5,* and *6,* and they match up in an obvious way. In other words, we can observe the states. All I say is that the set of things we can observe is equal to the set of states.

Now we need to define the observation function to say that what we are really observing is the state. For any particular state, there is a particular z, and no other z matches to that state. No other state goes with any other z. So I am going to say that the probability of you seeing z when you are in state s is *1* if $s = z$, which we can just shorten as *1* if and only if $s = z$:

$$O(s, z) = 1 \; if \; s = z$$

This works because probabilities have to add up to 1, but there are additional constraints on this function that make it an observation function. We get a probability distribution.

POMDP example

So here's a tiny little POMDP. We have got four underlying states and we have got two actions. The actions essentially move the agent left and right along this kind of hallway type thing, with some exceptions. So, from the green state, any action just resets you randomly to one of the blue states. Otherwise, things move left and right. At the end of the hallways here, at these two end states, if you try to go right when there's no more space to go, you just stick where you were. And if you try to go left when there's no more space to go, you stick where you were. Actions that take you to the green state give you a reward of *+1*.

I am showing the observations in the *Figure 10.2* and *Figure 10.3* with colors. So let me number the states just for ease of referring to them. We have got three states, **1**, **2**, and **4**. State **1** is blue, state **2** is blue, state **4** is blue. Based on the immediate observation alone, we don't know really where we are. We could be in a place that's to the right of the goal, so we should go left to get reward. Or we could be in a place that's to the left of the goal, which means we'd go right to get reward. And so we're in a tricky spot.

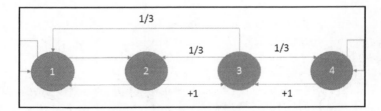

Figure 10.4: POMDP example

Let's imagine we took a left action and we saw blue. Then we took a right action and we saw blue. And then we took a left action. Now the question is: what's the probability that the color we see next is blue versus green?

Figure 10.5: State estimator

We have to think about all the different ways in which this might have been true and then figure out what is contradictory to what. But nonetheless, we can sort of intuitively work through this and then we will develop some kind of math in a systematic way of doing this next.

Let's say we know that we have started off in states *1, 2,* or *3* with equal probability, *1/3, 1/3* and *1/3*. We are definitely not starting off in state *4*.

Well, instead of keeping track of the states that we could be in, we can keep track of the probability that we were in each of those states because we're representing the start by probabilities. Now, we did end up with probability *1/3*, we have to thought that every time we were in some state, we go down the next state that we were likely to be into. And you kept track of all the different ways we could get to *1, 2, 3,* and *4*. We were actually keeping track of probabilities. First we go left and observe blue, what's the probability that we're now in state *1, 2, 3,* or *4*? We started off as *1/3, 1/3, 1/3,* and *0*:

$$State = [1, 2, 3, 4]$$
$$Probabilities = [1/3, 1/3, 1/3, 0]$$

So, can we just assume that we start out in state *1*, figure out where we would end up with the probabilities, then multiply that by *1/3*, and do the same thing with *2* and *3*. We were in state *1*, and if we go left, we would definitely see blue and be in state *1* of that point. Now assume we are in state *2*, it also sees blue and it will end up in state *1*. What about state *3*? Well, state *3*, no matter what it does, will end up seeing blue for sure. But it will end up in state *1, 2,* or *4* with equal probability. Let's figure out what our probability is after all this has happened. If you are in state *3*, what's the probability to get to state *3*? It is *0*; it is not possible to get there. Now let's figure out the probability to get to state *2*. We have *1/3* chance to get to state *2* and *1/3* chance of being in state *3*, so it's become *1/9*. The same argument works for state *4*; since the probabilities all have to add up to *1*, we can deduce that it's *7/9*:

$$Probability\ at\ state\ 1 = 7/9$$
$$Probability\ at\ state\ 2 = 1/9$$
$$Probability\ at\ state\ 3 = 0$$
$$Probability\ at\ state\ 4 = 1/9$$

State estimator

The next thing we need to worry about is the problem of state estimation. As we just discussed in the last section, we can make a POMDP into an MDP by expanding out the state space. What we are going to do is consider what we call belief states. So, the state that the decision maker is going to use in the context of a POMDP is going to be *a* belief state *b*. Belief state *b(s)* tells us the probability that we're actually in state *s* at the current time:

b(s) probability that we are in state s

It's a kind of vector. It's a probability distribution over states that is going to encode for us. It's going to retain for us information about the history that might be important for decision making. Here *b(s)* then, *b* is a vector and it's indexed by state *s*.

Now what we need to do is figure out how this belief state gets updated as we take actions in the world. So, think like this: we are in some belief state, we choose an action, the world gives us back an observation and we now need a new belief state to be formed from that.

b, a, z ---> b'

We are building up a notion of a belief MDP. So, we are going to turn the POMDP into a kind of MDP, specifically the belief MDP whose states are probability distributions over the states of the underlying MDP in the POMDP. Let's say if reward is a function of state, which it is sometimes, you should be able to use that to update your belief state. The reward is essentially not observed; but in reality, if you have a learner that is in some environment making observations and getting some reward back, if it knows something about how that reward is being generated, it can use that as a kind of observation. So, we can essentially assume that the observation has whatever information might be present in the reward in it. In fact, the observation is whatever sub teachers you get to see plus the reward:

r = f(z)

We say that the reward is actually something about the observable. We know that all of the reward we get is extracted from what we observe, and so it is anything that we model in the POMDP.

Now we need to derive this probability distribution over states b' from the old belief state, the action, the observation, and whatever quantities in the POMDP that we have. So, after we've taken action a and seen observation z, we need to figure out in this new belief state the probability that we are in state s'. Therefore, we have to do some kind of probabilistic inference or derivation to work that out:

$$b'(s') = probability\ of\ being\ in\ state\ s'\ after\ s,\ a,\ z$$

We ought to be able to do that right, because we have all the quantities that we need in the POMDP.

$$Pr(s'|\ b,\ a,\ z)$$

So we want the probability of the next state given that we were in a belief state and took an action and made an observation. Thus, we can manipulate this expression using the laws of probability.

What would be a piece of information that, if we knew it, would make it relatively straightforward to figure out the new state we were in? Well, if we knew what state we were in before, since we have a transition model, we'd know which states we are likely to be in next.

Let's break things down by the possible state that we started in and what exactly we want to know, that's the probability. We started in given b, a and z. So this is going to help us break things down successfully:

$$Pr(s'|\ b,\ a,\ z) = \sum_s Pr(s|\ b,\ a,\ z) \sum_s Pr(s'|\ b,\ a,\ z,\ s)$$

What do we know about the probability of being in a state, given a belief state that we took an action and we made some observation?

$$Pr(s'|\ b,\ a,\ z) = \sum_s b(s) \sum_s Pr(s'|\ b,\ a,\ z,\ s)$$

The main thing to point out here is that our observation is generated by the state we ended up in. So we are actually trying to figure out what state we are in based on the observation we got, whereas the generative model goes the other way. This is a prime situation to try to use Bayes' rule:

$$Pr(s'|\ b,\ a,\ z) = \sum_s b(s)\ [\sum_s Pr(z\ |\ s',\ a,\ s)\ Pr(s'\ |\ a,\ s)]\ /\ [Pr(z\ |\ a,\ s)]$$

Now we are getting really close to quantities that we recognize. In particular, the probability of an observation given the state that we just landed in is independent of the action and the state that we just discussed. From the previous equation, this is going to be the observation function:

$$Pr(z \mid s')$$

Here is the transition function, the probability of landing in some state as prime given that we were in state s and took action a:

$$Pr(s' \mid a, s)]$$

And then this is just going to be a normalization factor at the bottom:

$$[Pr(z \mid a, s)]$$

So substituting these quantities and rewriting out this normalization factor basically means the numerator divided by the sum of all possible next states s'. We get one component of the new belief state as prime if we apply the same idea over all possible states as prime. Then we get a probability distribution over all the states that represents the likelihood of being in those states given that we, in belief state b, took action a and made observation z:

$$b'(s') = \sum_s b(s)\, O(s', z)\, T(s, a, s') \,/\, \sum_s \sum_{s'} b(s)\, O(s', z)\, T(s, a, s')$$

My point here is that $b'(s')$ can be easily calculated from quantities that we have lying around because we have the model, the POMDP. We also know what the previous belief state is, what action we just took, and what observation we made. So all this can be updated and we can keep track of this notion of where we are. This is the belief state notion of the belief MDP.

This doesn't actually tell us how to do decision-making because we just turned a POMDP into an MDP. That, by the way, has an infinite number of states:

$$POMDP \rightarrow MDP\ (\infty\ states)$$

So we know we have a number of algorithms that we can run: linear programming, policy iteration, or value iteration. They all at best grow a polynomial in the number of states. So it's a polynomial in ∞. This is problematic; we can't just take this MDP now that we have defined it and just solve it using our existing algorithms! We have to be a bit more careful. So I want to show the algorithmic process to actually do that.

Value iteration in POMDP

The trick for executing algorithms such as value iteration in infinite state space, like what you get from the belief MDP, is going to come only by looking really carefully at the infinite case and then showing that it can be represented in a finite way. So what we are going to do now is step through what value iteration would look like in POMDP. Then, piece by piece, we are going to convert it to something that can actually be computed. At first, it's going to be math, and then it's going to be an algorithm.

So here's the value iteration written out and it's in POMDP, but that doesn't really matter yet. We are going to define the value function at step zero as a function of the belief to be just zero everywhere:

$$V_0(b) = 0$$

And then we will say, for t greater than zero, the value function for time stamp t as a function of belief state b is going to be the maximum overall actions--the reward for taking that action in the context of that belief state. We are going to sum over all the possible observations of the probability that we make that observation, multiplied by the value function at the previous time step for the resulting belief state b', which is what we get by doing what we discussed in the previous section (which we call the state estimation for b, a, z):

for t>0

$$V_t(b) = Max_a \, [R(b, a) + \gamma \sum_z Pr(z \mid b, a) \, V_{t-1}(b')]$$
where b' = SE(b, a, z)

In POMDP, our problem is to find a mapping between states to an action from probability distribution.

The following figure represents the two state POMDP in our running example. It introduces how we can represent the belief state. In POMDP, the belief state can be represented as a single number. As the belief state is actually a probability distribution, the sum is 1 for all the probabilities.

For a two-state POMDP, we can represent the belief state with a single number. Since a belief state is a probability distribution, the sum of all probabilities must be 1.

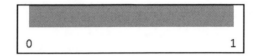

Figure 10.6 Belief space for a two-state POMDP

The key insight is that the finite horizon value function is **piecewise-linear and convex (PWLC)** for every horizon length. This means that for each iteration, we only need to find a finite number of linear segments that make up the value function.

The following figure shows a sample value function over belief space for a POMDP. The vertical axis is the value, while the horizontal axis is the belief state. The POMDP value function is the upper surface of a finite number of linear segments.

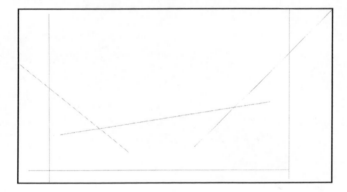

Figure 10.7: PWLC value function

These linear segments will completely specify the value function over the belief space that we desire. These amount to nothing more than lines, or more generally, hyper-planes through belief space. We can simply represent each hyper-plane with a vector of numbers that are the coefficients of the equation of the hyper-plane. The value at any given belief state is found by plugging in the belief state into the hyper-plane's equation. If we represent the hyper-plane as a vector (that is, the equation coefficients) and each belief state as a vector (the probability at each state), then the value of a belief point is simply the dot product of the two vectors:

$$V_t(b) = Max_{\text{alpha belongs vector } t}\ alpha.b$$

$$V_t(b) = Max_{\text{alpha belongs vector } t}\ \Sigma_s\ b(s).alpha(s)$$

We can now represent the value function for each horizon as a set of vectors. To find the value of a belief state, we simply find the vector that has the largest dot product with the belief state.

Instead of linear segments over belief space, another way to view the function is that it partitions belief space into a finite number of segments. We will be using both the value function and this partitioning representation to explain the algorithms. Keep in mind that they are more or less interchangeable:

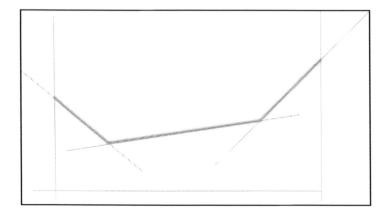

Figure 10.8: PWLC function and the belief space

The first issue we faced here was how we can represent a value function on a continuous space. Because each horizon's value function is PWLC, we solved this problem by representing the value function as a set of vectors.

Reinforcement learning for POMDP

So now that we have an idea of what POMDPs are about, we should discuss a little bit about what it might mean to do reinforcement learning in them because we've basically discussed planning. If we have a model of the POMDP, we can run some calculations and run value iteration to get a way of deciding what to do actually and how you get a value function. Is it clear how you would use a value function to get a policy? In the same way as you would for an MDP. If you have the model, then you can use one step look ahead with the value function to figure out what the optimal action is in any given belief state. Once we have run valuation and gotten an approximation of the optimal value function, then what will we do when that valuation doesn't actually converge? Well, we discussed earlier that the value iteration converges in the limit to the right value function, but after any finite number of steps, it need not have the optimal value function. It will, after some finite number of steps, have the optimal policy that is not going to be true in the POMDP case because there are an infinite number of states.

It is going to be the case that we get an arbitrarily good approximation after some finite number of iterations but not necessarily the optimal policy. If we do one step back up or one step look ahead with a near-optimal value function, we get a near-optimal policy.

Now that we have discussed planning in POMPDs, we should discuss reinforcement learning in POMPDs. What's the difference between planning and reinforcement learning? Well, in planning we know everything, but in a reinforcement learning we don't know everything and we have to explore and exploit. That makes the problem harder.

Is reinforcement learning harder than planning? Are POMDPs more difficult to deal with than MDPs? Actually planning in POMDPs is formally undecidable, in the sense that I give you a POMDP and ask, *Is this the optimal first action to take from this belief state?* If you can solve this problem, you can solve the halting problem. This has profound implications because we are human beings running around in the world and we are living in a POMDP because we can't know everything. So even if I could relive life an infinite number of times, I still don't know what is the right thing to do. It's undecidable; you may never know what to do.

Basically planning is hard, so I assume reinforcement learning is also hard. Thus, the results that we have for reinforcement learning in POMDPs are more empirical and algorithmic results; they are not really formal results. If you have some kind of robotic system or agent system that's trying to figure out what to do and the world that it's in is partially observable, then you have to do something like this.

So in particular, we had kind of two main flavors of reinforcement learning algorithms for MDPs. There's value iteration and policy iteration. Those are planning algorithms, but for reinforcement learning in an MDP, the two main branches are model-based RL and model-free RL. One learns a model and one doesn't. You can't use a model if you don't learn it or if you don't know it.

So learn a model and then use it, versus don't bother to learn the model and just do it. We can actually use this same kind of distinction, this model-based RL and model-free based RL in the POMDP setting. In model-based RL, we actually try to learn the POMDP and then plan in it, but in model-free RL, we try to map observations to actions and we do that iteratively over time. So we don't actually build the model but we do try to figure it out.

Summary

In this chapter, we first learned about IRL. We discussed that only if we have the knowledge of the behavior (policy) can we estimate the reward structure from a specific behavior in the environment. And this is the major problem of IRL, where, from the given optimal policy (we are assuming that it is optimal), we are trying to determine the underlying reward structure.

IRL is the problem of finding the environment's reward function given some observations of the behavior of an optimally behaving agent. Then we learned about the IRL algorithm. Later, we saw a complete implementation in the *Implementing a car obstacle avoidance problem* section.

We learned about POMDP and went into the details of what it is and how to solve it. In particular we discussed belief states, which represent the states we might be in and how much we believe that we are in them. We also discussed POMDP as a strict generalization of MDP. Then we discussed one of the unfortunate consequences of dealing with POMDP: they are hard to solve or are fundamentally difficult. Despite this, we did come up with some algorithms for solving MDPs, such as value iteration. We discussed PWLC, representing the value function as a PWLC function. One of the nice things here was that we showed we could build up these sets of linear functions. Because we care only about the maximum at a given point, we could throw away the bunch of them that might be unnecessary and keep the hard problem possibly manageable. Then we went on to solve POMDP in reinforcement learning.

In the next chapter, we will discuss the current research areas in reinforcement learning.

11

Current Research – Reinforcement Learning

This chapter focuses on current research activities in the field of reinforcement learning. To start with, we will discuss in detail hierarchical reinforcement learning; then we will look into reinforcement learning with hierarchies of abstract machines. We will end the chapter by discussing MAXQ value function decomposition.

Hierarchical reinforcement learning

Reinforcement learning systems with large state spaces are affected by a problem referred to as the curse of dimensionality, the fact that state spaces grow exponentially with the number of state variables they take into account. When the state space grows too large, the agent will not be able to find an optimal policy for a task, which affects its practical application in large systems. The best you can do in such situations is provide an approximate solution, such as a divide-and-conquer approach to optimization. To do this, we divide the generation task into several subtasks; they have smaller state spaces and can therefore find a solution more easily. In other words, we learn a hierarchy of policies for generation subtasks rather than a single policy for the whole task.

To address the challenges of incorporation of abstract actions faced by reinforcement learning in different ways, feasibly the major thing is the boost reward propagation throughout our tasks. Coming back to our example, let's think that the agent is in the bedroom and he needs to learn how to reach the refrigerator. To accomplish this task, he needs to perform a long sequence of actions; therefore he is facing a challenging credit assignment problem to decide the best actions he should take.

Now let's say the agent selects the *go to the kitchen* action; from there, he also performs some basic actions to go from center of the kitchen to the refrigerator. Rewards also propagate directly based on the actions from the kitchen to whatever he selects in the *go to the kitchen* action. He can learn very quickly whether selecting *go to the kitchen* action is a good choice or a bad choice, even though there are lots of other basic actions to help him reach the refrigerator. We can say that the complexity of learning a value from an abstract action is almost independent of other relevant action paths.

The **hierarchical reinforcement learning (HRL)** is the study done to decompose an RL problem into a hierarchy of subproblems or subtasks such that higher level parent tasks invoke lower level child tasks as if they were primitive actions. Decomposition can be a multilevel hierarchy. All or some of the them can be problems of reinforcement learning.

Any flat learning agent that is characterized by a single MDP can be decomposed into a set of subtasks:

$$\text{Each sub task} = M_i$$

Here, *i* and *j* are indexes that uniquely identify each subtask in a hierarchy of subtasks such that:

$$M = \{M^0_0, M^1_0, M^1_1, M^1_2, ..., M^X_Y\}$$

These indexes do not specify the order of execution of subtasks because the order is subject to learning. Each subtask, or agent in the hierarchy, is defined as a **Semi-Markov Decision Process (SMDP)**:

$$\{ M^i_j = S^i_j, A^i_j, T^i_j, R^i_j \}$$

in which

$$S^i_j = \{s_0, s_1, s_2, ..., s_N\}$$

Is a set of states of subtasks:

$$M^i_j. A^i_j = \{a_0, a_1, a_2, ..., a_M\}$$

Is a set of actions of subtask M_j^i that can be either primitive or composite. Primitive actions are single-step actions as in an MDP and receive single rewards. Composite actions are temporally extended actions that correspond to other subtasks in the hierarchy and are children of the current (parent) subtask, such as referring expression generation. Composite actions receive cumulative rewards.

The execution of a composite action, or subtask, takes a variable number of time steps τ to complete, which is characteristic of an SMDP model (and this distinguishes it from an MDP). The parent SMDP of a subtask passes control down to its child subtask and then remains in its current state s_t until control is transferred back to it, that is, until its child subtask has terminated execution. It then makes a transition to the next state s'. T_j^i is a probabilistic state transition function of subtask M_j^i, and R_j^i is a reward function:

$$R_j^i(s', \tau | s, a)$$

Discounted cumulative rewards of composite actions are computed according to:

$$r_{t+1} + \gamma r_{t+2} + \gamma 2 r_{t+3} + \cdots + \gamma^{\tau-1} r_{t+\tau}$$

Here, γ is called the discount rate, a parameter that is $0 \leq \gamma \leq 1$ and indicates the relevance of future rewards in relation to immediate rewards. As γ approaches 1, both immediate and future rewards are increasingly equally valuable. The equation for optimal hierarchical action selection is:

$$\pi^{*i} j(s) = arg\ max_{a \in A} Q^{*i} j(s, a)$$

Here, $Q^{*i} j(s, a)$ specifies the expected cumulative reward for executing action a in state s and then following π^{*i}_j. To learn hierarchical policies, we can use the HSMQ-learning algorithm; it is a hierarchical version of Q-learning. During policy learning, Q-values are updated according to the following update rule:

New Estimate ← Old Estimate + Step Size [Target – Old Estimate]

Using the aforementioned notation, this corresponds to:

$$Q_j^i(s, a) \leftarrow Q_j^i(s, a) + \alpha[r + \gamma^\tau max_{a'} Q_j^i(s', s') - Q_j^i(s, a)]$$

Here, α is a step-size parameter. It indicates the learning rate, which decays from 1 to 0; for example, in $\alpha = 1/(1 + visits(s, a))$, $visits(s, a)$ corresponds to the number of times the state-action pair (s, a) has been visited before time step t.

Advantages of hierarchical reinforcement learning

The major idea of HRL is the notion of an abstract action. What are abstract actions? You can think of abstract actions as shortcuts that encapsulate the complete sequence (list of basic actions) in a single choice. It is hierarchical because it is possible that some abstract actions themselves are part of other abstract actions. Let me give you an example to understand this better. Suppose an agent is roaming in a house. He takes some basic actions such as turn left, move forward, and turn right. Now there is a possible abstract action called *go to the kitchen*. Once the agent selects this option, it actually activates the subpolicy that contains a list of basic actions to take the agent to the kitchen. Now it is possible that there is another abstract policy called make dinner, itself containing the action *go to the kitchen*.

There is an another major advantage of HRL: it supports better exploration. The biggest weakness of reinforcement learning is that it requires long periods of time due to random action selection. The result is actually a kind of motion where the agent moves in a limited area rather than exploring the entire state space. In our last example, the agent going to the refrigerator took a significant amount of time and lots of random actions. The agent will be roaming around all areas of the bedroom by taking lots of basic actions.

Now suppose the agent selects an action, *go to dining room*. That will take a lot of basic actions and cover a significantly different area in the state space. We can say that the agent's random exploration results in broader coverage of the state space. Hence, it is generally within proximity of the goal.

A third advantage of HRL is that it advances itself to state abstraction. This means state abstraction is a process of ignoring portions of the state that are not relevant to the present task, thus dropping the size of the overall state space. In HRL, it is possible that unlike state abstractions are with unlike abstract actions. In our example, let's say the agent wants to learn a subpolicy to reach the door of the bedroom. It is not important to consider what is going on inside the house, so the subpolicy is just about the policy related to the bedroom and not entire state space of the house. Thus, it is much easier to learn the subpolicy.

Another important thing to discuss is transfer learning in hierarchical reinforcement learning; this is not a major benefit of HRL but is made easier by the hierarchical framework. Transfer learning is actually a process by which an agent gains knowledge in a task and makes use of it in a new task. This is possible in other reinforcement learning frameworks but is made much easier by HRL.

The SMDP model

We will very briefly look into the major features of the SMDP reinforcement learning model and later we will enhance this model to perform HRL.

The model's architecture is shown in the following diagram. The top represents the current state, which is a population of neurons. It's actually an abstract vector that can represent any desired information and it is encoded into neural activities. The state can change continuously over time, and if desired, the system can be an approximate discrete state. The vector space is used for restricting the state to a fixed point.

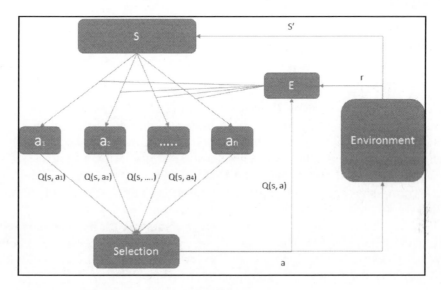

Figure 11.1: SMDP model

The output activity of the state neurons is passed to a second set of neural populations, corresponding to the different actions available to the agent a_n. Each of those populations attempts to output the value of its associated action given the current state (as represented by the activity of the s population). We can interpret the output of the a neurons as estimated Q values.

Next, the system needs to select an action to perform based on those Q values. The selection network performs this function, along with several memory components needed to preserve information across the SMDP time delay. The end result is that the highest valued action and the Q value of that action are produced as output.

The action is delivered to the environment, which computes a new state and reward. The system is designed to treat the environment as a black box; all of its processing occurs in a general, task-independent fashion so that different environments can be swapped out without affecting the rest of the model. The value of the selected action is delivered to the error calculation network, *E*. The output of this network is used to drive an error-modulated local learning rule on the connections between the *s* and *a* populations so that, over time, the output of the a populations will come to represent the correct Q values.

Hierarchical RL model

In order to extend this model for hierarchical reinforcement learning, the first step is to allow it to represent several different policies. That is, it needs to be able to represent one set of Q values if it is in the go to the grocery store context, and flexibly switch to a different set of Q values if the context changes to go to work.

One approach would be to have multiple sets of connections between the *s* and *a* populations, and switch between them using some gating mechanism. However, this is impractical for a number of reasons. It greatly increases the number of connections needed, it introduces a new problem of how to switch between connections, and it is inflexible in that the contexts must be directly encoded into the structure of the model. Thus, in our model, we accomplish this by including a representation of the current context in the vector input to the s population. The output of the s neurons then represents context-dependent activity, allowing the system to produce different Q values in different contexts with a single set of connection weights. This allows the system to represent and swap between different policies simply by changing the context representation in the s input, without changing any of the structural aspects of the model.

The next question is: how to organize the model into a hierarchy so that higher level decisions (for example, go to the grocery store) can control lower level decisions? Given the structure laid out earlier, this can be accomplished by allowing high-level systems to set the context in low-level systems. This architecture is shown in the following diagram. The key feature is that the action selected by the higher level system, rather than affecting the environment, is used to set the context of the lower level system. Thus, if the higher level system were to select the *go to the grocery store* action, it would set the lower level system to be in the grocery store context. The lower level system would then choose actions according to its grocery store policy, and the selected actions would be delivered to the environment to control the movement of the agent.

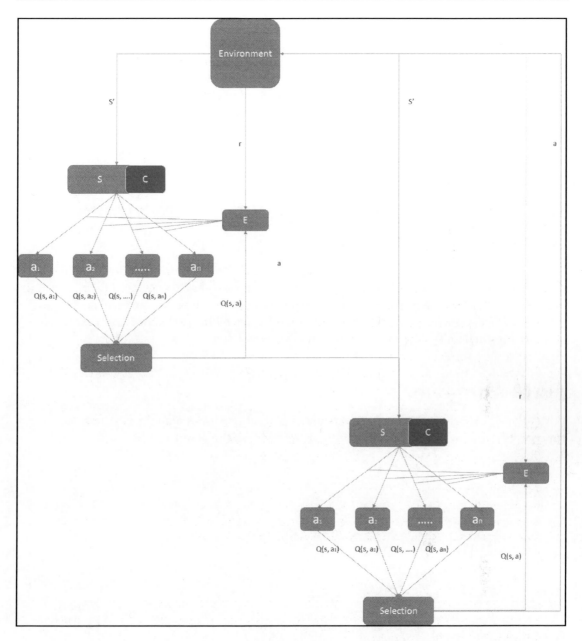

Figure 11.2: HRL model

Note that we have shown a system with two levels, but there is no theoretical restriction on the depth of the hierarchy. These systems can be chained together in this way to provide as many levels as desired, the only constraint being the number of neurons required. In addition, we have shown the architecture here such that all levels of the hierarchy receive the same environmental state and reward information, which is the simplest case. However, this system can also operate in the case where different hierarchical levels use different (for example, internally generated) state/reward values, an example of which is demonstrated in the results section.

Reinforcement learning with hierarchies of abstract machines

The basic idea of **hierarchies of abstract machines (HAM)** is to derive a partial policy based on hierarchical finite state machines without specifying the choice state, and then use RL to learn the optimal policy from the derived partial policy. In a deep hierarchical structure, when HAM is applied, there are sometimes lots of internal transitions where one machine calls another machine with an unchanged environment state.

HAM framework

Formally, a HAM $H = \{N_0, N_1, N_2, \ldots\}$ consists of a set of Moore machines, where N_0 represents a root machine, which is the starting point of the agent:

```
A machine N is a tuple {Λ, μ, δ, M, Σ} where,

Λ = output
δ = is the transition function machine
M = set of machine state
Σ = It is the input, which then coordinate with the environment state space
represent it as S

with
δ(s, m) being the next machine state given machine state
environment state s ∈ S and m ∈ M

μ = is the function machine output
with μ(m) ∈ Λ being the output of machine state m ∈ M
```

There are five types of machine states;

- **Start**: These are the initial states or entering states of the running machines
- **Action**: These run or perform any specific actions in the environment
- **Choose**: These select or determine the next state of the machine
- **Call**: These invoke other machine executions
- **Stop**: These return control to the calling machine and end the current execution

Let's say machine N has a start state (N-*Start*) and stop state (N-*Stop*). For both states, the output is not defined. Now, for the action state, associated primitive actions are the outputs. And for the call state, the output is specified as the call to another machine that runs the choose state. Here, the output is the set of all possible choices and each choice has to be made in the next machine state.

A runtime stack is required to run a HAM. It actually stores runtime information, such as machine state, local variables used in the machine, and the parameter passed to the machine.

Running a HAM algorithm

This algorithm gives the pseudocode for running a HAM, where the Execute function executes an action in the environment and returns the next state of the environment. The Choose function picks the next machine state given the updated stack z, the current environment state s, and the set of available choices $\mu(m)$.

For example, z means all possible states from a given HAM H. The agent running the HAM H over an MDP M becomes a joint SMDP $H \circ M$ as it is defined over the joint space of Z. S. $H \circ M$ is the only action and choice allowed at a choice point. A choice is a joint state (z, s), where an action needs to be selected and it is represented as z.Pop().

Here is an SMDP and it works like this: the choice is to be made at the choice point and the system will run automatically until we reach a position where we have to make another choice, called next choice point. See this algorithm:

```
Run(N : machine, z : stack, s : environment state):
z.Push(N )
m ← N.start

while m != N .stop do
    if Type(m) = action then
        s ← Execute(μ(m))
    else if Type(m) = call then
```

```
        s ← Run(μ(m), z, s, π)
    if Type(m) = choose then
        z.Push(m) m ← Choose(z, s, μ(m))
        z.Pop()
    else
        m ← δ(m, s)

  z.Pop()
  return s
```

HAM for mobile robot example

For an example, see the following diagram, which shows a HAM for a mobile robot navigating in a grid map. The navigate machine has a choice state, at which it has to choose between *Move Fast* and *Move Slow*. In this simple example, if the choice made at stack *[Navigate, Choose]* is *Move Fast*, then the stack of the next choice point must be *[Navigate, Choose, Move(Fast), Choose]*. There could be many such internal transitions in a HAM with arbitrary structure for a complex domain. It is easier for a human designer to come up with a deep HAM rather than a shallow HAM. In the setting of concurrent learning, where multiple HAMs are running concurrently, there are even more opportunities to have internal transitions defined over the resulting joint SMDP.

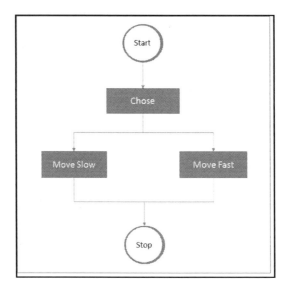

Figure 11.3: The navigate machine

In the following diagram, the move (speed) machine has to select repeatedly between East, West, South, and North with the specified speed parameter until the robot reaches its destination:

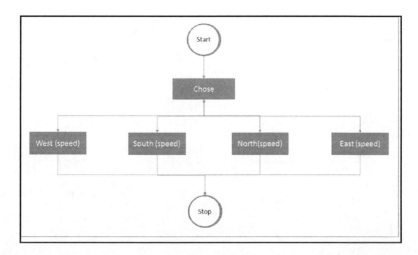

Figure 11.4: The move (speed) machine

You can think of a HAM as similar to a modern programming language, where we call a function, and after executing the logic it transfers control back to the calling function. In the execution logic, it executes the actions, gets new environment states, and so on. Here, HAM execution is exactly like running a code and it provides a very efficient way of running and designing a HAM.

For example, the HAM shown in *Figure 11.3* is equivalent to the pseudo code in the *Running a HAM algorithm* section, where a machine becomes a function. Here, Execute is the macro executing an action with specified parameters and returning the next environment state. The Choose macro extends the Choose function from running a HAM algorithm to choose among not only a set of machine states but also a set of parameters for the next machine:

```
Navigate(s : environment state):
  speed ← Choose₁(Slow, Fast)
  s ← Move(s, speed)
return s

Move(s : environment state, speed : parameter):
while not s.atDest() do
  a ← Choose₂(West, South, North, East)
  s ← Execute(a, speed)
return s
```

HAM for a RoboCup keepaway example

The RoboCup keepaway problem is actually a 2D game similar to RoboCup soccer. We called it keepaway because we have two teams, a team of takers and team of keepers. The team of keepers has to maintain the ball to themselves and a team of takers tries to get the ball from the keepers. There are a total of three keepers and two takers in the limited area of the field. This is represented in the following diagram.

Now here the system has action spaces and a continuous state. There are different primitive actions: turn, dash, or kick. The turn action changes the body angle of the player, kick gives an acceleration to the ball, and dash gives an acceleration to the player. Note that all the primitive actions are exposed to noise.

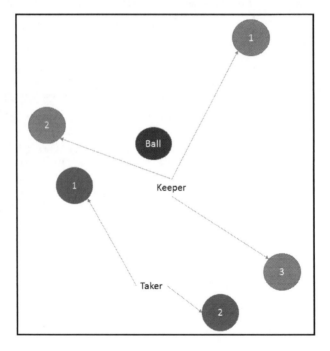

Figure 11.5: RoboCup example

Each game is an episode and the episode starts with the players and the ball at the fixed position. It ends when the ball goes outside the field or the taker kicks the ball. The total number of time steps makes up the cumulative reward for the keepers. The following are the actions in the game:

- `Stay()`: No change; remain in the same position
- `Move(v, d)`: Dash with speed v in direction d
- `Intercept()`: Here, the ball is being intercepted
- `Pass(v, k)`: Now pass the ball with speed v to the teammate k
- `Hold()`: Stay in the same position

As per the experiment, the taker's policy is fixed. When the ball is kickable, they need to hold it; otherwise they try to intercept the ball. The main goal in this game is to learn the best response policy while playing the game.

In this example, the policy of HAM is from the keeper's perspective; for each keeper, it runs multiple instances of HAM for the keeper to form a joint policy. Now, to run the HAM concurrently, they all have to be synchronized, and if any machine is at the choose state, then other machines have to wait. This means if multiple machines are at the choose state, then a joint choice has to be made and not an independent choice for each machine. To accomplish this, all the players must share the selected joint choice and learned value functions.

Now I will present the algorithm in pseudocode for the RoboCup keepaway game. Take note that the keeper is the root machine. There are lots of internal transitions in a single HAM. Let's assume that whenever the pass machine selects a choice *ChooseOption₁*, it is actually of the keeper machine. Then the available choice points for the pass machine are *ChooseOption₄*, and *ChooseOption₃*.

Let's say the joint machine states are *[ChooseOption₁, ChooseOption₂, ChooseOption₃]*, where each element is actually the state of the HAM machine. If the joint choice made is *[PassBall, MoveBall, StayOrPosition]*, then the next consecutive states of the machine must be *[Choose₃, Choose₅, StayOrPosition]* and *[Choose₄, Choose₆, StayOrPosition]*, following the joint HAM:

```
Keeper(state : environment as state):
while not state.Terminate() do
    if state.KickableBall() then
        m ← ChooseOption1(PassBall, HoldBall)
        state ← RunBall(m, state)
    else if state.FastestToBall() then
        state ← Intercept(state)
    else m ← ChooseOption2(StayOrPosition, MoveBall)
        state ← RunBall(m, state)
```

```
return state

PassBall(state : environment as state):
k ← ChooseOption3(1, 2, . . .)
v ← ChooseOption4(Normal, Fast)
while state.KickableBall() do
    state ← RunBall(PassBall, k, v)
return state

HoldBall(state : environment as state):
state ← RunBall(HoldBall)
return state

Intercept(state : environment as state):
state ← RunBall(Intercept)
return state

StayOrPosition(state : environment as state):
i ← state.ControlTheBall()
while i = state.ControlTheBall() do
    state ←RunBall(StayOrPosition)
return state

MoveBall(state : environment as state):
d ← ChooseOption5(0°  , 90° , 180° , 270°)
v ← ChooseOption6(Normal, Fast)
i ← state.ControlTheBall()
while i = state.ControlTheBall() do
    v ←RunBall(MoveBall, d, v)
return state
```

MAXQ value function decomposition

MAXQ describes how to decompose the overall value function for a policy into a collection of value functions for individual subtasks (and subtasks recursively).

The MAXQ decomposition takes a given MDP M and decomposes it into a set of subtasks $\{M_0, M_1, \ldots, M_n\}$, with the convention that M_0 is the root subtask (that is, solving M_0 solves the entire original MDP M).

An unparameterized subtask is a three-tuple subtask, $\{T_i, A_i, R_i\}$, defined as follows:

- **Ti(si)**: A termination predicate that partitions S into a set of active states, S_i and a set of terminal states, T_i. The policy for subtask M_i can be executed only if the current state s is in S_i.

- **Ai**: A set of actions that can be performed to achieve subtask M_i. These actions can be primitive actions from A, the set of primitive actions for the MDP, or other subtasks, which we will denote by their indexes i. We will refer to these actions as the children of subtask i. If a child subtask M_j has formal parameters, then it can occur multiple times in A_i, and each such occurrence must specify the actual values that will be bound to the formal parameters. The set of actions A_i may differ from one state to another, so technically, A_i is a function of s. However, we will suppress this dependence in our notation.

- **Ri(s' |s, a)**: This is the pseudo-reward function that specifies a pseudo-reward for each transition from a state $s \in S_i$ to a terminal state $s' \in T_i$. This pseudo-reward tells us how desirable each of the terminal states is for this subtask. It is typically employed to give goal terminal states a pseudo-reward of zero and any non-goal terminal state a negative reward.

Each primitive action a from M is a primitive subtask in the MAXQ decomposition such that a is always executable, it always terminates immediately after execution, and its pseudo-reward function is uniformly zero.

If a subtask has formal parameters, then each possible binding of actual values to the formal parameters specifies a distinct subtask. We can think of the values of the formal parameters as part of the name of the subtask. In practice, of course, we implement a parameterized subtask by parameterizing the various components of the task. If b specifies the actual parameter values for task M_i, then we can define a parameterized termination predicate $T_i(s, b)$ and a parameterized pseudo-reward function $R_i(s' | s, a, b)$. To simplify notation in the rest of the chapter, we will usually omit these parameter bindings from our notation.

Taxi world example

Let's consider the following simple example of the taxi world. The following diagram shows a 5 x 5 grid world inhabited by a taxi agent. Now there are four locations specially designated in this world, marked as R(ed), B(lue), G(reen), and Y(ellow). The taxi problem is episodic.

Each episode starts from a randomly chosen square; the passenger can be in any of the four designated locations (that is choosing randomly). Once he gets into the taxi, it is his wish where he wants to get down, out of any of the four designated locations. He cannot get down from the taxi at any other non-designated location. The taxi must reach the customer's location and drop him at a specific location.

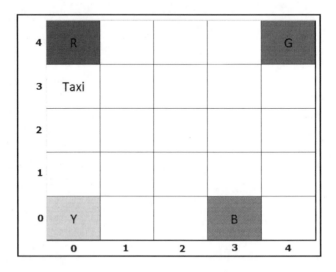

Figure 11.6: Taxi world example

There are three primitive actions in this domain:

- **Pickup**: A pickup action
- **Navigate**: Four navigation actions that move the taxi by one square—North, South, East, or West
- **Putdown**: A putdown action

Each action is deterministic. There is a reward of -1 for each action and an additional reward of +20 for successfully dropping the passenger. There is a reward of -10 if the taxi attempts to execute the putdown or pickup actions illegally. If a navigation action would cause the taxi to hit a wall, the action is a no-op, and there is only the usual reward of -1.

We seek a policy that maximizes the total reward per episode. There are 500 possible states: 25 squares x 5 locations for the passenger (counting the four starting locations and the taxi) x 4 destinations.

This task has a simple hierarchical structure in which there are two main subtasks: Get the passenger and deliver the passenger. Each of these subtasks in turn involves the subtask of navigating to one of the four locations and then performing a pickup or putdown action.

This task illustrates the need to support temporal abstraction, state abstraction, and subtask sharing. The temporal abstraction is obvious; for example, the process of navigating to the passenger's location and picking up the passenger is a temporally extended action that can take different numbers of steps to complete depending on the distance to the target. The top-level policy (get passenger, deliver passenger) can be expressed very simply if these temporal abstractions can be employed.

The need for state abstraction is perhaps less obvious. Consider the subtask of getting the passenger. While this subtask is being solved, the destination of the passenger is completely irrelevant. It cannot affect any of the navigation or pickup decisions. Perhaps more importantly, when navigating to a target location (either the source or destination of the passenger), only the identity of the target location is important. The fact that in some cases the taxi is carrying the passenger and in other cases it is not is irrelevant.

Finally, support for subtask sharing is critical. If the system could learn how to solve the navigation subtask once, then the solution could be shared by both the *Get the passenger* and *Deliver the passenger* subtasks. We will soon show that the MAXQ method provides a value function representation and learning algorithm that supports temporal abstraction, state abstraction, and subtask sharing.

To construct a MAXQ decomposition for the taxi problem, we must identify a set of individual subtasks that we believe will be important for solving the overall task. In this case, let us define the following four tasks:

- **Navigate(t)**: In this subtask, the goal is to move the taxi from its current location to one of the four target locations, which will be indicated by the formal parameter *t*
- **Get**: In this subtask, the goal is to move the taxi from its current location to the passenger's current location and pick up the passenger
- **Put**: The goal of this subtask is to move the taxi from the current location to the passenger's destination location and drop off the passenger
- **Root**: This is the whole taxi task

Each of these subtasks is defined by a subgoal, and each subtask terminates when the subgoal is achieved.

After defining these subtasks, we must indicate for each subtask which other subtasks or primitive actions it should employ to reach its goal. For example, the *Navigate(t)* subtask should use the four primitive actions: North, South, East, and West. The *Get* subtask should use the *Navigate* subtask and the pickup primitive action, and so on.

All of this information can be summarized by a directed acyclic graph called a task graph, which is shown in the following graph. In this graph, each node corresponds to a subtask or a primitive action, and each edge corresponds to a potential way in which one subtask can *call* one of its child tasks. The notation of formal/actual (for example, t/source) tells us how a formal parameter is to be bound to an actual parameter.

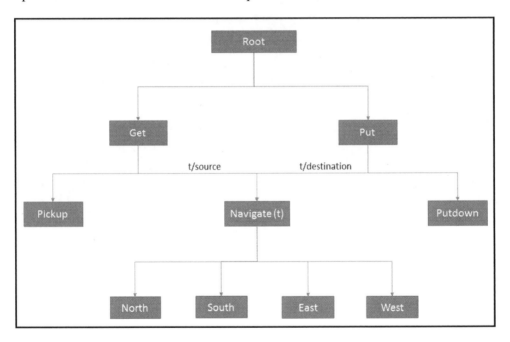

Figure 11.7: Task graph for taxi world

Suppose that for each of these subtasks, we write a policy (for example, as a computer program) to achieve the subtask. We will refer to the policy for a subtask as a subroutine, and we can view the parent subroutine as invoking the child subroutine via ordinary subroutine call-and-return semantics. If we have a policy for each subtask, then this gives us an overall policy for the taxi MDP. The Root subtask executes its policy by calling subroutines that are policies for the *Get* and *Put* subtasks. The *Get* policy calls subroutines for the pickup primitive action and the *Navigate(t)* subtask. And so on. We will call this collection of policies a hierarchical policy. In a hierarchical policy, each subroutine executes until it enters a terminal state for its subtask.

Decomposition of the projected value function

Now that we have defined a hierarchical policy and its projected value function, we can show how that value function can be decomposed hierarchically. The decomposition is based on the following theorem.

Given a task graph over tasks $M_0, \ldots, M_n$ and a hierarchical policy Π, each subtask M_i defines a semi-Markov decision process with states S_i, actions A_i, probability transition function $P^{\Pi}_i (s', N | s, a)$, and expected reward function $R(s, a) = V^{\Pi}(a, s)$, where $V^{\Pi}(a, s)$ is the projected value function for child task M_a in state s. If a is a primitive action, $V^{\Pi}(a, s)$ is defined as the expected immediate reward of executing a in s:

$$V^{\Pi}(a, s) = \Sigma_{s'}\, P(s' | s, a)\, R(s' | s, a)$$

To make it easier for programmers to design and debug MAXQ decompositions, we have developed a graphical representation called MAXQ graph. A MAXQ graph for the taxi domain is shown in the following diagram. The graph contains two kinds of nodes, max nodes and Q nodes. The max nodes correspond to the subtasks in the task decomposition. There is one max node for each primitive action and one max node for each subtask (including the root) task. Each primitive max node i stores the value of $V^{\pi}(i, s)$. The Q nodes correspond to the actions that are available for each subtask. Each Q node for parent task i, state s, and subtask a stores the value of $C^{\pi}(i, s, a)$.

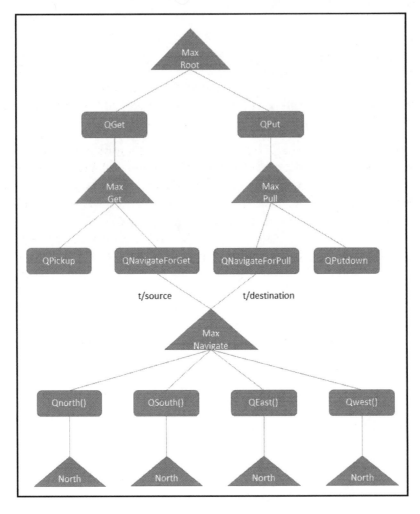

Figure 11.8: MAXQ graph for the taxi domain

In addition to storing information, the max nodes and Q nodes can be viewed as performing parts of the computation described by the decomposition equations. Specifically, each max node i can be viewed as computing the projected value function $V^{\Pi}(i, s)$ for its subtask. For primitive max nodes, this information is stored in the node. For composite max nodes, this information is obtained by *asking* the Q node corresponding to $\Pi_i(s)$. Each Q node with parent task i and child task a can be viewed as computing the value of $Q^{\Pi}(i, s, a)$. It does this by *asking* its child task a for its projected value function $V^{\Pi}(a, s)$ and then adding its completion function $C^{\Pi}(i, s, a)$.

As an example, consider the situation shown in Figure 11.6, which we will denote by s_1. Suppose the passenger is at R and wishes to go to B. Let the hierarchical policy we are evaluating be an optimal policy denoted by Π (we will omit the superscript * to reduce clutter in the notation). The value of this state under Π is *10*, because it will cost 1 unit to move the taxi to R, 1 unit to pick up the passenger, 7 units to move the taxi to B, and 1 unit to drop the passenger; so it's a total of 10 units (a reward of -10). When the passenger is delivered, the agent gets a reward of +20, so the net value is +10.

The following diagram shows how the MAXQ hierarchy computes this value. To compute the value $V^{\Pi}(Root, s_1)$, MaxRoot consults its policy and finds that $\Pi Root(s_1)$ is Get. Hence, it *asks* the Q node, QGet to compute $Q^{\Pi}(Root, s_1, Get)$. The completion cost for the *Root* task after performing a *Get*, $C^{\Pi}(Root, s_1, Get)$, is 12, because it will cost 8 units to deliver the customer (for a net reward of 20-8 = 12) after completing the *Get* subtask. However, this is just the reward after completing *Get*, so it must ask *MaxGet* to estimate the expected reward of performing *Get* itself. The policy for *MaxGet* dictates that in s_1, the navigate subroutine should be invoked with t bound to R, so *MaxGet* consults the Q node, QNavigateForGet, to compute the expected reward. *QNavigateForGet* knows that after completing the *Navigate(R)* task, one more action (pickup) will be required to complete *Get*, so $C^{\Pi}(MaxGet, s_1, Navigate(R)) = -1$. It then asks *MaxNavigate(R)* to compute the expected reward of performing navigate to location R. The policy for *MaxNavigate* chooses the North action, so *MaxNavigate* asks QNorth to compute the value. *QNorth* looks up its completion cost and finds that $C^{\Pi}(Navigate, s_1, North)$ is zero (that is, the navigate task will be completed after performing the North action). It consults MaxNorth to determine the expected cost of performing the *North* action itself. Because *MaxNorth* is a primitive action, it looks up its expected reward, which is -1.

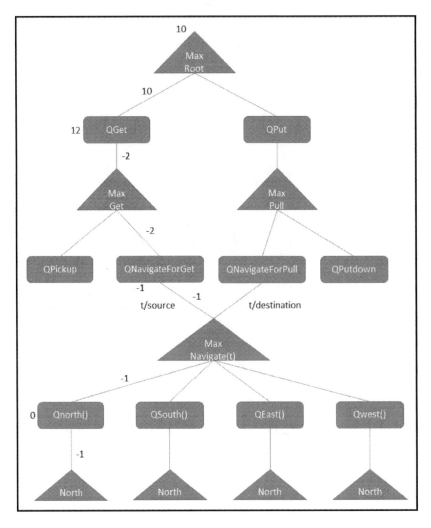

Figure 11.9: Computing the value of a state using the MAXQ hierarchy

Now this series of recursive computations can conclude as follows:

- Q^{Π} *(Navigate(R), s_1, North) = -1 + 0*
- V^{Π} *(Navigate(R), s_1) = -1*
- V^{Π} *(Get, s_1) = -2*
- Q^{Π} *(Root, s_1, Get) = -2 + 12*

The end result of all of this is that the value of $V''(Root, s_1)$ is decomposed into a sum of C terms plus the expected reward of the chosen primitive action:

$$V''(Root, s_1) = V''(North, s_1) + C''(Navigate(R), s_1, North) +$$

$$C''(Get, s_1, Navigate(R)) + C''(Root, s_1, Get)$$
$$= -1 + 0 + -1 + 12$$
$$= 10$$

Summary

In this chapter, we discussed the current research topics in the field of reinforcement learning. We started with hierarchical reinforcement learning and discussed a major issue with reinforcement learning: when the state space grows too large, the agent will not be able to find an optimal policy for a task, which affects its practical application in large systems. We divide the generation task into several subtasks, which have smaller state spaces and can therefore find a solution more easily. In other words, we learn a hierarchy of policies for generation subtasks rather than learning one single policy for the whole task.

We also saw the advantages of hierarchical reinforcement learning. Then we briefly discussed the SMDP model. We converted the SMDP model into hierarchical reinforcement learning.

We also went through reinforcement learning with HAM in detail. We discussed that HAM is used to write a partial policy as a set of hierarchical finite-state machines with unspecified choice states, and uses reinforcement learning to learn an optimal completion of this partial policy. Then we described the HAM framework and saw the five types of machine states. Furthermore, we discussed running a HAM algorithm. Later we covered a detailed example of HAM for a mobile robot, in which we saw the navigate machine and the move speed machine. We also wrote the pseudo code for this example. We discussed HAM for a RoboCup keepaway example and wrote its pseudo code as well.

The third topic we discussed was MAXQ value function decomposition. MAXQ describes how to decompose the overall value function for a policy into a collection of value functions for individual subtasks (and subtasks recursively). We covered a detailed example of a taxi world and discussed how to decompose the task.

Index

58188678R00188

Made in the USA
San Bernardino, CA
25 November 2017